THE THEATRE OF TENNESSEE WILLIAMS

Volume V

By TENNESSEE WILLIAMS

||||||||||||||||||||||||||||||||||||||||||||||||||||||||||||||||||||||||||||||||||||||||||||||||||||||||||||||||||

PLAYS

Baby Doll (a screenplay)
Camino Real
Cat on a Hot Tin Roof
Clothes for a Summer Hotel
Dragon Country
The Glass Menagerie
A Lovely Sunday for Creve Coeur
The Red Devil Battery Sign
Small Craft Warnings
A Streetcar Named Desire
Sweet Bird of Youth
THE THEATRE OF TENNESSEE WILLIAMS, VOLUME I
  Battle of Angels, A Streetcar Named Desire, The Glass Menagerie
THE THEATRE OF TENNESSEE WILLIAMS, VOLUME II
  The Eccentricities of a Nightingale, Summer and Smoke, The Rose Tattoo, Camino Real
THE THEATRE OF TENNESSEE WILLIAMS, VOLUME III
  Cat on a Hot Tin Roof, Orpheus Descending, Suddenly Last Summer
THE THEATRE OF TENNESSEE WLLIAMS, VOLUME IV
  Sweet Bird of Youth, Period of Adjustment, The Night of the Iguana
THE THEATRE OF TENNESSEE WILLIAMS, VOLUME V
  The Milk Train Doesn't Stop Here Anymore, Kingdom of Earth (The Seven Descents of Myrtle), Small Craft Warnings, The Two-Character Play
THE THEATRE OF TENNESSEE WILLIAMS, VOLUME VI
  27 Wagons Full of Cotton and Other Short Plays
THE THEATRE OF TENNESSEE WILLIAMS, VOLUME VII
  In the Bar of a Tokyo Hotel and Other Plays
27 Wagons Full of Cotton and Other Plays
The Two-Character Play
Vieux Carré

POETRY

Androgyne, Mon Amour
In the Winter of Cities

PROSE

Collected Stories
Eight Mortal Ladies Possessed
Hard Candy and Other Stories
The Knightly Quest and Other Stories
One Arm and Other Stories
The Roman Spring of Mrs. Stone
Where I Live: Selected Essays

THE THEATRE OF
TENNESSEE WILLIAMS

Volume V

The Milk Train Doesn't Stop Here Anymore

Kingdom of Earth (The Seven Descents of Myrtle)

Small Craft Warnings

The Two-Character Play

A NEW DIRECTIONS BOOK

Manufactured in the United States of America
New Directions books are printed on acid-free paper.

Published simultaneously in Canada by Penguin Books, Canada Limited

Fifth Printing

New Directions Books are published for James Laughlin
by New Directions Publishing Corporation
80 Eight Avenue, New York, NY 10011

ISBN 978-0-8112-0593-1

Contents

THE MILK TRAIN DOESN'T STOP HERE ANYMORE

"*Consume my heart away; sick with desire*
And fastened to a dying animal
It knows not what it is; and gather me
Into the artifice of eternity."
—FROM *Sailing to Byzantium*
BY WILLIAM BUTLER YEATS

AUTHOR'S NOTES

Sometimes theatrical effects and devices such as those I have adopted in the third (and I hope final) version of this play are ascribed to affectation or "artiness," so it may be helpful for me to explain a bit of my intention in the use of these effects and devices, and let the play's production justify or condemn them.

I have added to the cast a pair of stage assistants that function in a way that's between the Kabuki Theatre of Japan and the chorus of Greek theatre. My excuse, or reason, is that I think the play will come off better the further it is removed from conventional theatre, since it's been rightly described as an allegory and as a "sophisticated fairy tale."

Stage assistants in Japanese Kabuki are a theatrical expedient. They work on stage during the performance, shifting set pieces, placing and removing properties and furniture. Now and then in this play they have lines to speak, very short ones that serve as cues to the principal performers. . . . They should be regarded, therefore, as members of the cast. They sometimes take a balletic part in the action of the play. They should be dressed in black, very simply, to represent invisibility to the other players. The other players should never appear to see them, even when they speak or take part in the action, except when they appear "in costume."

THE SETTING represents the library and bedroom of the white villa, downstage, and the bedrooms of the pink and blue villinos: most importantly, the terrace of the white villa, I think, should extend the whole width of the proscenium, with a small apron for a white iron bench, a step down from the terrace.

3

Separations between interior and exterior should not be clearly defined except by lighting. When a single interior is being used, the other interior areas should be masked by light, folding screens, painted to blend with the cyclorama, that is, in sea-and-sky colors: they should be set in place and removed by the stage assistants. The cyclorama and these folding screens represent, preferably in a semi-abstract style, the mountain-sea-sky of Italy's Divina Costiera *in summer.*

Since the villas are, naturally, much farther apart than they can appear on the stage, the director could adopt a convention of having actors, who are to go from one villa to another, make their exits into the wings. They would wait till the stage assistants have removed the screens that mask the next interior to be used, and then come back out and enter that area.

August, 1963.

━━

THE PLAYERS

MRS. GOFORTH
CHRISTOPHER FLANDERS
BLACKIE
THE WITCH OF CAPRI
RUDY, a watchman
GIULIO
SIMONETTA

TWO STAGE ASSISTANTS
  (Sometimes appearing in
  costume for small parts)

MEMBERS OF THE KITCHEN STAFF

The Milk Train Doesn't Stop Here Anymore was presented at the Brooks Atkinson Theatre in New York on January 1, 1964, by David Merrick, with Neil Hartley as associate producer and Kermit Kegley as stage manager. Directed by Tony Richardson, the set design was by Rouben Ter-Artunian, the music by Ned Rorem, the lighting by Martin Aronstein, and the hair styles by Michel Kazan. The leads players were as follows.

MRS. GOFORTH	TALLULAH BANKHEAD
CHRISTOPHER FLANDERS	TAB HUNTER
BLACKIE	MARIAN SELDES
RUDY	RALPH ROBERTS
THE WITCH OF CAPRI	RUTH FORD
STAGE ASSISTANTS	BOBBY DEAN HOOKS, KONRAD MATTHAEI

An earlier version of *The Milk Train Doesn't Stop Here Anymore* was staged for the first time anywhere at the Festival of Two Worlds in Spoleto, Italy, on July 11, 1962. It reopened in New York on January 10, 1963, produced by Roger L. Stevens and directed by Herbert Machiz, with stage set and lighting by Jo Mielziner, costumes supervision by Fred Voelpel from sketches by Peter Hall, and music by Paul Bowles. The cast included Hermione Baddeley (Flora Goforth), Ann Williams (Francis Black), Clyde Ventura (Giulio), Paul Roebling (Chris Flanders), Maria Tucci (Angelina), Bruce Gibson (Rudy), and Mildred Dunnock (Vera Ridgeway Condotti).

PROLOGUE

At the rise of the curtain, the STAGE ASSISTANTS *are on stage. All the interior areas are masked by their individual screens. The light of the cyclorama suggests early dawn.*

ONE: Daybreak: flag-raising ceremony on Mrs. Goforth's mountain.

TWO: Above the oldest sea in the Western world.

ONE: Banner.

[TWO *hands it to him.* TWO *places the staff in a socket near the right wings and attaches the flag to it. A fan in the wings whips it out as it is being raised, so that the audience can see the device on it clearly.*]

ONE: The device on the banner is a golden griffin.

TWO: A mythological monster, half lion, and half eagle.

ONE: And completely human.

TWO: Yes, wholly and completely human, that's true.

ONE: We are also a device.

TWO: A theatrical device of ancient and oriental origin.

ONE: With occidental variations, however.

TOGETHER: We are Stage Assistants. We move the screens that mask the interior playing areas of the stage presentation.

ONE: We fetch and carry.

TWO: Furniture and props.

ONE: To make the presentation—the play or masque or pageant—move more gracefully, quickly through the course of the two final days of Mrs. Goforth's existence.

7

MRS. GOFORTH'S VOICE [*offstage; half sleeping*]: Ahhhhhhhh, Meeeeeeeeee . . .

[*There is heard the sound of distant church bells.*]

ONE: The actors will not seem to hear us except when we're in costume.

TWO: They will never see us, except when we're in costume.

ONE: Sometimes we will give them cues for speech and participate in the action.

MRS. GOFORTH'S VOICE [*off stage*]: Ahhhhhhh, Ahhhhhh, Ahhhhhh . . .

[ONE *and* TWO *show no reaction to this human cry.*]

MRS. GOFORTH'S VOICE [*off stage; more wakefully*]: Another day, Oh, Christ, Oh, Mother of Christ!

[*There is silence, a pause, as the cyclorama's lighting indicates the progress of the day toward the meridian.*]

ONE *and* TWO [*together*]: Our hearts are invisible, too.

[*The fan that whipped out the flag bearing the personal emblem, the griffin, of* MRS. GOFORTH, *dies down and the flag subsides with it, and will not whip out again till the flag-lowering ceremony which will take place during the last three lines of the play.*]

[*Now it is noon. Electric buzzers sound from various points on the stage. The* STAGE ASSISTANTS *cross rapidly up center and remove a screen, the middle panel of which is topped by* MRS. GOFORTH's *heraldic device, the gold griffin. The library of the white villa is unmasked and the play begins.*]

SCENE ONE

MRS. GOFORTH: I made my greatest mistake when I put a fast car in his hands, that red demon sports car, his fighting cock, I called it, which he drove insanely, recklessly, between my estate and the Casino at Monte Carlo, so recklessly that the Police Commissioner of Monaco came personally to ask me. Correction, *beg* me. Correction, *implore* me!— To insist that he go with me in the Rolls with a chauffeur at the wheel, as a protection of his life and of the lives of others.— M. le Commissionaire, I said, for me there are no others.— I know, Madame, he said, but for the others there are others.— Then I confessed to the Commissioner of Police that over this young poet with Romanov blood in his veins, I had no more control than my hands had over the sea-wind or the storms of the sea. At night he had flying dreams, he would thrash his arms like wings, and once his hand, on which he wore a signet ring with the heavy Romanov crest, struck me in the mouth and drew blood. After *that, necessarily*—twin beds . . .

BLACKIE: Mrs. Goforth, excuse me, but the last thing I have typed up is—oh, here it is.— "My first two husbands were ugly as apes and my third one resembled an ostrich."— Now if this passage you're dictating to me comes in direct sequence it will sound as if you had put the fast car in the hands of the ostrich.

[*There is a long, tempestuous pause.*]

MRS. GOFORTH: Aren't you the sly one, oh, you're sly as ten flies when you want to give me the needle, aren't you, Miss Blackie? My first three marriages were into Dun and Bradstreet's and the Social Register, both!— My first husband, Harlon Goforth, whose name I still carry after three later marriages— that dignified financier, *tycoon!*—was a man that Presidents

9

put next to their wives at banquets in the White House, and you sit there smoking in my face, when you know I've been told to quit smoking, and you make a joke of my work with a dead-pan expression on your Vassar-girl face, in your Vassar-girl voice, and *I will not tolerate it!*— You know goddamn well I'm talking about my *fourth* husband, the *last* one, the one I married for love, who plunged off the Grande Corniche between Monte Carlo and—died that night in my arms in a clinic at Nice: and my heart died with him! Forever! [*Her voice breaks.*]

BLACKIE: I'm sorry, Mrs. Goforth. [*Puts out cigarette.*] I'm no writer but I do think in writing there has to be some kind of logical—sequence, continuity—between one bit and the next bit, and the last thing you dictated to me—

MRS. GOFORTH: Was it something I put on the tape-recorder in my bedroom after I'd been given one of those injections that upset my balance at night?

BLACKIE: I took it off your bedroom tape this morning.

MRS. GOFORTH: Always check those night recordings with me before we begin to work the following morning. We're working against time, Blackie. Remember, try to remember, I've got two deadlines to meet, my New York publishers and my London publishers, both, have my memoirs on their Fall List. I said fall. It's already late in August. Now do you see why there's no time for goofing, or must I draw you a picture of autumn leaves falling?

BLACKIE: Mrs. Goforth, I think those publishers' deadlines are unrealistic, not to say cruel, and as for me, I not only have to function as a secretary but as an *editor*, I have to *collate* the material you dictate to me and I'm not being sly or cruel, I'm just being *honest* with you when I tell you—

MRS. GOFORTH [*cutting in*]: All cruel people describe themselves as paragons of frankness!

10

BLACKIE: I think we'd better stop now.

MRS. GOFORTH: *I* think we'd better go *on*, now!

BLACKIE: Mrs. Goforth, the Police Commissioner of Monaco was right when he told you that there were "others." I am one of those "others." I've had no sleep, scarcely any at all and—

MRS. GOFORTH: *You've* had no sleep? What about me, how much sleep do *I* get?

BLACKIE: You sleep till noon or after!

MRS. GOFORTH: Under sedation, with nightmares!

BLACKIE: Your broker is on the phone . . .

[*The* STAGE ASSISTANTS *have entered with phone.*]

MRS. GOFORTH [*immediately brightening*]: Chuck, baby, how're we doing? Ah-huh, glamour stocks still slipping? Don't hold on to 'em, dump them before they drop under what I bought 'em at, baby. We'll start buying back when they hit the basement level.— Don't give me an argument, Sell! *Sell! Hell!*— It's building into a crash! So, baby, I'm hitting the silk! High, low, jack and the game! Ho ho!

[*She bangs down the phone, exhilarated, and it is removed by one of the* STAGE ASSISTANTS. *The other* ASSISTANT *has rushed to the stage-right wings, and he now appears in a white doctor's jacket. This is one of the costumes that make the* ASSISTANTS *seen and heard by the other actors.*]

ASSISTANT [*as* DR. LULLO]: *Buon giorno!*

MRS. GOFORTH: What's he wheeling in here that looks like a baby-buggy for a baby from Mars?

[*He is pushing a "mock-up" of a portable X-ray machine.*]

BLACKIE: It's something your doctor in Rome, Dr.—what? Rengucci?—had sent up here to spare you the trouble of inter-

rupting your work to take a new set of pictures to show what
progress there is in the healing of the lesion, the lung abscess,
that—

MRS. GOFORTH: Oh, so you're having private consultations with
that quack in Rome?

BLACKIE: Just routine calls that he told me to make sure to
spare you the trouble of—

MRS. GOFORTH: Spare me no trouble, just spare me your goddamn *presumptions!*

DR. LULLO: *Forse più tardi, forse un po' più tardi?*

MRS. GOFORTH: Will you get your sneaky grin out of here?
Va, va. Presto!

[*He retires quickly from the lighted area.* MRS. GOFORTH *advances both fearfully and threateningly upon the medical
apparatus.*]

My outside is public, but my insides are private, and the Rome
quack was hired by my bitch daughter that wants to hang
black crepe on me. Wants to know if I'm going, and when I'll
go. Doesn't know that if and when I do go, she gets one dollar,
the rest goes to a—a *cultural foundation!*—named for *me!*
Blackie, wheel this thing off the terrace, to the cliff-side of the
mountain and shove it over!

BLACKIE: Mrs. Goforth, you mustn't ask me to do ridiculous
things.

MRS. GOFORTH: I don't do ridiculous things and don't ask anyone else to do 'em for me. But if you think it's ridiculous of me
to show my opinion of Rengucci's presumption and—*Look,
watch this! Here we go, perambulator from Mars. Out, down,
go!*

12

[*She thrusts it violently onto the forestage, where it is seized by the* STAGE ASSISTANTS *and rushed into the wings. She crosses onto the forestage, leaning forward to watch its fall off the cliff. After a couple of moments, we hear a muted crash that signifies its destruction on the rocky beach under the mountain. Then she straightens, dizzily, with a fierce laugh, and staggers back toward the library area, where* BLACKIE, *meanwhile, has closed her notebook and rushed off stage. Heartbeat sounds are heard amplified, as* MRS. GOFORTH *moves distractedly about the library area, calling out breathlessly for* BLACKIE. *She presses several buttons on the "intercom" box on the desk: electric buzzers sound from here and there on the stage but no one responds: She washes down a pill with a swig of brandy. The heart-beat sounds subside as her agitation passes. She sinks into the desk chair.*]

Ahhh . . .

[*She activates her tape-recorder and speaks into it with a voice that is plaintively childlike.*]

Blackie, the boss is sorry she took her nerves out on you. It's those night injections I take for my—neuralgia—neuritis—bursitis. The pick-up pills and the quiet-down pills: nerves shot . . .

[*A sea wave booms under the mountain.*]

Oh, God, Blackie, I'm *scared!* You know what I'm scared of? Possibly, maybe, the Boss is—dying this summer! On the *Divina Costiera*, under that, that—angry old lion, the sun, and the—insincere sympathy of the— [*Her mood suddenly reverses again.*] No, no, no, I don't want her goddamn sympathy, I'll take that slobbery stuff off the tape and— *Begin! Continue! Dictation!* [*She rises, paces the forestage with a portable "mike."*]

[*A phrase of lyrical music is heard. She stops short, lifting a jeweled hand as if to say "Listen!" Then suddenly the accre-*

tion of years is broken through. The stage dims out except for her follow-spot on the forestage.]

"Cloudy symbols of a—high romance . . ." Who said that, where is that from? Check tomorrow, Blackie, in the *Book of Familiar Quotations* . . . Begin, continue dictation.

[*A pause, while she paces back and forth.*]

The love of true understanding isn't something a man brings up the road to you every day or once in a blue moon, even. But it was brought to me once, almost too late but not quite. . . .

The hard shell of my heart, the calcium deposits grown around it, could still be cracked, broken through, and my last husband broke through it, and I was brought back to life and almost back to—what?—Youth. . . .

The nights, the nights, especially the first one I spent with Alex! The way that a lover undresses, removes his clothes the first night you spend together, is a clue, a definite clue, to your whole future relationship with him, you know. Alex unclothed himself *unconsciously gracefully*, as if before no one in a—room made of windows, and then, unclothed—*correction:* clothed in a god's perfection, his naked body!—he went from window to window, all the way round the bedroom, drawing the curtains together so that daybreak beginning wouldn't wake us early from the sleep after love, which is a heavenly sleep that shouldn't be broken early. Then came to rest in a god's perfection beside me: reached up to turn off the light: I reached up and turned it *back on!*

[*At this point,* MRS. GOFORTH'S *watchdogs* (lupos) *set up a great clamor on the inland side of the mountain. A* MAN *shouts.* WOMAN SERVANTS *scream in Italian. Somebody calls,* "Rudy, Rudy!" MRS. GOFORTH *is very annoyed by this disruption of her tender recollections: she presses various buttons on the intercom box on her desk.*]

14

MRS. GOFORTH [*shouting over the dogs*]: *Che succede! Che fa, Cretini! Stronzi!* [*etc.*]

[*The savage barking continues but diminishes a little in volume as a* YOUNG MAN, *who has just been assaulted by dogs, limps and stumbles onto the terrace. He bears a heavy white sack over his shoulder, looking back as if to make sure he's no longer pursued.* BLACKIE *appears behind him, panting, looking as if she'd also been roughed up by the dogs.*]

BLACKIE [*to the* YOUNG MAN]: Places go mad, it's catching, people catch it! [*She draws a breath.*] There's a doctor up here, I'll get him for you.

CHRIS: Can I see Mrs. Goforth?

BLACKIE: Sit down somewhere. I'll see if she can see you, and I'll—

[*The* YOUNG MAN, CHRIS, *limps out upon the forestage, sinks onto a white iron bench. A wave crashes below the mountain. He looks blankly out at the audience for a moment, then shakes his head and utters a desperate-sounding laugh.* BLACKIE *rushes into the library area.*]

Mrs. Goforth, I can't stand this sort of thing!

MRS. GOFORTH: *What?*

BLACKIE: Those dogs of Rudy's, those wolves, attacked a young man just now.

MRS. GOFORTH: What young man, doing what?

BLACKIE: He was climbing the mountain to see you!

MRS. GOFORTH: Who is he, what does he want?

BLACKIE: I didn't stop to ask that. I had to drive the dogs off to keep him from being torn to pieces before I—asked him questions. Look! [*She shows* MRS. GOFORTH *a laceration on her thigh, just over the knee.*] The others just watched and screamed like children at a circus!

MRS. GOFORTH: Sit down, have a brandy. A place like this is always protected by dogs.

[*There is the sound of another wave crashing.*]

CHRIS: Boom. [*He discovers that his leather pants, lederhosen, have been split down his thigh.*]

BLACKIE: That gangster's bodyguard, Rudy, just stood there and watched!

MRS. GOFORTH: Blackie, this estate contains things appraised by Lloyd's at over two million pounds sterling, besides my jewels and summer furs, and that's why it has to be guarded against trespassers, uninvited intruders. Have you had your anti-tetanus shot, or—whatever they call it?

BLACKIE: Yes, I'm all right but he isn't. [*She presses a button on the intercom box.*]

MRS. GOFORTH: Who're you calling?

BLACKIE: I'm calling Dr. Lullo.

MRS. GOFORTH: Stop that, leave that to me! Do you think I want to be sued by this trespasser? Get away from my desk. I'm going to buzz Rudy. [*She presses another button.*] Rudy, *dove* Rudy? *Io lo voglio in libreria, subito, presto! Capito?*

[*The* YOUNG MAN *staggers to his feet and calls:* "Mrs. Goforth!" MRS. GOFORTH *picks up a pair of binoculars and gazes out at the terrace.* BLACKIE *stares at her with consternation.*]

CHRIS: Mrs. Goforth?

[RUDY, *the watchman, in semi-military costume, appears on the terrace.*]

16

RUDY: Shut up, stop that shouting. [*He enters the library area.*]

MRS. GOFORTH: Aw. Rudy. What happened, what's the report?

RUDY: I caught this man out there climbing up here from the highway.

BLACKIE: He set the dogs on him.

MRS. GOFORTH: That's what the dogs are here for. Rudy, what's the sign say on the gate on the highway?

RUDY: "Private Property."

MRS. GOFORTH: Just "Private Property," not "Beware of Dogs"?

RUDY: There's nothing about dogs down there.

MRS. GOFORTH: Well, for Chrissake, put up "Beware of Dogs," too. Put it up right away. If this man sues me, I've got to prove *there was a "Beware of Dogs"* sign.

BLACKIE: How can you prove what's not true?

MRS. GOFORTH [*to* RUDY]: Go on, hurry it up!

[*Rudy leaves.*]

MRS. GOFORTH [to BLACKIE]: Now pull yourself together. What a day! It's too much for me, I'll have to go back to bed. . . .

[GIULIO, the gardener's son, a boy of seventeen, appears on the terrace.]

GIULIO [to the YOUNG MAN, who is applying an antiseptic to his lacerations]: *Come va? Meglio?*

CHRIS: *Si, meglio, grazie.* Do you understand English?

17

GIULIO: Yes, English.

CHRIS: Good. Would you please tell Mrs. Goforth that Mr. Christopher Flanders is here to see her, and— Oh, give her this book, there's a letter in it, and—ask her if I may see her, don't—don't mention the dogs, just say I—I want very much to see her, if she's willing to see me. . . .

[*During this exchange on the forestage,* MRS. GOFORTH *has picked up a pair of binoculars.* GIULIO *knocks at the screen that represents the door between the terrace and the library.*]

MRS. GOFORTH: Come in, come in, *avanti!*

[*The* BOY *enters, excitedly.*]

GIULIO: Man bring this up road.

MRS. GOFORTH [*gingerly accepting the book in her hand*]: Young man that dogs bite bring this—[*squints at book*]—to me?

GIULIO: This, this, brings! Up mountains!

[*She turns the book and squints at a photograph of the author.*]

MRS. GOFORTH: Man resemble this photo?

[BLACKIE *is still quietly weeping at the desk.*]

GIULIO: *Non capisco.*

MRS. GOFORTH: Man!—*Uomo!*—resemble, look like—this photo?

GIULIO: Yes, this man. This man that dogs bite on mountain. [*Points out excitedly toward the* YOUNG MAN *on the bench.*]

MRS. GOFORTH: Well, go back out—*vada fuori e dica*— Blackie! Tell him to go back out there and say that I am very upset over the accident with the dogs, but that I would like to know why he came here without invitation, and that I am not responsible for anybody that comes here without invitation!

18

BLACKIE [*strongly, as she rises*]: No, I will not. I will not give a man nearly killed by dogs such an inhuman message.

MRS. GOFORTH: He hasn't been seriously hurt, he's standing up now. Listen he's shouting my name.

[*The* YOUNG MAN *has called, "Mrs. Goforth?" in a hoarse, panting voice. His shirt and one leg of his lederhosen have been nearly stripped off him. He has the opposite appearance to that which is ordinarily encountered in poets as they are popularly imagined. His appearance is rough and weathered; his eyes wild, haggard. He has the look of a powerful, battered, but still undefeated, fighter.*]

CHRIS: *Mrs. Goforth!*

[*His call is almost imperious. A wave crashes under the mountain:* CHRIS *closes his eyes, opens them, crosses to the lounge chair on the terrace and throws himself down in it, dropping a large canvas sack on the terrace tiles. The excited, distant barking of the dogs has now died out. Female voices are still heard exclaiming at a distance, in Italian.*]

MRS. GOFORTH [*looking again through her binoculars*]: Pull yourself together. The continent has been overrun by beatniks lately, I've been besieged by them, Blackie. Writers that don't write, painters that don't paint. A bunch of free-loaders, Blackie. They come over here on a Jugoslavian freighter with about a hundred dollars in travelers' checks and the summer addresses of everybody they think they can free-load on. That's why I'm not so sympathetic to them. Look, I made it, I got it because I made it, but they'll never work for a living as long as there is a name on their sucker list, Blackie. Now cut the hysterics now, and go out there and—

BLACKIE: *What?*

MRS. GOFORTH: Interrogate him for me!

BLACKIE: Interrogate? A badly injured young man?

MRS. GOFORTH: Trespasser! Get that straight in case he tries to sue me. [*She continues inspecting him through the binoculars.*] Hmm, he's not bad-looking, in a wild sort of way, but I'm afraid he's a beatnik. He has a beard and looks like he hasn't seen water for bathing purposes in a couple of weeks.

BLACKIE: You would, too, if a pack of wild dogs had attacked you.

MRS. GOFORTH: *Watchdogs, lupos,* defending private property: get that straight. He has on lederhosen. Hmm.— The first time I saw Alex, in the Bavarian Alps, he had on lederhosen and the right legs for 'em, too. And it's odd, it's a coincidence that I was dictating some recollections of Alex, who was a poet, when this young—*trespasser*—got here. Now if the sweat and the filthy appearance just come from the dogs' attack on him, I mean from *meeting* the dogs, you can tell by the smell of him while you're talking to him.

BLACKIE: You want me to go out and smell him? I'm not a dog, Mrs. Goforth.

MRS. GOFORTH: You don't have to be a dog to smell a beatnik. Sometimes they smell to high heaven because not washing is almost a religion with 'em. Why, last summer one of those ones you see in *Life* and *Look*, came up here. I had to talk to him with a handkerchief held to my nose. It was a short conversation and the last one between us.

[CHRIS *staggers up from the lounge chair and shouts: "Mrs. Goforth."*]

MRS. GOFORTH: What impudence, going on shouting at me like that!

BLACKIE: I think the least you could do is go out there your-

20

self and show some decent concern over the dogs' attack on him.

MRS. GOFORTH: I'm not going to see him till I've checked with my lawyers about my liability, if any. So be a good scout, a nice Brownie den-mother, and go out there and—

BLACKIE: *Interrogate* him?

MRS. GOFORTH: Ask him politely what he wants here, why he came to see me without invitation, and if you get the right answers, put him in the pink villino. And I'll see him later, after my siesta. He might be O.K. for a while, and I could use some male companionship up here since all I've got is you and Generalissimo Rudy for company this summer. I do need male company, Blackie, that's what I need to be me, the old Sissy Goforth, high, low, jack and the game!

BLACKIE: I'll go see if he's seriously hurt.

[*She crosses out, to the terrace, and approaches* CHRIS *limping about the forestage.*]

BLACKIE [to CHRIS]: How are you, are you all right, now?

CHRIS: Not all right, but better. Could I see Mrs. Goforth?

BLACKIE: Not yet, not right now, but she told me to put you in the little pink guest house, if you can—walk a little. It's a little way down the mountain.

CHRIS: Well, thank God, and— [*He tries to lift his sack and stumbles under its weight.*] Mrs. Goforth, of course . . .

BLACKIE: [*calling*]: *Giulio! Vieni qui!*

[GIULIO *comes on to the terrace.*]

BLACKIE: *Porta questo sacco al villino rosa.*

GIULIO [*lifting sack*]: *Pesante!—Dio* . . .

21

BLACKIE: *Tu sei pesante nella testa!* [*Then to* CHRIS] You can bathe and rest till Mrs. Goforth feels better and is ready to see you.

CHRIS: Oh.—Thanks . . .

[*He follows her off the terrace. The* STAGE ASSISTANTS *fold and remove the screen masking a bed upstage. The bed is small but rococo, and all pink. The* STAGE ASSISTANTS *return downstage with the screen and wait near* MRS. GOFORTH, *who is still watching the terrace scene through her binoculars.*]

MRS. GOFORTH [*to herself*]: Ah, God . . . [*Raises a hand unconsciously to a pain in her chest.*]

[*The* STAGE ASSISTANTS *unfold the screen before her, as the library area is dimmed out.*]

SCENE TWO

The area representing the pink villino is lighted: the light is warm gold afternoon light and striated as if coming through half-open shutters. A cupid is lowered over the bed by a wire: there are smaller cupids on the four posts of the bed. BLACKIE, CHRIS, *and* GIULIO *enter the narrow lighted area, the young poet limping.* GIULIO *bears the canvas sack with difficulty, muttering* "Pesante!"

BLACKIE: Here you are, this is it. Now!

CHRIS: What?

BLACKIE: How are your legs? Mrs. Goforth keeps a doctor on the place, a resident physician, and I think he ought to come here and do a proper job on those dog-bites.

CHRIS: They're not that bad, really.

BLACKIE: Have you had shots?

CHRIS: Shots?

BLACKIE: For tetanus?

CHRIS: Yes, yes, sometime or other. I'm actually just—tired out.

BLACKIE: Giulio, see if the water's running in the bathroom. I'm sure you want to bathe before you rest, Mr. Flanders. Oh, oh, no covers on the bed.

CHRIS: Don't bother about covers on it.

BLACKIE: I think, I have an idea, you're going to sleep a good while, and you might as well sleep comfortably. Giulio. Covers for bed.

GIULIO: *Dove?*

BLACKIE: *Cerca nell' armadio del bagno.*

[GIULIO *goes out.* CHRIS *sits down on the foot of the narrow bed. His head falls forward.*]

Mr. Flanders! [*He pulls himself up.*] Please try to stay awake till the bed's made up and you've bathed.

CHRIS: Your name is—? [*He rises, unsteadily.*]

BLACKIE: Frances Black, called Blackie.

CHRIS: How do you do. Mine's Flanders, Christopher Flanders.

[GIULIO *enters.*]

GIULIO: *Non c'è acqua.*

BLACKIE: Well, tell your papa to turn the water on.

[GIULIO *tosses some pink silk sheets on the bed and runs back out.*]

I hope you don't mind camphor, the smell of camphor.

[*He shakes his head slightly, holding onto a bed post.*]

The water ought to be running in a minute.

CHRIS: I hope there's a shower. A tub wouldn't be safe for me. I don't think even drowning would wake me up.

24

BLACKIE: I'll wait here till you've bathed.

CHRIS: It's wonderful here after—yesterday in—Naples . . .

BLACKIE: Would you please get on the other side of the bed and help me spread these sheets?

[*He staggers around the bed. They make it up.*]

CHRIS: You—

BLACKIE: What?

CHRIS: I wondered if you're related to Mrs. Goforth or if you're—

BLACKIE: Not related. I'm working for Mrs. Goforth: secretarial work. She's writing a sort of—all right, you can sit down, now—she's writing her memoirs and I'm helping her with it, the little, as best I—can. . . .

[*He sinks back onto the bed and drops his head in his hands.*]

Mr. Flanders, the water's turned on, now.

CHRIS [*staggering up*]: Oh. Good. Thank you. This way? [*Starts off.*]

BLACKIE: I'll fill the tub for you. Do you want warm or cold water, or—

CHRIS: Cold, please. Let me do it.

BLACKIE: No, just stay on your feet till it's ready for you.

[*She passes him and goes off. There is the sound of running water. He sits exhaustedly on the bed and sways. His forehead strikes the newel-post which is topped by a cupid. The room is full of painted and carved cupids. He looks up at the cupid on the post, shakes his head with a sad, wry grimace, drops his head in his hands, and slumps over again.*]

25

BLACKIE *returns from the bathroom with a towel-robe. She claps her hands.*]

BLACKIE: I told you to stay on your feet.

CHRIS [*struggling up*]: Sorry. What is—I almost said "Where am I?"

BLACKIE: Here's a towel-robe for you. You'd better just duck in and out.

CHRIS [*crossing to door and looking back at her from the threshold*]: Is this called the Cupid Room?

BLACKIE: I don't know if it's called that but it should be.

CHRIS [*starting to leave but on threshold*]: What a remarkable bathtub, it's almost the size of a deck pool on a steamship.

BLACKIE [*dryly*]: Yes, Mrs. Goforth thinks a bathtub should be built for at least two people.

CHRIS [*entering*]: She must have been to Japan.

BLACKIE: Yes. She probably owns it.

[CHRIS *enters the bathroom: There is a splash, a loud gasp.*]

BLACKIE: Oh, I should have warned you, it's mountain spring water.

CHRIS: Does it come from a glacier?

[BLACKIE *picks up the cords of his rucksack to drag it away from the bedside. She finds it startlingly heavy. She kneels beside it to loosen the drawstrings, draws out a silvery section of some metalwork. She rises guiltily as* CHRIS *reappears in the towel-robe.*]

BLACKIE: You're—shivering.

CHRIS: For exercise. Shivering's good exercise.

BLACKIE: I don't think you need any more exercise for a while. How did you get this sack of yours up the mountain?

CHRIS: Carried it—from Genoa.

BLACKIE: I could hardly drag it away from the bed.

CHRIS: Yes, it's heavy with metal. I work in metal, now. I construct mobiles, but it's not the mobiles that are heavy, it's the metalsmith tools.

BLACKIE: You, uh—sell—mobiles, do you?

CHRIS: No, mostly give 'em away. Of course I—

BLACKIE: What?

CHRIS: Some things aren't made to be sold. Oh, you sell them, but they're not made for that, not for selling, they're made for—

BLACKIE: Making them?

CHRIS: Is there something buzzing in the room or is the buzz in my head? Oh, a wasp. It'll fly back out the shutter. Is this a cigarette box? [*Opens box on small bedside table.*] Empty.

BLACKIE: Have a *Nazionale*. [*She offers him the pack.*]

CHRIS: Thank you.

BLACKIE: I'll leave the pack here, I have more in my room.— Your hair's not dry, it's still wet. [*He shakes his head like a spaniel.*] Dry it with the towel and get right into bed. I have to get back to work now. I work here, I do secretarial work and I—

CHRIS: Don't go right away.

BLACKIE: You need to rest, right away.

CHRIS: The ice water woke me up.

BLACKIE: Just temporarily, maybe.

CHRIS: I'll rest much better if I know a bit more, such as—Did Mrs. Goforth remember who I was?

BLACKIE: I don't know about that but she liked your looks, if that's any comfort to you.

CHRIS: I didn't see her. She saw me?

BLACKIE: She inspected you through a pair of military field-glasses before she had me take you to the pink villa with the—king-size bathtub, the pink silk sheets, and the cupids.

CHRIS: Do they, uh—signify something?

BLACKIE: Everything signifies something. I'll—I'll shut the shutters and you get into bed. [*She turns away from him.*]

CHRIS [*sitting on the bed*]: What is the program for me when I awake?

BLACKIE [*with her back still toward him*]: Don't you make out your own programs?

CHRIS: Not when I'm visiting people. I try to adapt myself as well as I can to their programs, when I'm—visiting people.

BLACKIE: Is that much of the time?

CHRIS: Yes, that's—*most* of the time. . . .

BLACKIE: Well, I think you're in for a while, if you play your cards right. You do want to be in, don't you? After hauling that sack all the way from Genoa and up this mountain to Mrs. Goforth? Or have the pink silk sheets and the cupids scared you, worse than the dogs you ran into?

CHRIS: You have a sharp tongue, Blackie.

BLACKIE: I'm sorry but I was mistaken when I thought I had

28

strong nerves. They're finished for today if not for the season, for—years. . . . [*She starts away.*]

CHRIS: Have a cigarette with me. [*He extends the pack to her.*]

BLACKIE: You want to get some more information from me?

CHRIS: I'd sleep better if I knew a bit more.

BLACKIE: I wouldn't be too sure of *that.*

CHRIS: I've heard, I've been told, that Mrs. Goforth hasn't been well lately.

[BLACKIE *laughs as if startled.*]

CHRIS: She's lucky to have you with her.

BLACKIE: Why?

CHRIS: I can see you're—sympathetic and understanding about Mrs. Goforth's—condition, but—not sentimental about it. Aren't I right about that?

BLACKIE: I'm not understanding about it, and I'm afraid I've stopped being sympathetic. Mrs. Goforth is a dying monster. [*Rises.*] Sorry, *I'm talking too much!*

CHRIS: No, not enough. Go on.

BLACKIE: Why do you want to hear it?

CHRIS: I've climbed a mountain and fought off a wolf pack to see her.

BLACKIE: *Why?*

CHRIS: No where else to go, now.

BLACKIE: Well, that's an honest admission.

CHRIS: Let's stick to honest admissions.

BLACKIE [*sitting back down by the bed*]: All right. I'll give you something to sleep on. You'll probably wish I hadn't but here it is. She eats nothing but pills: around the clock. And at night she has nightmares in spite of morphine injections. I rarely sleep a night through without an electric buzzer by my bed waking me up. I tried ignoring the buzzer, but found out that if I did she'd come stumbling out of her bedroom, onto the terrace, raving into a microphone that's connected to a tape-recorder, stumbling about and raving her—

CHRIS: Raving?

BLACKIE: Yes, her demented memoirs, her memories of her career as a great international beauty which she thinks she still is. I'm here, employed here, to—take down and type up these—

CHRIS: Memories?

BLACKIE: That's enough for you now. Don't you think so?

CHRIS: She doesn't know she's—

BLACKIE: Dying? Oh, no! Won't face it! Apparently never thought that her—legendary—existence—could go on less than forever! Insists she's only suffering from neuralgia, neuritis, allergies, and bursitis! Well? Can you still sleep? After this—bedtime story?

CHRIS: Blackie, I've had a good bit of experience with old dying ladies, scared to death of dying, ladies with lives like Mrs. Goforth's behind them, which they won't think are over, and I've discovered it's possible to give them, at least to offer them, something closer to what they need than what they think they still want. Yes. . . . Would you please throw me the strings of my sack, Blackie?

[*She tosses the strings to the bedside. He hauls the rucksack over, leans out of the bed to open it: removes a mobile.*]

30

Give her this for me, Blackie. It took me six months to make it. It has a name, a title. It's called "The Earth Is a Wheel in a Great Big Gambling Casino."

[*Music is heard playing softly.*]

BLACKIE:—"The Earth Is—"?

CHRIS: ". . . a Wheel in a Great Big Gambling Casino." I made it on hinges, it has to be unfolded before it's hung up. I think you'd better hang it up before you show it to her, if you don't mind, and in a place where it will turn in the wind, so it will make a—more impressive—impression. . . . And this is for you, this book. [*He hands a book to her.*]

BLACKIE: Poems?

CHRIS: It's a verse-adaptation I made of the writings of a Swami, a great Hindu teacher, my—teacher. Oh. One thing more. I'd like to make a phone call to a friend, an invalid lady, in Sicily—Taormina, a mountain above Taormina.— Would Mrs. Goforth object if I—?

BLACKIE: Not if she doesn't know. What's the number?

[*He gives her the number in Italian and is told that it will not go through for some time.*]

There'll be a delay. Is it very important?

CHRIS: Yes, it is. She's dying. Blackie? You're the kindest person I've met in a long, long time. . . .

BLACKIE [*Drawing a sheet over him*]: This sort of thing is just automatic in women.

CHRIS: Only in some of them, Blackie. [*His eyes fall shut.*]

BLACKIE: You're falling asleep.

CHRIS: Yes, automatic—like kindness in some women. . . . [*He

31

drops his cigarette and she picks it up and crosses to the phone.]

BLACKIE [*into the phone*]: Mariella? Bring a tray of food up to the pink villa. Better make it cold things. The guest's asleep and won't wake up for hours. [*She hangs up, looks at* CHRIS *and exits with book.*]

[*Lights dim on this area and a spot of light immediately picks up* MRS. GOFORTH *on the terrace. The* STAGE ASSISTANTS *have set a screen before this area and light is brought up on the forestage which represents the terrace of the white villa. The* STAGE ASSISTANTS *remove a wide screen and we see* MRS. GOFORTH *with two servants,* GIULIO *and* SIMONETTA. MRS. GOFORTH *is preparing to take a sun bath on the terrace. Her appearance is bizarre. She has on a silk robe covered with the signs of the zodiac, and harlequin sunglasses with purple lenses.*]

MRS. GOFORTH [*in her very "pidgin" Italian*]: Table here. *Capito? Tabolo.* [*Points.*] *Qui.* On *tabolo,* I want— What are you grinning at?

GIULIO [*very Neapolitan*]: *Niente, niente ma scusa!* [*He places table by chaise.*]

SIMONETTA [*giggling*]: *Tabolo.*

MRS. GOFORTH: On *tabolo voglio—una bottiglia d'acqua minerale, San Pellegrino, capite, molto ghiacciata: capite?*

[SIMONETTA *giggles behind her hand at* GIULIO's *antic deference to the Signora.* MRS. GOFORTH *glares suspiciously from one to the other, turning from side to side like a bull wondering which way to charge.* BLACKIE *enters the terrace area with the mobile, folded.*]

Che stronzi! Both of 'em.

BLACKIE: You mustn't call them that, it has an insulting meaning.

MRS. GOFORTH: I know what it means and that's what I mean it to mean. Generalissimo Rudy says they sleep together and carry on together some nights right here on my terrace.

BLACKIE: They're from Naples, and—

MRS. GOFORTH: What's that got to do with it?

BLACKIE: —and Generalissimo Rudy wants the girl for himself, so he—

MRS. GOFORTH: *Will you please tell them what I want on the table by this chaise. Here?*

BLACKIE: What do you want on the table?

MRS. GOFORTH: I—want a cold bottle of *acqua minerale,* cigarettes, matches, my Bain-Soleil, my codeine and empirin tablets, a shot of cognac on the rocks, the Paris *Herald-Tribune,* the Rome *Daily American,* the Wall Street *Journal,* the London *Times* and *Express,* the— Hey, what did you do with the—

BLACKIE: The visitor?

MRS. GOFORTH: The beatnik trespasser, yes, and what the hell have you got there that rattles like a string of boxcars crossing a railyard switch?

BLACKIE: The young man's in the pink villa, where you told me to put him. This is something he gave me for me to give you. It seems he constructs mobiles.

MRS. GOFORTH: Mobiles? Constructs?

BLACKIE: Yes, those metal decorations. He gives them titles. This one's called "The Earth Is a Wheel in a Great Big Gambling Casino."

33

MRS. GOFORTH: Is it a present—or something he hopes he can sell me?

BLACKIE: It's a present. He wanted me to suspend it before you saw it, but since you've already seen it—shall I hang it up somewhere?

MRS. GOFORTH: No, just put it down somewhere and help me up. The sun is making me dizzy. I don't know why I came out here. What am I doing out here?

BLACKIE: I was going to remind you that Dr. Rengucci warned you not to expose yourself to the sun, till the chest abscess, the lesion, has healed completely.

MRS. GOFORTH: *I don't have a chest abscess!*— Stop putting bad mouth on me! Open the door, I'm going in the library. . . .

[*The* STAGE ASSISTANTS *rush out and remove the screen masking that area as* MRS. GOFORTH *starts toward it, lifting a hand like a Roman Empress saluting the populace.*]

MRS. GOFORTH [*as she enters the library area*]: What did he have to say?

BLACKIE: The—?

MRS. GOFORTH: *Trespasser,* what did he have to say?

BLACKIE: About what?

MRS. GOFORTH: *Me.*

BLACKIE: He wondered if you remembered him or not.

MRS. GOFORTH: Oh, I might have met him somewhere, sometime or other, when I was still meeting people, interested in it, before they all seemed like the same person over and over and I got tired of the person.

34

BLACKIE: This young man won't seem like the same person to you.

MRS. GOFORTH: That remains to be— Blackie, y'know what I need to shake off this, this—depression, what would do me more good this summer than all the shots and pills in the pharmaceutical kingdom? I need me a lover.

BLACKIE: What do you mean by "a lover"?

MRS. GOFORTH: I mean a lover! What you *you* mean by a lover, or is that word outside your Vassar vocabulary?

BLACKIE: I've only had one lover, my husband Charles, and I lost Charles last spring.

MRS. GOFORTH: What beats me is how you could have a husband named Charles and not call him Charlie. I mean the fact that you called him Charles and not Charlie describes your whole relationship with him, don't it?

BLACKIE [*flaring*]: *Stop about my husband!*

MRS. GOFORTH: The dead are dead and the living are living!

BLACKIE: Not so, I'm not dead but not living!

MRS. GOFORTH: Giulio! [*He has entered the library area with the mineral water.*] *Va al villino rosa e portami qui* the sack— *il sacco!—dell' ospite là.*

BLACKIE: Oh, no, you mustn't do that, that's too undignified of you!

[GIULIO *goes out to perform this errand.*]

MRS. GOFORTH: Take care of your own dignity and lemme take care of mine. It's a perfectly natural, legitimate thing to do, to go through the luggage of a trespasser on your place for— possible—weapons, and so forth. . . . [*She sits at the desk.*] Pencil, notebook, dictation.

[BLACKIE *pays no attention to these demands, but lights a cigarette behind* MRS. GOFORTH's *back as she begins dictating.*]

—Season of '24, costume ball at Cannes. Never mind the style, now. Polish up later. . . .

—Went as Lady Godiva. All of me, gilded, my whole body painted gold, except for—green velvet fig leaf. Breasts? Famous breats? Nude, nude completely!

—Astride a white horse, led into the ballroom by a young nigger. Correction. A Nubian—slave-boy. Appearance created a riot. Men clutched at my legs, trying to dismount me so they could *mount* me. Maddest party ever, ever imaginable in those days of mad parties. This set the record for madness. —In '29, so much ended, but not for me. I smelt the crash coming, animal instinct—very valuable asset. Put everything into absolutely indestructible utilities such as—Tel. and Tel., *electric power.* . . .

[GIULIO *enters with the rucksack.*]

GIULIO: *Ecco, il sacco!* [*Drops it before* MRS. GOFORTH *with a crash that makes her gasp.*]

BLACKIE: May I be excused? I don't want to take part in this.

MRS. GOFORTH: Stay here. You heard that noise, that wasn't just clothes, that was metal.

BLACKIE: Yes, I suppose he's come here to seize the mountain by force of arms.

MRS. GOFORTH [*to* GIULIO]: Giulio, open, *aprite!*

[GIULIO *opens the sack and the inspection begins.*]

BLACKIE: I told you he made mobiles. The sack's full of metalsmith's tools.

MRS. GOFORTH: He hauled this stuff up the mountain?

36

BLACKIE: It didn't fly up.

MRS. GOFORTH: He must have the back of a dray horse. Tell this idiot to hold the sack upside down and empty it all on the floor, he's taking things out like it was a Christmas stocking.

BLACKIE: I'll do it. He'd break everything. [*She carefully empties the contents of the sack onto the floor.*]

MRS. GOFORTH: See if he's got any travelers' checks and how much they amount to.

BLACKIE [*ignoring this order and picking up a book*]: He offered me this book, I forgot to take it.

MRS. GOFORTH [*glaring at the book through her glasses*]: *Meanings Known and Unknown.* It sounds like something religious.

BLACKIE: He says it's a verse-adaptation he did of a—

MRS. GOFORTH: Swami Something. See if you can locate the little book they always carry with names and addresses in it. Sometimes it gives you a clue to their backgrounds and—inclinations. Here. This is it. [*Snatches up an address book.*]— Christ, Lady Emerald Fowler, she's been in hell for ten years.— Christabel Smithers, that name rings a long-ago church bell for a dead bitch, too. Mary Cole, *dead!* Laurie Emerson, *dead!* Is he a graveyard sexton? My God, where's his passport?

BLACKIE [*picking it up*]: Here.

MRS. GOFORTH: Date of birth: 1928. Hmmm, no chicken, Blackie. How old's that make him?

BLACKIE: —Thirty-five.

[*She lights a cigarette.* MRS. GOFORTH *snatches the cigarette from* BLACKIE's *hand. She sets it on the desk and in a moment starts smoking it herself.*]

37

MRS. GOFORTH: No travelers' checks whatsoever. Did he have some cash on him?

BLACKIE: I don't know, I neglected to frisk him.

MRS. GOFORTH: Did you get him to bathe?

BLACKIE: Yes.

MRS. GOFORTH: How'd he look in the bathtub?

BLACKIE: I'm afraid I can't give you any report on that.

MRS. GOFORTH: Where's his clothes? No clothes, *niente vestiti in sacco?*

GIULIO [*produces one shirt, laundered but not ironed*]: *Ecco una camicia, una bella camicia!*

MRS. GOFORTH: One shirt!

BLACKIE: He probably had to check some of his luggage somewhere, in order to get up the—goatpath . . . and the clothes he had on were demolished by Rudy's dogs.

MRS. GOFORTH: Well, put a robe in his room. I know—the Samurai warrior's robe that Alex wore at breakfast. We always wore robes at breakfast in case we wanted to go back to bed right after. . . .

[A STAGE ASSISTANT *enters with an ancient Japanese robe, with a belt and sword attached.*]

BLACKIE: Did he keep the sword on him at breakfast?

MRS. GOFORTH: Yes, he did and sometimes he'd draw it out of the scabbard and poke me with it. Ho ho. Tickle me with the point of it, ho ho ho ho!

BLACKIE: You weren't afraid he'd—accidentally—?

MRS. GOFORTH: Sure, and it was exciting. I had me a little revolver. I'd draw a bead on him sometimes and I'd say, you

38

are too beautiful to live, and so you have to die, now, tonight—
tomorrow—

[*The* STAGE ASSISTANT *hands the robe to* BLACKIE, *who accepts it without a glance at him.*]

—put the robe in the pink villino, and then call the Witch of Capri.

BLACKIE: Which witch?

MRS. GOFORTH: The one that wired me last month: "Are you still living?" Tell her I am. And get her over for dinner, tell her it's *urgentissimo!* Everything's *urgentissimo* here this summer. . . .

[*Phone buzzes on desk. As* BLACKIE *starts off,* MRS. GOFORTH *answers the phone.*]

Pronto, pronto, chi parla?—Taormina? Sicilia?—I've placed no call to that place. [*She slams down the phone.*] —Hmmm, the summer is coming to life! I'm coming back to life with it!

[*She presses buttons on her intercom system. Electric buzzers sound from various points on the stage as the* STAGE ASSISTANTS *cover the library area with the griffin-crested screen.*]

THE SCENE DIMS OUT.

SCENE THREE

*That evening. The setting is the terrace of the white villa and
a small section of* MRS. GOFORTH's *bedroom, upstage left. In this
scene, the* STAGE ASSISTANTS *may double as* BUTLERS, *with or
without white jackets. At the curtain's rise, the two screens are
lighted, one masking the small dinner table on the forestage,
the other* MRS. GOFORTH; *a* STAGE ASSISTANT *stands beside each
screen so that they can be removed simultaneously when a chord
provides the signal. The middle panel of* MRS. GOFORTH's *screen
is topped by a gold-winged griffin to signify that she is "in
residence" behind it.*

MRS. GOFORTH'S VOICE [*asthmatically*]: Simonetta, la roba.

[SIMONETTA *rushes behind the screen with an elaborate
Oriental costume.*]

Attenzione, goddamn it, *questa roba molto, molto valore. Va
bene. Adesso, parruca!**

SIMONETTA [*emerging from the screen*]: *A parruca bionda?*

MRS. GOFORTH: *Nera, nera!*

[*There is heard a reedy chord as on a harmonium. The screens
are whisked away. In the stage-left area, we see* MRS. GOFORTH
in the Oriental robe, on the forestage, RUDY *in his semi-military
outfit pouring himself a drink, and a small section of balustrade
on which is a copper brazier, flickering with blue flame.*
BLACKIE *enters, stage right, with a napkin and silver and sets a
third place at the table,* RUDY *hovers behind her.*]

BLACKIE: Stop breathing down my neck.

MRS. GOFORTH: *Ecco!*

[*She puts on a black Kabuki wig with fantastic ornaments*

* Wig.

40

stuck in it. Her appearance is gorgeously bizarre. As she moves, out upon the forestage, there is Oriental music.]

Well, no comment, Blackie?

BLACKIE: The Witch of Capri has just gotten out of the boat and is getting into the funicular.

MRS. GOFORTH: You kill me, Blackie, you do, you literally kill me. I come out here in this fantastic costume and all you say is the Witch of Capri has landed.

BLACKIE: I told you how fantastic it was when you wore it last week-end, when that Italian screen star didn't show up for dinner, so I didn't think it would be necessary to tell you again, but what I do want to tell you is that I wish you'd explain to Rudy that I find him resistible, and when I say resistible I'm putting it as politely as I know how.

MRS. GOFORTH: What's Rudy doing to you?

BLACKIE: Standing behind me, and—

MRS. GOFORTH: You want him in front of you, Blackie?

BLACKIE: I want him off the terrace while I'm on it.

MRS. GOFORTH: Rudy, you'd better go check my bedroom safe. These rocks I've put on tonight are so hot they're radioactive. [*to* BLACKIE] Guess what I'm worth on the hoof in this regalia?

BLACKIE: I'm no good at guessing the value of—

MRS. GOFORTH: I can't stand anything false. Even my kidney stones, if I had kidney stones, would be genuine diamonds fit for a Queen's crown, Blackie.

[BLACKIE *lights a cigarette.* MRS. GOFORTH *takes the cigarette from her.*]

A witch and a bitch always dress up for each other, because

otherwise the witch would upstage the bitch, or the bitch would upstage the witch, and the result would be havoc.

BLACKIE: Fine feathers flying in all directions?

MRS. GOFORTH: That's right. The Witch has a fairly large collection of rocks herself, but no important pieces. [*She crosses, smoking, to the table.*] Hey. The table's set for three. Are you having dinner with us?

BLACKIE: Not this evening, thanks, I have to catch up on my typing.

MRS. GOFORTH: Then who's this third place set for?

BLACKIE: The young man in the pink villa, I thought he'd be dining with you.

MRS. GOFORTH: That was presumptuous of you. He's having no meals with me till I know more about him. The Witch of Capri can give me the low-down on him. In fact, the only reason I asked the Witch to dinner was to get the low-down on this mountain climber.

THE WITCH [*at a distance*]: Yoo-hoo!

MRS. GOFORTH: Yooo-hooo! She won't be here more than a minute before she makes some disparaging comment on my appearance. Codeine, empirin, brandy, before she gets here. She takes a morbid interest in the health of her friends because her own's on the downgrade.

THE WITCH [*nearer*]: Yoo-hoo!

MRS. GOFORTH: Yooo-hooo! Here she comes, here comes the Witch.

[THE WITCH OF CAPRI, *the Marchesa Constance Ridgeway-Condotti, appears on the terrace. She looks like a creature out of a sophisticated fairy tale, her costume like something*

42

that might have been designed for Fata Morgana. Her dress is gray chiffon, paneled, and on her blue-tinted head she wears a cone-shaped hat studded with pearls, the peak of it draped with the material of her dress. Her expressive, claw-like hands are aglitter with gems. At the sight of MRS. GO-FORTH, *she halts dramatically, opening her eyes very wide for a moment, as if confronted by a frightening apparition, then she utters a dramatic little cry and extends her arms in a counterfeit gesture of pity.]*

THE WITCH: *Sissy! Love!*

MRS. GOFORTH: Connie . . .

[They embrace ritually and coolly, then stand back from each other with sizing-up stares.]

THE WITCH: Sissy, don't tell me we're having a Chinese dinner.

MRS. GOFORTH: This isn't a Chinese robe, it's a Kabuki dancer's, a Japanese national treasure that Simon Willingham bought me on our reconciliation trip to Japan. It's only some centuries old. I had to sneak it through customs—Japanese customs—by wearing it tucked up under a chinchilla coat. Y'know I studied Kabuki, and got to be very good at it. I was a guest artist once at a thing for typhoon relief, and I can still do it, you see.

[She opens her lacquered fan and executes some Kabuki dance movements, humming weirdly. The effect has a sort of grotesque beauty, but she is suddenly dizzy and staggers against the table. THE WITCH *utters a shrill cry;* BLACKIE *rushes to catch her and support the table.* MRS. GOFORTH *tries to laugh it off.]*

Ha, ha, too much codeine, I took a little codeine for my neuralgia before you got here.

THE WITCH: Well, I'm suffering, too. We're suffering together.

Will you look at my arm. [*She draws up her flowing sleeve to expose a bandaged forearm.*] The sea is full of Medusas.

MRS. GOFORTH: Full of what?

THE WITCH: Medusas, you know, those jellyfish that sting. The Latins call them Medusas, and one of them got me this morning, a giant one, at the *Piccola Marina*. I want a martini. . . . I've got to stay slightly drunk to bear the pain. [*She tosses her parasol to* BLACKIE *and advances to the liquor cart.*] Sissy, your view is a *meraviglia, veramente una meraviglia!* [*She drains a martini that* BLACKIE *pours her, then swings full circle and dizzily returns to a chair at the table.*] Do we have to eat?— I'm so full of canapés from Mona's cocktail do . . .

MRS. GOFORTH: Oh, is that what you're full of? We're having a very light supper, because the smell of food after codeine nauseates me, Connie.

BLACKIE: Mrs. Goforth, shouldn't I take something to your house guest since he's not dining with you?

MRS. GOFORTH: No, meaning no, but you can leave us now, Blackie. Oh, excuse me, this is my secretary, Miss Black. Blackie, this is—what's your latest name, Connie?

THE WITCH: I mailed you my wedding invitation the spring before last spring to some hospital in Boston, the Leahey Clinic, and never received a word of acknowledgment from you.

MRS. GOFORTH: Oh, weddings and funerals're things you show up at or you don't according to where you are and—

[*She rings bell for service: the* STAGE ASSISTANTS *appear with white towels over their forearms or colored mess-jackets. Note: Although they sometimes take part in the action of the play, the characters in the play never appear to notice the* STAGE ASSISTANTS.]

—*other* circumstances: Have a gull's egg, Connie.

THE WITCH: No, thank you, I can't stand gulls.

MRS. GOFORTH: Well, eating their eggs cuts down on their population.

THE WITCH: What is this monster of the deep?

MRS. GOFORTH: *Dentice, dentice freddo.*

THE WITCH: It has a horrid expression on its face.

MRS. GOFORTH: Don't look at it, just eat it.

THE WITCH: Couldn't possibly, thank you.

MRS. GOFORTH: Are you still living on blood transfusions, Connie? That's not good, it turns you into a vampire, a *pipistrella,* ha, ha. . . . Your neck's getting too thin, Connie. Is it true that you had that sheep embryo—plantation in—Switzerland? I heard so. I don't approve of it. It keys you up for a while and then you collapse, completely. The human system can't stand too much stimulation after—sixty. . . .

THE WITCH: What did they find out at the Leahey Clinic, Sissy?

MRS. GOFORTH: Oh, *that,* that was just a little—routine check-up. . . .

THE WITCH: When you called me today I was so relieved I could die: shouted "Hallelujah" silently, to myself. I'd heard such distressing rumors about you lately, Sissy.

MRS. GOFORTH: Rumors? Hell, what rumors?

THE WITCH [*crossing to the bar cart for a refill*]: I can't tell you the rumors that have been circulating about you since your house party last month. The ones you brought over from Capri came back to Capri with stories that I love you too much to repeat.

MRS. GOFORTH: Repeat them, Connie, repeat them.

THE WITCH: Are you sure you feel well enough to take them? [*She returns to her chair.*] Well—they said you were, well, that you seemed to be off your rocker. They said you spent the whole night shouting over loudspeakers so nobody could sleep, and that what you shouted was not to be *believed!*

MRS. GOFORTH: Oh, how *nice* of them, Connie. Capri's turned into a nest of vipers, Connie—and the sea is full of Medusas? Mmm. The Medusas are spawned by the bitches. You want to know the truth behind this gossip? Or would you rather believe a pack of malicious inventions?

THE WITCH: You know I love you, Sissy. What's the truth?

MRS. GOFORTH: Not that.—I'll tell you the truth. [*She rises and indicates the intercom speaker.*] I'm writing my memoirs this summer. I've got the whole place wired for sound, a sort of very elaborate intercom or walkie-talkie system, so I can dictate to my secretary, Blackie. I buzz my secretary any time of the day and night and continue dictating to her. That's the truth, the true story. [*She goes over to* THE WITCH.]

THE WITCH [*taking her hand*]: I'm so glad you told me, Sissy, love!

MRS. GOFORTH: Has it ever struck you, Connie, that life is all memory, except for the one present moment that goes by you so quick you hardly catch it going? It's really all memory, Connie, except for each passing moment. What I just now said to you is a memory now—recollection. Uh-hummm . . . [*She paces the terrace.*] —I'm up now. When I was at the table is a memory, now. [*She arrives at the edge of lighted area downstage right, and turns.*] —when I turned at the other end of the terrace is a memory, now. . . .

[THE WITCH *gets up and goes toward her.*]

46

Practically everything is a memory to me, now, so I'm writing my memoirs. . . . [*She points up.*] Shooting star: it's shot:—a memory now. Four husbands, all memory now. All lovers, all memory now.

THE WITCH: So you're writing your memoirs.

MRS. GOFORTH: Devoting all of me to it, and all of my time. . . . At noon today, I was dictating to Blackie on a tape-recorder: the beautiful part of my life, my love with Alex, my final marriage. Alex . . .

THE WITCH [*going to the bar cart*]: Oh, the young Russian dancer from the Diaghilev troupe?

MRS. GOFORTH [*returning to her chair*]: Oh, God, no, I never married a dancer. Slept with a couple but never married a one. They're too narcissistic for me; they love only mirrors. Nope, Alex was a young poet with a spirit that was as beautiful as his body, the only one I married that wasn't rich as Croesus. Alex made love without mirrors. He used my eyes for his mirrors. The only husband I've had, of the six I've had, that I could make love to with a bright light burning over the bed. Hundred-watt bulbs overhead! To see, while we loved. . . .

THE WITCH [*going back to the table with the pitcher of martinis*]: Are you dictating this. Over a loudspeaker?

MRS. GOFORTH: Ah, God—Alex . . .

THE WITCH: Are you in pain? Do you have a pain in your chest?

MRS. GOFORTH: Why?

THE WITCH: You keep touching your chest.

MRS. GOFORTH: Emotion. I've been very emotional all day. . . . At noon today, a young poet came up the goatpath from the

47

highway just as I was in the emotional—throes—of dictating my memories of young Alex. . . .

THE WITCH [*draining her martini*]: Ah-ha.

MRS. GOFORTH: He came up the goatpath from the Amalfi Drive wearing lederhosen like Alex was wearing the first time I set eyes on him.

THE WITCH [*starting to pour another martini*]: Ahh-ha!

MRS. GOFORTH [*snatching the pitcher from* THE WITCH *and placing it on the floor*]: Do you want to hear this story?

THE WITCH: Liquor improves my concentration. Go on. You've met a new poet. What was the name of this poet?

MRS. GOFORTH: His name was on the book.

THE WITCH: Yes, sometimes they do put the author's name on a book.

MRS. GOFORTH [*unamused*]: Sanders? No. Manders? No.

THE WITCH: Flanders. Christopher Flanders. [*Makes large eyes.*] Is he still in circulation?

MRS. GOFORTH: I don't know if he's in circulation or not but I do know he came up here to see me and not by the boat and funicular, he—

THE WITCH [*moving toward* MRS. GOFORTH]: Well, God help you, Sissy.

MRS. GOFORTH: Why, is something wrong with him?

THE WITCH: Not if you're not superstitious. Are you superstitious?

MRS. GOFORTH: What's superstition got to do with—

THE WITCH: I've got to have a wee drop of brandy on this! [*She crosses over to the bar cart.*] This is really uncanny!

48

MRS. GOFORTH: *Well, come out with it, what?*

THE WITCH [*selecting the brandy bottle*]: I think I'd rather not tell you.

MRS. GOFORTH [*commandingly*]: *What?*

THE WITCH: Promise me not to be frightened?

MRS. GOFORTH: When've I ever been frightened? Of what? Not even that stiletto you've got for a tongue can scare me! [*She downs her own martini at a gulp.*] So what's the—

THE WITCH: Chris, poor Chris Flanders, he has the bad habit of coming to call on a lady just a step or two ahead of the undertaker. [*She sits down.*] Last summer, at Portofino, he stayed with some Texas oil people, and at supper one night that wicked old Duke of Parma, you know the one that we call the Parma Violet, he emptied a champagne bottle on Christopher's head and he said, "I christen thee, Christopher Flanders, the Angel of Death." The name has stuck to him, Sissy. Why, some people in our age bracket, we're senior citizens, Sissy, would set their dogs on him if he entered their grounds, but since you're not superstitious— Why isn't he dining here with us?

MRS. GOFORTH: I wanted some information about him before I—

THE WITCH: Let him stay here?

MRS. GOFORTH: He's here on probation. [*She rings for* GIULIO, *and then crosses center.*] I put him in the pink villa where he's been sleeping since noon, when he climbed up a goatpath to see me.

THE WITCH [*following* MRS. GOFORTH]: I hope he's not playing his sleeping trick on you, Sissy.

MRS. GOFORTH: Trick? Sleeping?

THE WITCH: Yes, last summer when he was with that Portofino

49

couple from Texas, they were thrown into panic when they heard his nickname, "Angel of Death," and told him that night to check out in the morning. Well, that night, he swallowed some sleeping pills that night, Sissy, but of course he took the precaution of leaving an early morning call so he could be found and revived before the pills could—

[MRS. GOFORTH *abruptly begins to leave.*]

Where're you going, Sissy?

MRS. GOFORTH: Follow me to the pink villa, hurry, hurry, I better make sure he's not playing that trick on me.

[*She rushes off.* THE WITCH *laughs wickedly as she follows. The* STAGE ASSISTANTS *immediately set a screen before this acting area and the light dims. Then they remove a screen upstage, and we see* CHRIS *asleep in the pink villa. A lullaby, perhaps the Brahms one is heard.* MRS. GOFORTH *and* THE WITCH *appear just on the edge of the small lighted area.*]

MRS. GOFORTH: Everything's pink in this villa, so it's called the pink villa.

THE WITCH: I see. That's logical, Sissy. Hmmm. There he is, sleeping.

MRS. GOFORTH [*in a shrill whisper as they draw closer to the bed*]: Can you tell if he's—?

[THE WITCH *removes her slippers, creeps to the bedside and touches his wrist.*]

—Well?

THE WITCH: Hush! [*She slips back to* MRS. GOFORTH.] You're lucky, Sissy. His pulse seems normal, he's sleeping normally, and he has a good color. [*She slips back to the bed, and bends her face to his.*] Let me see if there's liquor on his breath. No. It's sweet as a baby's.

MRS. GOFORTH: Don't go to bed with him!

THE WITCH: No, that's your privilege, Sissy.

MRS. GOFORTH [*moving downstage from the lighted area in a follow-spot*]: Come out here.

THE WITCH [*reluctantly following*]: You must have met him before.

MRS. GOFORTH: Oh, somewhere, sometime, when I was still meeting people, before they all seemed like the same person over and over, and I got tired of the—person.

THE WITCH: You know his story, don't you?

[*The* STAGE ASSISTANTS *place a section of balustrade, at an angle, beside them, and a copper brazier with the blue flame in it. The flame flickers eerily on* THE WITCH'*s face as she tells what she knows of* CHRIS. *Music plays against her stylized recitation.*]

Sally Ferguson found him at a ski lodge in Nevada where he was working as a ski instructor.

MRS. GOFORTH: A poet, a ski instructor?

THE WITCH: Everything about him was like that, a contradiction. He taught Sally skiing at this Nevada lodge where Sally was trying to prove she was a generation younger than she was, and thought she could get away with it. Well, she should have stuck to the gentle slopes, since her bones had gone dry, but one day she took the ski lift to the top of the mountain, drank a hot buttered rum, and took off like a wild thing, a crazy bird, down the mountain, slammed into a tree, and broke her hip bone. Well, Christopher Flanders carried her back to the ski lodge. We all thought she was done for, but Chris worked a miracle on her that lasted for quite a while. He got her back on her pins after they'd pinned her broken hip together with steel pins.

51

They traveled together, to and from Europe together, but then one time in rough weather, on the promenade deck of one of the *Queen* ships, the *Mary*, he suddenly let go of her, she took a spill and her old hip bone broke again, too badly for steel pins to pin her back together again, and Sally gave up her travels except from one room to another, on a rolling couch pushed by Chris. We all advised her to let Chris go, like Chris had let go of her on the promenade deck of the *Mary*. Would She? Never! She called him "my saint," "my angel," till the day she died. And her children contested her will, so that Chris got nothing, just his poems published, dedicated to Sally. The book won a prize of some kind, and *Vogue* and *Harper's Bazaar* played it up big with lovely photos of Chris looking like what she called him, an angel, a saint. . . .

MRS. GOFORTH: Did he sleep with that old Ferguson bitch? Or was he just her Death Angel?

[*The phone rings on the bedside table: the area has remained softly lighted.* CHRIS *starts up, drops back, feigning sleep, as* MRS. GOFORTH *rushes to the phone and snatches it up.*

—*Pronto, dica.*— Taormina, Sicily? No, *sbagliato!*

[MRS. GOFORTH *looks with angry suspicion at* CHRIS, *who murmurs as if in sleep. She notices the food tray by the bed, and snatches it up, then returns to* THE WITCH, *downstage.*]

He's already making long-distance calls on the phone and look at this! He's had them bring him a food tray, and I am going to remove it, I can't stand guests, especially not invited, that act like they're in a hotel, charging calls and calling for room service. Come on, I'm turning out the lights.

THE WITCH: My slippers.

[*She slips back to the bed and picks up her slippers, lingering over* CHRIS. *Suddenly she bends to kiss him on the mouth. He*

52

rolls over quickly, shielding his lower face with an arm and uttering a grunt of distaste.

Possum!

[*The lights dim in the area, as* THE WITCH *moves downstage.* MRS. GOFORTH *has disappeared.*]

Siss? Sissy! Yoo-hoo!

MRS. GOFORTH [*from a distance*]: Yoo-hoo!

THE WITCH [*following*]: Yooooooooo-hoooooooooo . . .

[*The* STAGE ASSISTANTS *replace the screen that masked the pink villa bed. Then they fold and remove the screen before* BLACKIE's *bed in the blue villa. The area remains dark until a faint dawn light appears on the cyclorama. Then* BLACKIE's *bed is lighted, and we see her seated on it, brushing her dark hair with a silver-backed brush.*]

THE SCENE DIMS OUT.

SCENE FOUR

It is later that night. The terrace of the white villa. The Watchman, RUDY, sweeps the audience with the beam of his flashlight. We hear a long, anguished "Ahhhh" from behind the screen masking MRS. GOFORTH's bed. RUDY, as if he heard the outcry, turns the flashlight momentarily on the screen behind which it comes. He chuckles, sways drunkenly, then suddenly turns the light beam on CHRIS who has entered quietly from the wings, stage right.

CHRIS [*shielding his eyes from the flashlight*]: Oh. Hello.

RUDY: You still prowling around here?

CHRIS [*agreeably*]: No, I'm—Well, yes, I'm— [*His smile fades as RUDY moves in closer.*] I just now woke up hungry. I didn't want to disturb anybody, so I—

RUDY: You just now woke up, huh?

CHRIS: Yes, I—

RUDY: Where'd you just now wake up?

CHRIS: In the, uh, guest house, the—

RUDY: Looking for the dogs again, are you? [*He whistles the dogs awake. They set up a clamor far away.*]

CHRIS: I told you I just now woke up hungry. I came out to see if—

RUDY: [*moving still closer and cutting in*]: Aw, you woke up *hungry?*

CHRIS: Yes. Famished.

RUDY: How about this, how'd you like to eat this, something like this, huh?

[*He thrusts his stick hard into* CHRIS's *stomach.* CHRIS *expells his breath in a "hah."*]

'Sthat feel good on your belly? Want some more of that, huh? huh?

[*He drives the stick again into* CHRIS's *stomach, so hard that* CHRIS *bends over, unable to speak.* BLACKIE *rushes onto the terrace in a dressing gown, her hair loose.*]

BLACKIE: *Rudy! What's going on here?*

[*The dogs, roused, are barking, still at a distance.*]

This young man is a guest of Mrs. Goforth. He's staying in the pink villa. Are you all right, Mr. Flanders?

[CHRIS *can't speak. He leans on a section of balustrade, bent over, making a retching sound.*]

Rudy, get off the terrace!—you drunk gorilla!

RUDY [*grinning*]: He's got the dry heaves, Blackie. He woke up hungry and he's got the dry heaves.

CHRIS: *Can't—catch—breath!*

[*From her bed behind the griffin-crested screen,* MRS. GOFORTH *cries out in her sleep, a long, anguished "Ahhhhhh!" The dogs' barking subsides gradually. The "Ahhhhh" is repeated and a faint light appears behind her screen.* BLACKIE *turns on* RUDY, *fiercely.*]

BLACKIE: I said get off the terrace, now get off it.

RUDY: You shoulda told me you—

BLACKIE: Off it, off the terrace!

RUDY [*overlapping* BLACKIE's *speech*]: You got yourself a boy friend up here, Blackie! You should've let me know that.

BLACKIE: Mr. Flanders, I'll take you back to your place.

CHRIS [*gasping*]: Is there—anywhere closer—I could catch my breath?

[*She stands protectively near him as* RUDY *goes off the terrace, laughing.*

[*The* STAGE ASSISTANTS *rush out to remove a screen masking* BLACKIE's *bed in the blue villa, indicating "Blackie's bedroom."* CHRIS *straightens slowly, still gasping. The* STAGE ASSISTANTS *leave. Then* CHRIS *and* BLACKIE *cross to her villino, represented only by a narrow blue-sheeted bed with a stand beside it that supports an intercom box.*]

BLACKIE: Now tell me just what happened so I can give a report to Mrs. Goforth tomorrow.

CHRIS: The truth is I was looking for something to eat. I've had no food for five days, Blackie, except some oranges that I picked on the road. And you know what the acid, the citric acid in oranges, does to an empty stomach, so I—I woke up feeling as if I had a—a bushel of burning sawdust in my stomach, and I—

BLACKIE: I had food sent to your room. You didn't find it?

CHRIS: No. God, no!

BLACKIE: Then the cook didn't send it, or it was taken out while you were sleeping, and I'm afraid you'll have to wait till morning for something to eat. You see, the only kitchen is in Mrs. Goforth's villa. It's locked up like a bank vault till Mrs. Goforth wakes up and has it opened.

CHRIS: How long is it till morning?

BLACKIE: Oh, my—watch has stopped. I'm a watch-winding person, but I forgot to wind it.

[*The sky has lightened a little and there is the sound of church bells at a distance.*]

CHRIS: The church-bells are waking up on the other mountains.

BLACKIE: Yes, it's, it must be near morning, but morning doesn't begin on Mrs. Goforth's mountain till she sleeps off her drugs and starts pressing buttons for the sun to come up. So—

CHRIS: What?

[*The intercom box comes alive with a shrill electric buzz.*]

BLACKIE: Oh, God, she's awake, buzzing for me!

CHRIS: Oh, then, could you ask her to open the kitchen? A glass of milk, just some milk, is all I—

BLACKIE: Mrs. Goforth isn't buzzing for morning, she's buzzing for me to take dictation and, oh, God, I don't think I can do it. I haven't slept tonight and I just couldn't take it right now, I—

CHRIS: Let me take it for you.

BLACKIE: No. I'll have to answer myself, or she'll come stumbling, raving out, and might fall off the cliff.

[*She presses a button on the intercom box.*]

Mrs. Goforth? Mrs. Goforth?

[*The* STAGE ASSISTANTS *remove the screen masking* MRS. GOFORTH's *bed, upstage left. We see her through the gauze curtains enclosing the bed. She pulls a cord, opening the curtains, and speaks hoarsely into a microphone.*]

MRS. GOFORTH: *Blackie? It's night, late night!*

BLACKIE: Yes, it's late, Mrs. Goforth.

MRS. GOFORTH: Don't answer: this is dictation. Don't interrupt me, this is clear as a vision. The death of Harlon Goforth, just now—clearly—remembered, clear as a vision. It's night, late night, without sleep. He's crushing me under the awful weight of his body. Then suddenly he stops trying to make love to me. He says, "Flora, I have a pain in my head, a terrible pain in my head." And silently, to myself, I say, "Thank God," but out loud I say something else: "Tablets, you want your tablets?" He answers with the groan of—I reach up and turn on the light, and I see—death in his eyes! I see, I know. He has death in his eyes, and something worse in them, terror. I see terror in his eyes. I see it, I feel it, myself, and I get out of the bed, I get out of the bed as if escaping from quicksand! I don't look at him again, I move away from the bed. . . .

[*She rises from the bed, the microphone gripped in her hand.*

I move away from death, terror! I don't look back, I go straight to the door, the door onto the terrace!

[*She moves downstage with the microphone.*]

It's closed, I tear it open, I leave him alone with his death, his—

BLACKIE: She's out of bed, she's going out on the —

[*She rushes into the wings. The light dims on the blue villa bed.*]

MRS. GOFORTH [*dropping the microphone as she moves out on white villa terrace*]: I've gone out, now, I'm outside, I'm on the terrace, twenty-five stories over the high, high city of Goforth. I see lights blazing under the high, high terrace but not a light blazing as bright as the blaze of terror that I saw in his eyes!

[*She staggers to the edge of the forestage.*

Wind, cold wind, clean, clean! Release! Relief! Escape from—

[*She reaches the edges of the orchestra pit. A wave crashes loudly below.*]

I'm lost, blind, dying! I don't know where I—

BLACKIE [*rushing out behind her*]: Mrs. Goforth! Don't move! You're at the edge of the cliff!

MRS. GOFORTH [*stopping, her hands over her eyes*]: Blackie!

[*She sways.* BLACKIE *rushes forward to catch her.*] Blackie, don't leave me alone!

[*The stage is blacked out.*]

INTERMISSION.

SCENE FIVE

The scene is the terrace of the white villa the following morning.
MRS. GOFORTH *is standing on the terrace while dictating to*
BLACKIE, *who sits at a small table. Above the table and about the*
balustrade are cascades of bougainvillaea. Coins of gold light,
reflected from the sea far below, flicker upon the playing area,
which is backed by fair sky. There has been a long, reflective
pause in the dictation. MRS. GOFORTH *stands glaring somberly out*
at the sea.

MRS. GOFORTH: Blackie, I want to begin this chapter on a more
serious note.

[*She moves around to the right of the table. Then continues*
emphatically and loudly.]

Meaning of life!

BLACKIE: Dictation?

MRS. GOFORTH: Not yet, wait, don't rush me. [*Repeats in a*
softer tone.] Meaning of life . . .

[CHRIS *appears at the far end of the terrace. He wears the*
Samurai robe. BLACKIE *sees him, but* MRS. GOFORTH *doesn't.*
BLACKIE *indicates by gesture that he should not approach*
yet.]

Yes, I feel this chapter ought to begin with a serious comment
on the meaning of life, because y'know, sooner or later, a person's obliged to face it.

BLACKIE: Dictating now, Mrs. Goforth?

MRS. GOFORTH: No, no, thinking—reflecting, I'll raise my hand
when I begin the dictation. [*She raises a jeweled hand to demon-*
strate the signal that she will use.]

BLACKIE: Begin now?

60

[CHRIS *smiles at her tone of voice.* BLACKIE *shrugs and closes her notebook, rises quietly, and goes up to* CHRIS, *who lights her cigarette.*]

MRS. GOFORTH: One time at Flora's Folly, which was the name of the sixteenth-century coach house, renovated, near Paris where I had my salon, my literary evenings, I brought up the question, "What is the meaning of life?" And do you know they treated it like a joke? Ha ha, very funny, Sissy can't be serious!— but she *was*, she *was*. . . .

CHRIS: I think she's started dictating. Is there something to eat?

BLACKIE: Black coffee and saccharine tablets.

CHRIS: That's *all?!*

BLACKIE: Soon as I get a chance, I'll raid the kitchen for you.

MRS. GOFORTH [*almost plaintively*]: Why is it considered ridiculous, bad taste, *mauvais gout*, to seriously consider and discuss the possible meaning of life, and only stylish to assume it's just—what?

[*The* STAGE ASSISTANTS *have come out of the wings.*]

ONE: Charade. Game.

TWO [*tossing a spangled ball to his partner*]: Pastime.

ONE [*tossing the ball back*]: Flora's Folly.

TWO [*tossing the ball back*]: Accident of atoms.

ONE [*returning ball*]: Resulting from indiscriminate copulation.

[BLACKIE *throws her cigarette away and returns to her former position. The* STAGE ASSISTANTS *withdraw.*]

MRS. GOFORTH: I've often wondered, but I've wondered *more* lately . . . meaning of *life.*

[*The* STAGE ASSISTANTS *reappear with a small table and two chairs. They wait in the wings for a moment before placing them. They then retire.*]

Sometimes I think, I suspect, that everything that we do is a way of—*not* thinking about it. Meaning of life, and meaning of death, too. . . . *What in hell are we doing?* [*She raises her jeweled hand.*] Just going from one goddamn frantic distraction to another, till finally one too many goddamn frantic distractions leads to disaster, and blackout? Eclipse of, total of sun?

[*She keeps staring out from the terrace, her head turning slowly right and left, into the swimming gold light below her, murmuring to herself, nodding a little, then shaking her head a little. Her small jeweled hands appear to be groping blindly for something. She coughs from time to time.*]

There's a fog coming in. See it over there, that fog coming in?

BLACKIE: No. It's perfectly clear in all directions this morning.

MRS. GOFORTH: When I woke up this morning, I said to my-self—

BLACKIE: Dictation?

MRS. GOFORTH: Shut up! I said to myself, "Oh, God, not morning again, oh, no, no, I can't bear it." But I *did*, I bore it. You really don't see that mist coming in out there?

BLACKIE [*closing her notebook*]: Mrs. Goforth, the young man in the pink villa, Mr. Flanders, is waiting out here to see you. He has on the Samurai robe you gave him to wear while his clothes are being repaired, and it's very becoming to him.

MRS. GOFORTH: Call him over.

62

BLACKIE: Mr. Flanders!

MRS. GOFORTH: Hey, Samurai! *Banzai!*

[*Approaching,* CHRIS *ducks under a brilliant cascade of bougainvillaea vine.*]

BLACKIE: You certainly had a long sleep.

CHRIS: Did I ever!

MRS. GOFORTH [*sitting*]: Did he ever, ho ho. He slept round the clock, but still has romantic shadows under his eyes! There was a chorus girl in the Follies—I used to be in the Follies, before my first marriage—when she'd show up with circles under her eyes, she'd say, "The blackbirds kissed me last night," meaning she's been too busy to sleep that night, ho ho. . . .

CHRIS: I was busy sleeping, just sleeping. [*He bends over her hand.*]

MRS. GOFORTH: No, no, none of that stuff. Old Georgia swampbitches don't go in for hand kissing but—*setzen Sie doon,* and— Are you coming out here for battle with that sword on?

CHRIS [*sitting*]: Oh. No, but—I ran into a pack of wild dogs on the mountain, yesterday, when I climbed up here.

MRS. GOFORTH: Yes, I heard about your little misunderstanding with the dogs. You don't seem much the worse for it. You're lucky they didn't get at— [*grins wickedly*] your *face.*

CHRIS: I'm sorry if it disturbed you, but their bite was worse than their bark.

MRS. GOFORTH: The Italians call them *lupos* which means wolves. These watchdogs, they're necessary for the protection of estates like this, but—didn't you notice the "Private Property" sign in English and Italian, and the "Beware of Dogs" sign when you started up that goatpath from the highway?

63

CHRIS: I don't think I noticed a reference to dogs, no. I don't remember any mention of dogs, in English or Italian.

BLACKIE [*quickly*]: Naturally not, the "Beware of Dogs" sign was put up *after* Mr. Flanders' "little misunderstanding with the dogs."

MRS. GOFORTH: Blackie, that is not so.

BLACKIE: Yes, it *is* so, I heard you ordering the sign put up after, just after the—

MRS. GOFORTH [*trembling with fury*]: Blackie! You have *work* to do, don't you?

BLACKIE: I've never taken a job that called for collusion in—falsehood!

MRS. GOFORTH [*mocking her*]: Oh, what virtue, what high moral character, Blackie.

CHRIS [*cutting in quickly*]: Mrs. Goforth, Miss Black, I obviously *did* enter and trespass on private property at my own risk.

MRS. GOFORTH: If that statement's typed up—Blackie, type it up—would you be willing to sign it, Mr. Flanders?

CHRIS: Certainly, yes, of course, but let me write it up in my own handwriting and sign it right now. I'd hate for you to think I'd—

BLACKIE: He was attacked again last night.

MRS. GOFORTH: Again, by dogs?

BLACKIE: Not by dogs, by a dog. Your watchman, Rudy, attacked him because he woke up hungry and came outside to—

MRS. GOFORTH [*rising*]: *Blackie, get off the terrace!*

BLACKIE: I want to get off this mountain gone mad with your

madness! I try to help you, I try to feel sorry for you because you're—

MRS. GOFORTH: What? What am I?

CHRIS: Please. [*He tears a page out of* BLACKIE's *notebook and speaks to her quietly.*] It's all right. Go in.

MRS. GOFORTH: What did you say to that woman?

CHRIS: I said you're very upset, I said you're trembling.

MRS. GOFORTH: *I've been up here surrounded by traitors all summer!* [*She staggers.*] Ahhhhh!

[CHRIS *helps her into her chair.*]

God! God . . .

CHRIS: Now. [*He scribbles rapidly on the sheet of paper.*] Here. "I, Christopher Flanders, entered a gate marked 'Private' at my own risk and am solely responsible for a—misunderstanding with—dogs." Witnesses? Of the signature?

MRS. GOFORTH: Can you unscrew this bottle? [*She has been trying to open her codeine bottle.*]

CHRIS [*taking it from her and removing the cap*]: One?

MRS. GOFORTH: Two.— Thank you.— Brandy on that— [*She indicates liquor cart.*]

CHRIS: Courvoisier?

MRS. GOFORTH: Rémy-Martin.— Thank you.

CHRIS: Welcome. [*He resumes his seat and smiles at her warmly.*] Let me hold that glass for you.

[*She has spilled some of the brandy, her hand is shaking so violently.*]

MRS. GOFORTH: Thank you.— Ahh . . . [*She draws a deep*

breath, recovering herself.] You have nice teeth. Are they capped?

[CHRIS *shakes his head, smiling.*]

Well, you got beautiful teeth. In that respect nature's been favorable to you.

CHRIS: Thank you.

MRS. GOFORTH: Don't thank me, thank your dentist. [*She puts on lipstick, dabbing her nostrils with a bit of disposable tissue.*]

CHRIS: I've never been to a dentist—honestly not.

MRS. GOFORTH: Well, then, thank the Lord for the calcium that you got from your mother's milk. Well, I have a pretty wonderful set of teeth myself. In fact, my teeth are so good people think they are false. But look, look here! [*She takes her large incisors between thumb and forefinger to demonstrate the firmness of their attachment.*] See? Not even a bridge. In my whole mouth I've had exactly three fillings which are still there, put in there ten years ago! See them? [*She opens her mouth wide.*] This tooth here was slightly chipped when my daughter's third baby struck me in the mouth with the butt of a water pistol at Murray Bay. I told my daughter that girl would turn into a problem child, and it sure as hell did.— A little pocket-size bitch, getting bigger! I'm allergic to bitches. Although some people regard me as one myself . . . Sometimes *with* some justification. Want some coffee, Mr. Trojan Horse Guest?

CHRIS: Thanks, yes. Why do you call me that, a Trojan Horse Guest?

MRS. GOFORTH: Because you've arrived here without invitation, like the Trojan Horse got into Troy.

[*She rises shakily to pour him a cup of coffee from a silver urn on the smaller, upstage table. While her back is turned,*]

CHRIS *quietly crumples the sheet from* BLACKIE'*s notebook and throws it into the orchestra pit.*]

CHRIS: Don't you remember our meeting and conversation at the Ballet Ball, some years ago, quite a few, when you asked me to come here whenever I was in Europe?

MRS. GOFORTH: Passports expire and so do invitations. They've got to be renewed every couple of years.

CHRIS: Has my invitation expired?

MRS. GOFORTH: Coffee. We'll see about that, that remains to be seen. Don't you smoke with your coffee?

CHRIS: Usually, but I—

[*He indicates he has no cigarettes.* MRS. GOFORTH *smiles knowingly and opens a cigarette box on the table.*]

How does it feel, Mrs. Goforth, to be a legend in your own lifetime?

MRS. GOFORTH [*pleased*]: If that's a serious question, I'll give it a serious answer. A legend in my own lifetime, yes, I reckon I am. Well, I had certain advantages, endowments to start with: a face people naturally noticed and a figure that was not just sensational, but very durable, too. Some women my age, or younger, 've got breasts that look like a couple of mules hangin' their heads over the top rail of a fence. [*Touches her bosom.*] This is natural, not padded, not supported, and nothing's ever been lifted. Hell, I was born between a swamp and the wrong side of the tracks in One Street, Georgia, but not even that could stop me in my tracks, wrong side or right side, or no side. Hit show-biz at fifteen when a carnival show, I mean the manager of it, saw me and dug me on that *one street* in One Street, Georgia, I was billed at the Dixie Doxy, was just supposed to move my anatomy, but was smart enough to keep my tongue moving, too, and the verbal comments I made on my anatomical motions while in motion were a public delight. So I breezed through show-biz like a tornado, rising from one-week "gigs" in the sticks to star billing in the Follies while still in m'teens, ho ho . . . and I was still in my teens when I married Harlon Goforth, a marriage into the Social Register and Dun and Bradstreet's, both. Was barely out of my teens when I became his widow. Scared to make out a will, he died intestate, so everything went to me.

CHRIS: Marvelous. Amazing.

MRS. GOFORTH: That's right. All my life was and still is, except here, lately I'm a little run down, like a race horse that's been entered in just one race too many, even for me. . . . How do *you* feel about being a legend in your own lifetime? Huh?

CHRIS: Oh, *me!* I don't feel like a—mythological—griffin with gold wings, but this strong fresh wind's reviving me like I'd had a—terrific breakfast!

MRS. GOFORTH: Griffin, what's a griffin?

CHRIS: A force in life that's almost stronger than death. [*He springs up and turns to the booming sea.*] The sea's full of white race horses today. May I—would you mind if I—suggested a program for us? A picnic on the beach, rest on the rocks in the sun till nearly sundown, then we'd come back up here revitalized for whatever the lovely evening had to offer?

MRS. GOFORTH: What do you think it would have to offer?

CHRIS: Dinner on the terrace with the sea still booming? How is that for a program? Say, with music, a couple of tarantella dancers brought up from the village, and—

[RUDY *appears on the terrace.*]

RUDY: Mrs. Goforth, I've taken care of that for you. They're going—on the way out.

MRS. GOFORTH: No trouble?

RUDY: Oh, yeah, sure, they want to see the Signora.

MRS. GOFORTH: No, no, no. I won't see them!

[*But "they" are appearing upstage: the members of her kitchen staff, who have been discharged.*]

Here they come, hold them back!

[*She staggers up, turns her back on them. They cry out to her in Italian.* RUDY *rushes upstage and herds them violently off. A wave crashes.*]

CHRIS [*quietly*]: Boom. What was their—?

MRS. GOFORTH: What?

CHRIS: —transgression?

MRS. GOFORTH: They'd been robbing me blind. He caught them at it. We had—an inventory and discovered that—they'd been robbing me blind like I was—blind. . . .

CHRIS [*his back to her, speaking as if to himself*]: When a wave breaks down there, it looks as delicate as a white lace fan, but I bet if it hit you, it would knock you against the rocks and break your bones. . . .

MRS. GOFORTH. What?

CHRIS: I said it's so wonderful here, after yesterday in Naples. . . .

MRS. GOFORTH: What was wrong with yesterday in Naples? Were you picked up for vagrancy in Naples?

CHRIS: I wasn't picked up for anything in Naples.

MRS. GOFORTH: That's worse than being picked up for vagrancy, baby.

69

[*She chuckles. He grins agreeably.*]

CHRIS: Mrs. Goforth, I'm going to tell you the truth.

MRS. GOFORTH: The truth is all you could tell me that I'd believe—so tell me the truth, Mr. Flanders.

CHRIS: I'll go back a little further than Naples, Mrs. Goforth. I'd drawn out all my savings to come over here this summer on a Jugoslavian freighter that landed at Genoa.

MRS. GOFORTH: You're leading up to financial troubles, aren't you?

CHRIS: Not so much that as—something harder, much harder, for me to deal with, a state of— Well, let me put it this way. Everybody has a sense of *reality* of some kind or other, some kind of sense of things being real or not real in his, his—particular —world. . . .

MRS. GOFORTH: I know what you mean. Go on.

CHRIS: I've lost it lately, this sense of reality in my particular world. We don't all live in the same world, you know, Mrs. Goforth. Oh, we all see the same things—sea, sun, sky, human faces and inhuman faces, but—they're different in *here!* [*Touches his forehead.*] And one person's sense of reality can be another person's sense of—well, of madness!—chaos!—and, and—

MRS. GOFORTH: Go on. I'm still with you.

CHRIS: And when one person's sense of reality, or loss of sense of reality, disturbs another one's sense of reality—I know how mixed up this—

MRS. GOFORTH: Not a bit, clear as a bell, so keep on, y'haven't lost my attention.

CHRIS: Being able to talk: wonderful! When one person's sense of reality seems too—disturbingly different from another person's, uh—

70

MRS. GOFORTH: Sense of reality. Continue.

CHRIS: Well, he's—avoided! Not welcome! It's—*that simple.*
. . . And—yesterday in Naples, I suddenly realized that I was
in that situation. [*He turns to the booming sea and says "Boom."*]
I found out that I was now a—*leper!*

MRS. GOFORTH: Leopard?

CHRIS: *Leper!*—Boom!

[*She ignores the "boom."*]

Yes, you see, they hang labels, tags of false identification on
people that disturb their own sense of reality too much, like
the bells that used to be hung on the necks of—lepers!—Boom!

The lady I'd come over to visit, who lives in a castle on the top
of Ravello, sent me a wire to Naples. I walked to Naples on foot
to pick it up, and picked it up at American Express in Naples,
and what it said was: "Not yet, not ready for you, dear—Angel
of—Death. . . ."

[*She regards him a bit uncomfortably. He smiles very warmly
at her; she relaxes.*]

MRS. GOFORTH: Ridiculous!

CHRIS: Yes, and inconvenient since I'd—

MRS. GOFORTH: Invested all your remaining capital in this standing invitation that had stopped standing, collapsed, ho, ho, ho!

CHRIS: —Yes . . .

MRS. GOFORTH: Who's this bitch at Ravello?

CHRIS: I'd rather forget her name, now.

MRS. GOFORTH: But you see you young people, well, you
reasonably young people who used to be younger, you get in
the habit of being sort of—professional house guests, and as you

71

get a bit older, and who doesn't get a bit older, some more than just a *bit* older, you're still professional house guests, and—

CHRIS: Yes?

MRS. GOFORTH: Oh, you have charm, all of you, you still have your good looks and charm and you all do something creative, such as writing but not writing, and painting but not painting, and that goes fine for a time but—

CHRIS: You've made your point, Mrs. Goforth.

MRS. GOFORTH: No, not yet, quite yet. Your case is special. You've gotten a special nickname, "dear Angel of Death." And it's lucky for you I couldn't be less superstitious, deliberately walk under ladders, think a black cat's as lucky as a white cat, am only against the human cats of this world, of which there's no small number. So! What're you looking around for, Angel of Death, as they call you?

CHRIS: I would love to have some buttered toast with my coffee.

MRS. GOFORTH: Oh, no toast with *my* coffee, buttered, un-buttered—no toast. For breakfast I have only black coffee. Any-thing solid takes the edge off my energy, and it's the time after breakfast when I do my best work.

CHRIS: What are you working on?

MRS. GOFORTH: My memories, my memoirs, night and day, to meet the publisher's deadlines. The pressure has brought on a sort of nervous breakdown, and I'm enjoying every minute of it because it has taken the form of making me absolutely frank and honest with people. No more pretenses, although I was always frank and honest with people, comparatively. But now much more so. No more pretenses at all . . .

CHRIS: It's wonderful.

MRS. GOFORTH: What?

CHRIS: That you and I have happened to meet at just this time, because I have reached the same point in my life as you say you have come to in yours.

MRS. GOFORTH [suspiciously]: What? Which? Point?

CHRIS: The point you mentioned, the point of no more pretenses.

MRS. GOFORTH: You say you've reached that point, too?

[CHRIS *nods, smiling warmly.*]

Hmmmm.

[*The sound is skeptical and so is the look she gives him.*]

CHRIS: It's *true*, I *have*, Mrs. Goforth.

MRS. GOFORTH: I don't mean to call you a liar or even a phantasist, but I don't see how you could afford to arrive at the point of no more pretenses, Chris.

CHRIS: I probably couldn't afford to arrive at that point any more than I could afford to travel this summer.

MRS. GOFORTH: Hmmm. I see. But you traveled?

CHRIS: Yes, mostly on foot, Mrs. Goforth—since—Genoa.

MRS. GOFORTH [*rising and walking near the balustrade*]: One of the reasons I took this place here is because it's supposed to be inaccessible except from the sea. Between here and the highway there's just a goatpath, hardly possible to get down, and I thought impossible to get up. Hmm. Yes. Well. But you got yourself up.

CHRIS [*pouring the last of the coffee*]: I had to. I had to get up it.

73

MRS. GOFORTH [*turning back to him and sitting*]: Let's play the truth game. Do you know the truth game?

CHRIS: Yes, but I don't like it. I've always made excuses to get out of it when it's played at parties because I think the truth is too delicate and, well, *dangerous* a thing to be played with at parties, Mrs. Goforth. It's nitroglycerin, it has to be handled with the—the carefulest care, or somebody hurts somebody and gets hurt back and the party turns to a—devastating explosion, people crying, people screaming, people even fighting and throwing things at each other. I've seen it happen, and there's no truth in it—that's true.

MRS. GOFORTH: But you say you've reached the same point that I have this summer, the point of no more pretenses, so why can't we play the truth game together, huh, Chris?

CHRIS: Why don't we put it off till—say, after—supper?

MRS. GOFORTH: You play it better on a full stomach, do you?

CHRIS: Yes, you have to be physically fortified for it as well as —morally fortified for it.

MRS. GOFORTH: And you'd like to stay for supper? You don't have any other engagement for supper?

CHRIS: I have no engagements of any kind now, Mrs. Goforth.

MRS. GOFORTH: Well, I don't know about supper. Sometimes I don't want any.

CHRIS: How about after—?

MRS. GOFORTH: —What?

CHRIS: After lunch?

MRS. GOFORTH: Oh, sometimes I don't have lunch, either.

CHRIS: You're not on a healthful regime. You know, the spirit

74

has to live in the body, and so you have to keep the body in a state of repair because it's the home of the—spirit. . . .

MRS. GOFORTH: Hmmm. Are you talking about your spirit and body, or mine?

CHRIS: Yours.

MRS. GOFORTH: One long-ago meeting between us, and you expect me to believe you care more about my spirit and body than your own, Mr. Flanders?

CHRIS: Mrs. Goforth, some people, some people, most of them, get panicky when they're not cared for by somebody, but I get panicky when I have no one to care for.

MRS. GOFORTH: Oh, you seem to be setting yourself up as a— as a saint of some kind. . . .

CHRIS: All I said is I need somebody to care for. I don't say that— [*He has finished his coffee and he crosses to the warmer for more.*] I'm playing the truth game with you. Caring for somebody gives me the sense of being—sheltered, protected. . . .

MRS. GOFORTH: "Sheltered, protected" from what?

CHRIS [*standing above her*]: Unreality!—lostness? Have you ever seen how two little animals sleep together, a pair of kittens or puppies? All day they seem so secure in the house of their master, but at night, when they sleep, they don't seem sure of their owner's true care for them. Then they draw close together, they curl up against each other, and now and then, if you watch them, you notice they nudge each other a little with their heads or their paws, exchange little signals between them. The signals mean: we're not in danger . . . sleep: we're close: it's safe here. Their owner's house is never a sure protection, a reliable shelter. Everything going on in it is mysterious to them, and no matter how hard they try to please, how do they know if they please? They hear so many sounds, voices, and see so many things they

75

can't comprehend! Oh, it's ever so much better than the petshop window, but what's become of their mother?—who warmed them and sheltered them and fed them until they were snatched away from her, for no reason they know. We're all of us living in a house we're not used to . . . a house full of—voices, noises, objects, strange shadows, light that's even stranger— We can't understand. We bark and jump around and try to—be—*pleasingly playful* in this big mysterious house but—in our hearts we're all very frightened of it. Don't you think so? Then it gets to be dark. We're left alone with each other. We have to creep close to each other and give those gentle little nudges with our paws and our muzzles before we can slip into—sleep and—rest for the next day's—playtime . . . and the next day's mysteries.

[*He lights a cigarette for her.* THE WITCH *enters dramatically on the terrace.*]

THE WITCH: The next day's mysteries! *Ecco, sono qui.*

MRS. GOFORTH [*with unconcealed displeasure*]: My Lord, are you still here?

THE WITCH [*as if amazed*]: Christopher! Flanders!

CHRIS: How do you do, Mrs.— Oh, I started to say Mrs. Ridgeway but that isn't it, now, is it?

THE WITCH: What a back number you are!

CHRIS [*drawing away from her*]: Yes.

MRS. GOFORTH: How'd you miss your return trip to Capri last night? I thought you'd gone back there last night. I had the boatman waiting up for you last night.

THE WITCH: Oh, last *night!* What confusion! [*She puts down her hat and follows* CHRIS.] When was the last time I saw you?

MRS. GOFORTH: If *you* don't know, why should he?

76

THE WITCH: Oh, at the wedding banquet those Texas oil people gave me in Portofino, oh, yes, you were staying with them, and so depressed over the loss of—

CHRIS [*cutting in*]: Yes. [*He moves toward the balustrade.*]

THE WITCH: You'd taken such beautiful care of that poor old ridiculous woman, but couldn't save her, and, oh, the old Duke of Parma did such a wicked thing to you, poured champagne on your head and—called you—what did he call you?

MRS. GOFORTH: Let him forget it, Connie.

[THE WITCH *gives her a glance and moves up to* CHRIS.]

THE WITCH: Something else awful happened and you were involved in some way but I can't remember the details.

CHRIS: Yes, it's better forgotten, Mrs. Goforth is right. Some of the details are much better forgotten if you'll let me—forget them. . . .

[MRS. GOFORTH *rises and starts to go inside.*]

THE WITCH: Are you leaving us, Sissy?

MRS. GOFORTH: I'm going to phone the boat house t'make sure there's a boat ready for your trip back to Capri, because I know you want back there as soon as possible, Connie. [*She goes into the library.*]

THE WITCH [*going to the table*]: Chris, you're not intending to *stay* here!?

CHRIS: Yes, if I'm invited: I would like to.

THE WITCH: Don't you know, can't you tell? Poor Sissy's going, she's gone. The shock I got last night when I—I had to drink myself blind!—when I saw her condition! [*She comes closer to him.*] You don't want to be stuck with a person in her appalling condition. You're young, have fun. Oh, Chris, you've been

77

foolish too long. The years you devoted to that old Ferguson bitch, and what did you get?

CHRIS [*lighting a cigarette*]: Get?

THE WITCH: Yes, get? She *had* you, you were *had!—left* you? *Nothing!*—I bet, or why would you be here?

CHRIS: Please don't make me be rude. We don't understand each other, which is natural, but don't make me say things to you that I don't want to say.

THE WITCH: What can you say to me that I haven't heard said?

CHRIS: Have you heard this said to your face about you: that you're the heart of a world that has no heart, the heartless world you live in—has anyone said that to you, Mrs. Ridgeway?

THE WITCH: Condotti, Marchesa Ridgeway-Condotti, Mr. Death Angel Flanders.

CHRIS: Yes, we both have new titles.

THE WITCH [*throwing back her head*]: Sally! Laurie! Sissy! It's time for death, old girls, beddy-bye! [*Less shrilly.*] Beddy-bye, old girls, the Death Angel's coming, no dreams . . .

CHRIS: I'm sorry you forced me to say what I feel about you.

THE WITCH: Oh, that. My heart pumps blood that isn't my own blood, it's the blood of anonymous blood donors. And as for the world I live in, you know it as well as I know it. Come to Capri, it's a mountain, too.

CHRIS [*moving away*]: You're not afraid of the nickname I've been given?

THE WITCH: No, I think it's a joke that you take seriously, Chris. You've gotten too solemn. [*She follows him.*] Let me take that curse off you. Come to Capri and I'll give you a party, decorated with your mobiles, and—

MRS. GOFORTH [*to* BLACKIE]: *See? She's out there putting the make on—*

[BLACKIE *leaves as* MRS. GOFORTH *comes from the library toward the terrace.*]

THE WITCH [*to* CHRIS]: You're pale, you look anemic, you look famished, you need someone to put you back in the picture, the social swim. Capri?

[MRS. GOFORTH, *on the terrace, advances behind* CHRIS *and* THE WITCH.]

MRS. GOFORTH: What picture? What swim? Capri?

THE WITCH: It's marvelous there this season.

MRS. GOFORTH: The sea is full of Medusas. Didn't you tell me the sea is full of Medusas, and a giant one got you?

THE WITCH [*crossing to her*]: Oh, they'll wash out, they'll be washed out by tomorrow.

MRS. GOFORTH: When are *you* going to wash out? I thought you'd washed out last night. I've ordered a boat to take you back to Capri.

THE WITCH: I can't go back to Capri in a dinner gown before sundown. [*She sits at the table and stares at* CHRIS.]

MRS. GOFORTH: Well, try my hot sulphur baths, or just look the place over, it's worth it. It's worth looking over. Me, I'm about to start work, so I can't talk to you right now. [*She gets* THE WITCH's *hat and brings it to her.*] I'm right on the edge of breaking through here today, I'm on a strict discipline, Connie, as I explained last night to you, and—[*She coughs, falls into her chair.*]

THE WITCH: Sissy, I don't like that cough.

MRS. GOFORTH: Hell, do you think I like it? Neuralgia, nerves, overwork, but I'm going to beat it, it isn't going to beat *me*, or it'll be the first thing that ever *did* beat me!

THE WITCH [*rising and going to her*]: Be brave, Sissy.

MRS. GOFORTH: Leave me alone, go, Connie, it'll do you in, too. [*She fumbles for a tissue.*]

THE WITCH [*looking wide-eyed at* CHRIS *and moving close to him*]: Watch out for each other!— Chris, give her the Swami's book you translated. *Ciao!* [*She throws him a kiss and moves off, calling back.*] *Questo è veramente una meraviglia . . . Ciao, arrivederci. . . . Amici!*

[THE WITCH *goes out of the lighted area and down the goat-path.* CHRIS *goes to the table and sits, looking about.*]

MRS. GOFORTH: What are you looking for now?

CHRIS: I was just looking for the cream and sugar.

MRS. GOFORTH: Never touch it. Y'want a saccharine tablet?

CHRIS: Oh, no, thanks, I—don't like the chemical taste.

MRS. GOFORTH [*coming to the table*]: Well, it's black coffee or else, I'm afraid, Mr. What?—Chris!

CHRIS: You have *three* villas here?

MRS. GOFORTH: One villa and two villinos. Villino means a small villa. I also have a little grass hut, very Polynesian—[*moving in front of the table*]—down on my private beach too. I have a special use for it, and a funny name for it, too.

CHRIS: Oh?

MRS. GOFORTH: Yes, I call it "the Oubliette." Ever heard of an oubliette?

CHRIS: A place where people are put to be forgotten?

80

MRS. GOFORTH: That's right, Chris. You've had some education along that line. [*She returns to where he sits.*]

CHRIS: Yes, quite a lot, Mrs. Goforth, especially lately.

MRS. GOFORTH: As for the use of it, well, I've been plagued by imposters lately, the last few summers. The continent has been overrun by imposters of celebrities, writers, actors, and so forth. I mean they arrive and say, like "I am Truman Capote." Well, they look a bit like him so you are taken in by the announcement, "I am Truman Capote," and you receive him cordially only to find out later it isn't the true Truman Capote, it's the false Truman Capote. Last summer I had the false Truman Capote, and the year before that I had the false Mary McCarthy. That's before I took to checking the passports of sudden visitors. Well—[*She moves to the opposite chair and sits facing him.*] as far as I know they're still down there in that little grass hut on the beach, where undesirables are transferred to, when the villas are overcrowded. The Oubliette. A medieval institution that I think, personally, was discarded too soon. It was a dungeon, where people were put for keeps to be forgotten. You say you know about it?

[CHRIS *stares straight at her, not answering by word or gesture. His look is gentle, troubled.*]

So that's what I call my little grass shack on the beach, I call it "the Oubliette" from the French verb *"oublier"* which means to forget, to forget, to put away and—

CHRIS: —forget. . . .

MRS. GOFORTH: And I do really forget 'em. Maybe you think I'm joking but it's the truth. Can't stand to be made a Patsy. Understand what I mean?

[*He nods.*]

This is nothing personal. You came with your book—[*picks up*

81

his book of poetry] with a photograph of you on it, which still looks like you just, well, ten years younger, but still unmistakably you. You're not the false Chris Flanders, I'm sure about that.

CHRIS: Thank you. I try not to be.

MRS. GOFORTH: However, I don't keep up with the new personalities in the world of art like I used to. Too much a waste of vital energy, Chris. Of course you're not exactly a new personality in it: would you say so?

[CHRIS *smiles and shakes his head slightly.*]

You're almost a veteran in it. I said a veteran, I didn't say a "has been—[*She sneezes violently.*] I'm allergic to something around here. I haven't found out just what, but when I do, oh, brother, watch it go!

CHRIS [*rising and bringing her a clean tissue*]: I hope it isn't the bougainvillaea vines.

MRS. GOFORTH: No, it isn't the bougainvillaea, but I'm having an allergy specialist flown down here from Rome to check me with every goddamn plant and animal on the place, and whatever it is has to go.

CHRIS: Have you tried breathing sea water?

MRS. GOFORTH: Oh, you want to drown me?

CHRIS [*returning to his chair and sitting*]: Ha ha, no. I meant have you tried snuffing it up in your nostrils to irrigate your nasal passages, Mrs. Goforth, it's sometimes a very effective treatment for—

MRS. GOFORTH: Aside from this allergy and a little neuralgia, sometimes more than a little, I'm a healthy woman. Know how I've kept in shape, my body, the way it still is?

CHRIS: Exercise?

MRS. GOFORTH: Yes! In bed! Plenty of it, still going on! . . . But there's this worship of youth in the States, this Whistler's Mother complex, you know what I mean, this idea that at a certain age a woman ought to resign herself to being a sweet old thing in a rocker. Well, last week-end, a man, a *young* man, came in my bedroom and it wasn't too easy to get him out of it. I had to be very firm about it.

[BLACKIE *appears on the terrace with a plate of food for* CHRIS. MRS. GOFORTH *rises.*]

What've you got there, Blackie?

BLACKIE: Mr. Flanders' breakfast. I'm sure he would like some.

MRS. GOFORTH: Aw, now, isn't that thoughtful. Put it down there.

[*As* BLACKIE *starts to put it down on the table,* MRS. GOFORTH *indicates the serving table.*

I said down there. And get me my menthol inhaler and Kleenex. I have run out.

[BLACKIE *sets the plate on the serving table and retires from the lighted area.*

Simonetta!

[MRS. GOFORTH *rings and hands the tray to* SIMONETTA *as she enters.*]

Take this away. I can't stand the smell of food now.

[SIMONETTA *goes out.*]

CHRIS [*who has moved toward the serving table and stands stunned*]: Mrs. Goforth, I feel that I have, I must have disturbed

83

you, annoyed you—disturbed you because I—[*He crosses back to the table.*]

MRS. GOFORTH: Don't reach for a cigarette till I offer you one.

CHRIS: May I have one, Mrs. Goforth?

MRS. GOFORTH: Take one. Be my Trojan Horse Guest. Wait.

[*She moves beside him.*]

Kiss me for it.

[CHRIS *doesn't move.*]

Kiss me for it, I told you.

CHRIS [*putting the cigarette away*]: Mrs. Goforth, there are moments for kisses and moments not for kisses.

MRS. GOFORTH: This is a "not for kiss" moment?

[*He turns away, and she follows and takes his arm.*]

I've shocked *you* by my ferocity, have I? Sometimes I shock myself by it.

[*They move together toward the balustrade.*]

Look: a coin has two sides. On one side is an eagle, but on the other side is—something else. . . .

CHRIS: Yes, something else, usually some elderly potentate's profile.

[*She laughs appreciatively at his riposte and touches his shoulder. He moves a step away from her.*]

MRS. GOFORTH: Why didn't you grab the plate and run off with it?

CHRIS: Like a dog grabs a bone?

MRS. GOFORTH: Sure! Why not? It might've pleased me to see you show some fight.

CHRIS: I can fight if I have to, but the fighting style of dogs is not my style.

MRS. GOFORTH: *Grab, fight, or go hungry!* Nothing else works.

CHRIS: How is it possible for a woman of your reputation as a patron of arts and artists, to live up here, with all this beauty about you, and yet be—

MRS. GOFORTH: A bitch, a swamp-bitch, a devil? Oh, I see it, the view, but it makes me feel ugly this summer for some reason or other—bitchy, a female devil.

CHRIS: You'd like the view to be ugly to make you feel superior to it?

MRS. GOFORTH: [*turning to him*]: Why don't we sing that old church hymn:
"From Greenland's icy mountains to India's coral Isle
Everything is beautiful . . ."

CHRIS: "Man alone is vile."

MRS. GOFORTH: Hmm. Devils can be driven out of the heart by the touch of a hand on a hand, or a mouth on a mouth. Because, like Alex said once, "Evil isn't a person: evil is a thing that comes sneaky-snaking into the heart of a person, and takes it over: a mean intruder, a *squatter!*"

CHRIS: May I touch your hand, please?

MRS. GOFORTH [*as he does*]: Your hand's turned cold. I've shocked the warm blood out of it. Let me rub it back in.

CHRIS: Your hand's cold, too, Mrs. Goforth.

MRS. GOFORTH: Oh, that's just—nervous tension, never mind

85

that. I'll tell you something, Chris, you came here at a time unusually favorable to you. Now we're going to talk turkey. At least *I'm* going to talk turkey. You can talk ducks and geese, but I am going to talk turkey, cold turkey. You've come here at a time when I'm restless, bored, and shocked by the news of deaths of three friends in the States, one, two, three, like fire-crackers going off, right together almost, like rat-a-tat-tat blindfolded against the wall.— Well, you see I— [*She moves down to the lower terrace.*] I had a bad scare last winter. I was visiting relatives I'd set up on a grand estate on Long Island when some little psychosomatic symptom gave me a scare. They made a big deal of it, had me removed by a seaplane to the East River where they had an ambulance waiting for me, and whisked me off to a— Know what I said when I was advised to go under the knife the next day? Ha, I'll tell you, ha ha!— Called my law firm and dictated a letter cutting them off with one dollar apiece in my will. . . .

CHRIS [*who has come down to her*]: Mrs. Goforth, are you still afraid of— [*He hesitates.*]

MRS. GOFORTH: Death—never even think of it. [*She takes his arm and they move down to a bench, and sit.*]

CHRIS: Death is one moment, and life is so many of them.

MRS. GOFORTH: A million billion of them, if you think in terms of a lifetime as rich as mine's been, Chris.

CHRIS: Yes, life is something, death's nothing. . . .

MRS. GOFORTH: Nothing, nothing, but nothing. I've had to refer to many deaths in my memoirs. Oh, I don't think I'm immortal—I still go to sleep every night wondering if I'll—wake up the next day . . . [*Coughs and gasps for breath.*] —face that angry old lion.

CHRIS: Angry old—?

MRS. GOFORTH: —lion!

CHRIS: The sun? You think it's angry?

MRS. GOFORTH: Naturally, of course—looking down on—? Well, you know what it look down on. . . .

CHRIS: It seems to accept and understand things today. . . .

MRS. GOFORTH: It's just a big fire-ball that toughens the skin, including the skin of the heart.

CHRIS: How lovely the evenings must be here—when the fishing boats go out on the Gulf of Salerno with their little lamps shining.

MRS. GOFORTH: Well, they call this coast the *Divina Costiera*. That means the divine coast, you know.

CHRIS: Yes, I know. I suppose . . .

MRS. GOFORTH: You suppose what?

CHRIS: I suppose you dine on the terrace about the time the fishing boats go out with their little lamps and the stars come out of the—

MRS. GOFORTH: Firmament. Call it the firmament, not the sky, it's much more classy to call it the firmament, baby. How about spring? You write about spring and live in it, you write about love in the spring, haven't you written love-poems for susceptible—patrons?— Well! How many books of poems have you come out with?

CHRIS: Just the one that I brought you.

MRS. GOFORTH: You mean you burnt out as a poet?

CHRIS: —Pardon?

MRS. GOFORTH: You mean you burnt out as a poet?

[CHRIS *laughs uncomfortably.*]

Why're you laughing? I didn't say anything funny.

CHRIS: I didn't know I was laughing. Excuse me, Mrs. Goforth. But you are very—direct.

MRS. GOFORTH: Is that shocking?

CHRIS: No. No, not really. In fact I like that about you.

MRS. GOFORTH: But you give that little embarrassed laugh, like I'd made you uncomfortable.

CHRIS: My nerves are—

MRS. GOFORTH: Gone through like your list of suckers. [MRS. GOFORTH *sneezes and gets up to look for another tissue.*]

CHRIS [*standing*]: Mrs. Goforth—if you want me to go—

MRS. GOFORTH: That depends.

CHRIS: What does it depend on?

MRS. GOFORTH: Frankly, I'm very lonely up here this summer.

CHRIS: I can understand that.

MRS. GOFORTH: Now, you're not stupid. You're attractive to me. You know that you are. You've deliberately set out to be attractive to me, and you are. So don't be a free-loader.

[CHRIS *doesn't speak for a moment.*]

CHRIS [*gently*]: Mrs. Goforth, I think you've been exposed to the wrong kind of people and—

MRS. GOFORTH [*cutting in*]: I'm sick of moral blackmail! You know what that is. People imposing on you by the old, old trick of making you feel it would be unkind of you not to permit them to do it. In their hearts they despise you. So much they can't quite hide it. It pops out in sudden little remarks

88

and looks they give you. Busting with malice—because you have what they haven't. You know what some writer called that? "A robust conscience, and the Viking spirit in life!"

CHRIS [*going back on the terrace*]: Oh? Is that what he called it?

MRS. GOFORTH [*following*]: He called it that, and I have it! I give away nothing, I sell and I buy in my life, and I've always wound up with a profit, one way or another. You came up that hill from the highway with an old book of poems that you got published ten years ago, by playing on the terrible, desperate loneliness of a rich old broken-hipped woman, who, all she could do, was pretend that someone still loved her. . . .

CHRIS: You're talking about Mrs. Ferguson.

MRS. GOFORTH: Yes, I am.

CHRIS [*moving away from her*]: I made her walk again. She published my poems.

MRS. GOFORTH: How long after she published your poems did you let go of her arm so she fell on the deck of a steamship and her hip broke again?

CHRIS: I didn't let her go. She broke away from me—

[MRS. GOFORTH *laughs uproariously*]

—if you'll allow me to make a minor correction in the story. We were walking very slowly about the promenade deck of the *Queen Mary*, eight summers ago, more than a year after my poems were published. A young man called to her from a deck chair that we'd just passed, and she wheeled around and broke away from my hand, and slipped and fell, and her hip was broken again. Of course some malicious "friends" blamed me, but—I wouldn't leave her.

MRS. GOFORTH: No? She was still your meal-ticket?

89

CHRIS: Not at all.

MRS. GOFORTH: Who *was*?

CHRIS [*sitting*]: I was fashionable, then.

MRS. GOFORTH: Do you sit down while a lady is standing?

CHRIS [*springing up with a rather ferocious smile*]: Sorry, won't you sit down!

[*His tone is so commanding, abruptly, that she does sit down in the chair he jerks out for her.*]

May I tell you something about yourself? It may seem presumptuous of me to tell you this, but I'm going to tell you this: you're suffering more than you need to.

MRS. GOFORTH: I am—

CHRIS [*cutting through her protest*]: You're suffering from the worst of all human maladies, of all afflictions, and I don't mean one of the body, I mean the thing people feel when they go from room to room for no reason, and then they go back from room to room for no reason, and then they go *out* for no reason and come back *in* for no reason—

MRS. GOFORTH: You mean I'm alone here, don't you?

[CHRIS *takes hold of her hand. She snatches it away from him.*]

I'm *working* up here this summer, *working! Ever heard of it?*

[*A* STAGE ASSISTANT *appears in the wings as if she had shouted for him. He hands her a letter.*]

This morning's mail brought me this! My London publisher's letter! "Darling Flora: Your book of memoirs, *Facts and a Figure*, will, in my opinion, rank with and possibly—"

[*She squints, unable to decipher the letter further.* CHRIS *re-*

SCENE FIVE

*moves it from her trembling, jeweled hand, and completes
the reading.*]

CHRIS: "—rank with and possibly even out-rank the great
Marcel Proust's *Remembrance of Things Past* as a social docu-
mentation of two continents in three decades. . . ."

MRS. GOFORTH: Well?

CHRIS: A letter like this should fall on a higher mountain.

MRS. GOFORTH: Huh?

CHRIS: A letter like this should be delivered above the snow
line of an Alpine peak because it's snow, a snow job.

[*She snatches it back from him.*]

MRS. GOFORTH [*raging*]: For you, a blond beatnik, coming
from Naples on foot up a goddamn goatpath, wearing at this
table a Japanese robe because dogs tore your britches, I think
your presumption is not excusable, Mister! It lacks the excuse
of much youth, you're not young enough for your moxey.
This publisher's not a lover. A lover might snow me, but this
man's a business associate, and they don't snow you, not *me*,
not *Sissy Goforth!* They don't snow me—*snow me!* They don't
get up that early in the morning—

[*Her agitation somehow touches him. His smile turns warm
again.*]

—that they could— [*coughs*] snow me. . . .

[*The STAGE ASSISTANTS lean, whispering together, as they
retire from the stage.*]

CHRIS: Of course, without having your publisher's advantage
of knowing *Facts and a Figure*—

MRS. GOFORTH: Nothing, not a word of it!

91

CHRIS: No, not a word, but what I was going to say was that I think you need *companionship*, not just employees about you, up here, but— How often do you see old friends or new friends this summer, Mrs. Goforth? Often or not so often?

MRS. GOFORTH: Hell, all I have to do is pick up a phone to crowd this mountain with—

CHRIS: Crowds? Is it that easy this summer? You're proud. You don't want to ask people up here that might not come, because they're pleasure-seekers, frantic choosers of silly little distractions, and—and—

MRS. GOFORTH: "and—and" *what?*

CHRIS: Your condition, the terrible strain of your work, makes you seem—eccentric, disturbing!— To those sea-level, those lower-than-sea-level, people. . . .

MRS. GOFORTH: *Get to whatever you're leading up to, will you!*

CHRIS: I notice you have trouble reading. I've been told I have a good reading voice.

MRS. GOFORTH: Most human voices are very monotonous to me. Besides, I'm more interested in producing literature this summer than having it read to me.

CHRIS: Mmm—but you do need some agreeable companionship.

MRS. GOFORTH: Right you are about *that*, but how do I know your idea of agreeable companionship is the same as mine? You purr at me like a cat, now, but a cat will purr at you one minute and scratch your eyes out the next.

[*He leans back, smiling, working the sword up and down in its scabbard.*]

I think you better take off that old sword belt.

CHRIS: There're no buttons on the robe, so without the belt on it—

MRS. GOFORTH: Take it off you!

CHRIS: The *robe?*

MRS. GOFORTH: The *sword* belt. You grin and fiddle with the hilt—the sword—like you had—evil—intentions.

CHRIS: Oh. You suspect I'm a possible assassin?

MRS. GOFORTH: *Take it off, give it here!*

CHRIS: All right. Formal surrender, *unconditional . . . nearly.* [*He takes the sword belt off and hands it to her.*]

MRS. GOFORTH: *O.K., Robert E. Lee! At Appomattox . . .*

[*She hurls the sword belt to the terrace tiles behind her. A* STAGE ASSISTANT *darts out of the wings to remove it. The other* ASSISTANT *laughs off stage.*]

CHRIS: Now what can I use for a sash to keep things proper?

MRS. GOFORTH: See if this goes around you, if being proper's so important to you.

[*She hands him a brilliant scarf she has been wearing about her throat. He turns upstage to tie the scarf about him. A phone is heard ringing, off stage.* BLACKIE *appears from behind the library screen.*]

MRS. GOFORTH [*to* BLACKIE]: Who's calling? My broker again, with the closing quotations?

BLACKIE: The call's for *Mr. Flanders.*

CHRIS: *Me*, for *me?* But who could know I'm up here!

MRS. GOFORTH: Cut the bull. You got a call up here last night. Business is picking up for you.

CHRIS: This is—mystifying!

BLACKIE: The phone's in the library.

CHRIS: Excuse me.

[*He goes quickly behind the library screen.* MRS. GOFORTH *crosses toward it but remains, listening, outside it.*]

CHRIS [*behind screen*]: Pronto, pronto. Madelyn!— How are you, how's your dear mother?— Oh, my God!— I meant to come straight down there but—was it, uh, what they call peaceful? [*Pause.*] Oh, I'm so glad, I prayed so hard that it *would* be! And I'm so relieved that it *was*. I did so long to be with you but had to stop on the way. And you? Will you be all right? Yes, I know, *expected*, but still I could be some use in making the necessary arrangements? I'm at Flora Goforth's place, but if you could send a car to pick me up I could— Oh?— Oh?— Well, Madelyn, all I can say is *accept* it.— Bless you, goodbye. *Accept* it.

[MRS. GOFORTH *is shaken. She moves to the table as if she had received a personal shock.* CHRIS *comes back out. At the same moment, church bells ring in a village below the mountain.*]

CHRIS: —Church bells? In the village?

MRS. GOFORTH: Yes, appropriate, aren't they? Ringing right on a dead cue . . .

CHRIS: I just received news that's—*shocked* me. . . .

MRS. GOFORTH: Another name you have to scratch off the list?

CHRIS: Did you say "list"?

MRS. GOFORTH [*smiling at him cunningly, fiercely*]: I went to a spiritualist once. She said to me, "I hear many dead voices calling, 'Flora, Flora.'" I knew she was a fake, then, since all my close friends call me Sissy. I said, "Tell them to mind their own business, play their gold harps and mind their own harp-playing. Sissy Goforth's not ready to go forth yet and won't go forth till she's ready. . . ."

[CHRIS *extends a hand to her. The bells stop ringing.*]

What are you reaching out for?

CHRIS: Your hand, if I may, Mrs. Goforth. [*He has taken hold of it.*]

MRS. GOFORTH: Hold it but don't squeeze it. The rings cut my fingers.

CHRIS: I'm glad we've talked so frankly, so quickly today. The conversation we had at the ball at the Waldorf in 1950 was a long conversation but not as deep as this one.

MRS. GOFORTH: Who said anything deep? I don't say anything deep in a conversation, not this summer, I save it for my memoirs. Did you say anything deep, in your opinion? If you did, it escaped me, escaped my notice completely. Oh, you've known Swanees. Excuse me, Swamis. You've been exposed to the—intellectual scene, and it's rubbed off on you a little, but only skin-deep, as deep as your little blond beard. . . .

CHRIS: Perhaps I used the wrong word.

[*She places a cigarette in her mouth and waits for him to light it. He turns deliberately away from her, and places a foot on the low balustrade, facing seaward.*]

This "wine-dark sea," it's the oldest sea in the world. . . . Know what I see down there?

MRS. GOFORTH: The sea.

CHRIS: Yes, and a fleet of Roman triremes, those galleys with three banks of oars, rowed by slaves, commanded by commanders headed for conquests. Out for loot. *Boom!* Out for

95

conquering, pillaging, and collecting more slaves. *Boom!* Here's where the whole show started, it's the oldest sea in the Western world, Mrs. Goforth, this sea called the Mediterranean Sea, which means the middle of the earth, was the cradle, of life, not the grave, but the cradle of pagan and Christian—civilizations, this sea, and its connecting river, that old water snake, the Nile.

MRS. GOFORTH: I've been on the Nile. No message. Couple of winters ago I stayed at the Mena House, that hotel under the pyramids. I could see the pyramids, those big–big calcified fools–caps from my breakfast balcony. No message. Rode up to 'em on a camel so I could say I'd done the whole bit.

CHRIS: No message?

MRS. GOFORTH: No message, except you can get seasick on a camel. Yep, you can get mighty seasick on the hump of a camel. Went inside those old king-size tombstones.

CHRIS: No message inside them, either?

MRS. GOFORTH: No message, except the Pharaohs and their families had the idiotic idea they were going to wake up hungry and thirsty and so provided themselves with breakfasts which had gone very stale and dry, and the Pharaohs and families were still sound asleep, ho ho. . . .

[*He still has his back to her. She is obviously annoyed by his loss of attention.*]

And if you look this way, you'll notice I've got a cigarette in my mouth and I'm waiting for you to light it. Didn't that old Sally Ferguson bitch teach you to light a cigarette for a lady?

CHRIS [*facing her*]: She wasn't a bitch, unless all old dying ladies are bitches. She was dying, and scared to death of dying, which made her a little—eccentric . . .

96

[*He has picked up* MRS. GOFORTH'S *diamond-studded lighter. He lights her cigarette but doesn't return the lighter to the table. He tosses it in the palm of his hand.*]

MRS. GOFORTH: Thanks. Now put it down.

[*He sits down, smiling, on the low balustrade. There has occurred a marked change in his surface attitude toward her: the deferential air has gone completely.*

I meant my Bulgari lighter, not your—*backside!*

[*He studies the lighter as if to calculate its value. There is a pause.*]

If you don't put that lighter back down on the table, I'm going to call for Rudy! You know Rudy. You've made his acquaintance, I think.

CHRIS: If I don't put it down on the table but in my pocket, and if I were to run down the goatpath with it—how fast can Rudy run?

MRS. GOFORTH: How fast can *you* run? Could you outrun the dogs? Yesterday you didn't outrun the dogs.

CHRIS: That was—uphill, on the other side of your mountain. I think I could get down this side, yes, by the—funicular, I could operate it.

MRS. GOFORTH: Can you outrun a bullet?

CHRIS: Oh, would you have Rudy shoot at me for this lighter.

MRS. GOFORTH: You bet I would. That's a very valuable lighter.

[CHRIS *laughs and tosses the lighter on the table.*]

CHRIS: Hmmm. On a parapet over the Western world's oldest sea, the lady that owns it had a gangster—

MRS. GOFORTH: The bodyguard of a syndicate gangster!

CHRIS: Yes, the lady that owns it had her bodyguard shoot down a—what?—burnt-out poet who had confiscated a diamond-studded lighter because he was unfed and hungry. He'd been on a five-day fast for—nonsecular reasons, and it had upset his reason.

[MRS. GOFORTH *rings the bell on the table.* CHRIS *seizes her hand and wrests the bell away from it. She rises from the table and shouts: "Rudy!"*]

CHRIS [*louder than she*]: Rudy!

MRS. GOFORTH: You couldn't get away with it!

CHRIS: Oh, yes, I could, if I wanted. [*He tosses the bell back on the table with a mocking grin.*]

MRS. GOFORTH: What a peculiar—puzzlesome young man you are! You came out here like a dandy, kissed my hand, and now you're coming on like a young hood all of a sudden, and I don't like the change, it makes me nervous with you, and now I don't know if I want you around here or not, or if I'm—not superstitious. See? You've made me shaky.

CHRIS: You didn't know I was teasing?

MRS. GOFORTH: No. You're too good at it.

CHRIS: [*looking seaward*]: I see it, your oubliette on the beach, it looks attractive to me.

MRS. GOFORTH: Help me into my bedroom. [*She tries to rise but falls back into the chair.*] It's time for my siesta.

CHRIS: Could I stay there, a while?

MRS. GOFORTH: Later maybe. Not now. I need to rest.

CHRIS: I meant the grass hut on the beach, not your bedroom.

MRS. GOFORTH: Be still, she's coming back out, my secretary, and I'm not sure I trust her.

CHRIS: Do you trust anybody?

MRS. GOFORTH: Nobody human, just dogs. All except poodles, I never trusted a poodle. . . .

[BLACKIE *comes onto the terrace.*]

In again, out again, Finnegan! What's it *this* time, Blackie?

BLACKIE: Is it true you've discharged the kitchen staff again, Mrs. Goforth?

MRS. GOFORTH: Yes, it's true. . . . Haven't you heard about the inventory?

BLACKIE: What inventory, inventory of what?

MRS. GOFORTH: I had an intuition that things were disappearing and had Rudy check my list of fabulous china, my Sèvres, Limoges, Lowestoff, against what was still on the mountain. Half of it gone, decimated! And my Medici silver, banquet silver used by the Medicis hundreds of years ago, *gone!*—That's what the inventory disclosed!

BLACKIE: Mrs. Goforth, is it possible you don't remember—

MRS. GOFORTH: *What?*

BLACKIE: You had it removed to a storage house in Naples, in an armored truck.

MRS. GOFORTH: *Me?*

BLACKIE: *You!*

MRS. GOFORTH: *Not true!*

99

BLACKIE: Mrs. Goforth, when people are very ill and taking drugs for it, they get confused, their memories are confused, they get delusions.

MRS. GOFORTH: *This mountain has been systematically pillaged!* — That's what the inventory—

BLACKIE: An inventory made by the bodyguard of a syndicate gangster?

MRS. GOFORTH: How dare you suggest— *I have a guest at the table!*

BLACKIE: *I will always dare to say what I know to be true!*

MRS. GOFORTH: *Go in, find my checkbook and write out a check for yourself for whatever's coming to you, and bring it out here and I'll sign it for cash, at the Naples branch of my bank! You wanted out, now you got it, so take it! Take it!*

BLACKIE: *Gladly! Gladly!*

MRS. GOFORTH: Mutually *gladly! Go in!*

[BLACKIE *starts to go.* MRS. GOFORTH'S *shouting has brought on a coughing spasm. She covers her mouth with her hands and rushes, in a crouched position, toward the upstage area of the library.*]

CHRIS: —*Boom* . . .

BLACKIE: *Release!*

CHRIS [*pointing at the terrace pavement*]: Blackie? Look!— Blood, she's bleeding. . . .

MRS. GOFORTH'S VOICE [*off stage, hoarsely*]: *Dottore, chiama il dottore! Giulio, Simonetta!*

CHRIS: You'd better go in there with her.

100

BLACKIE: I can't yet. They'll get the doctor for her. [*She moves downstage, gasping.*] You see, she's made me *inhuman!*

[SIMONETTA *explodes onto the forestage.*]

SIMONETTA: *Signorina, la Signora é molto, molto malata!*

BLACKIE [*going toward her*]: *Dov'è la Signora, in camera da letto?*

SIMONETTA: *No, nella biblioteca, con il dottore! [She sits on a bench and sobs hysterically.*]

BLACKIE: Well, I'd better go in there.

CHRIS: What shall I do? Anything?

BLACKIE: Yes, stay here, don't go. [*Then, to* SIMONETTA, *who is now crying theatrically*] *Ferma questa—commedia.*

[SIMONETTA *stops crying, and begins straightening up the table.*]

[*To* CHRIS] Call the hospital in Rome, Salvatore Mundi, and ask for Dr. Rengucci. Tell him what's happening here and a nurse is needed at once. Then come in there, the library, and we'll—

[GIULIO *rushes out onto the forestage.*]

GIULIO: *La Signora Goforth vuol' vedere il Signore, presto, molto presto!*

BLACKIE [*to* CHRIS]: She's calling for *you.* I'd better go in first. Make the call and then come to the library.

[*She goes out one way,* CHRIS *the other.*]

GIULIO [*to* SIMONETTA]: She's dying?

SIMONETTA: No one's been paid this week. Who will pay us if she dies today?

101

GIULIO: *Guarda!*

[*He shows her a gold bracelet.* SIMONETTA *snatches at it.* GIULIO *pockets it with a grin, and starts off as she follows.*]

THE SCENE DIMS OUT.

SCENE SIX

Later the same day, toward sundown. The interiors of the white villa are screened and the terrace is lighted more coolly. BLACKIE *is seated at the downstage table, jotting in a notebook memoranda of things to be done before leaving. The* STAGE ASSISTANTS *stand by the flagstaff ready to lower the banner of* MRS. GOFORTH.

ONE: Cable her daughter that the old bitch is dying.

TWO: The banner of the griffin is about to be lowered.

BLACKIE [*as if translating their speech into a polite paraphrase*]: Cable Mrs. Goforth's daughter at Point Goforth, Long Island, that her mother is not expected to survive the night, and I'm waiting for—immediate—instructions.

ONE: Fireworks tonight at Point Goforth, Long Island.

TWO: A champagne fountain.

ONE *and* TWO [*together*]: Death: celebration.

BLACKIE: Call police in Amalfi to guard the library safe till Rudy has gone.

ONE: Rudy's root-a-toot-tooting through that safe right now.

TWO: He's disappointed to discover that the old bitch still has on her most important jewels.

ONE: And she's still conscious—fiercely!

BLACKIE: Contact mortuary. Amalfi.

TWO: That Blackie's a cool one.

[CHRIS *comes onto the terrace, now wearing his repaired lederhosen and a washed, but unironed, white shirt.*]

CHRIS: Blackie?

BLACKIE [*glancing up*]: Oh. I'm making out a list of things to do before leaving.

CHRIS: You're not leaving right away, are you?

BLACKIE: Soon as I get instructions from her daughter.

CHRIS: I called the Rome doctor and told him what had happened. He said he's expected it sooner, and there's nothing more to be done that can't be done by the doctor on the place.

BLACKIE: The little doctor, Lullo, has given her a strong shot of adrenalin which was a mistake, I think. She won't go to bed, keeps pressing electric buzzers for Simonetta who's run away, and she's put on all her rings so they won't be stolen. She's more afraid of being robbed of her jewelry than her life. What time would it be in the States?

CHRIS: What time is it here?

BLACKIE: Sundown, nearly.

CHRIS: About seven-thirty here would make it—about two-thirty there.

BLACKIE: Maybe a phone call would get through before a cable.

[*She rises. One of the* STAGE ASSISTANTS *brings a phone from the table by the chaise lounge, a little upstage.* BLACKIE *takes the phone.*

Try her daughter's husband at Goforth, Faller and Rush, Incorporated, Plaza 1-9000, while I—

[*She gives* CHRIS *the phone, and pours herself a brandy.* RUDY *comes out with a strongbox from the safe.*]

Who's that? Oh! *You!* What are you taking out?

RUDY: Just what I was told to take out.

104

BLACKIE: Well, take it out, but don't forget that everything's been listed.

RUDY: I don't forget nothing, Blackie. [*He goes off.*]

STAGE ASSISTANT ONE [*removing the crested screen*]: Her bedroom in the white villa.

TWO: The griffin is staring at death, and trying to outstare it.

[*We see* MRS. GOFORTH *seated. She wears a majestic ermine-trimmed robe to which she has pinned her "most important jewels," and rings blaze on her fingers that clench the chair arms.*]

ONE: Her eyes are bright as her diamonds.

TWO: Until she starts bleeding again, she'll give no ground to any real or suspected adversary. . . .

ONE: And *then*?

[*During this exchange between the* ASSISTANTS, *who now back into the wings on their soundless shoes,* BLACKIE *has made several other notations. Without looking up at* CHRIS, *she asks him:*]

BLACKIE: You're still very hungry, aren't you?

CHRIS: Yes, very.

BLACKIE: The new kitchen staff has arrived. I've put a bottle of milk in your rucksack, and your rucksack is in the library. You'd better just have the milk now. We'll have dinner later together.

CHRIS: Blackie, I've seen her grass hut on the beach, her oubliette, as she calls it. And—I wonder how long I could stay down there before I'd be discovered and—evicted?

105

BLACKIE: Long as you want to. Indefinitely, I guess. But how would you live down there with the villas all closed?

CHRIS: Oh, on—*frutti di mare:* shellfish. And I'd make a spear for spear-fishing.

BLACKIE: There's no fresh water down there, just the sea water.

CHRIS: I know how to make fresh water out of sea water.

BLACKIE: Why would you want to stay down there?

CHRIS [*as a wave crashes under the mountain*]: Boom! I'd like to make a mobile. I'd call it "Boom." The sea and the sky are turning the same color, dissolving into each other. Wine-dark sea and wine-dark sky. In a little while the little fishing boats with their lamps for night fishing will make the sea look like the night sky turned upside down, and you and I will have a sort of valedictory dinner on the terrace.

BLACKIE: Yes, it sounds very peaceful. . . .

[*The bedroom of the white villa is now brightened.* MRS. GOFORTH *staggers from her chair, knocking it over. The* STAGE ASSISTANTS *dart out to snatch the small chair and move it farther away, as she leans on a bed post, gasping. Then she draws herself up, advances to the chair's new position a little farther back. She reaches out for it. The* ASSISTANTS *pull it farther. She staggers dizzily after it. The* ASSISTANTS *exchange inquiring looks. They silently agree to allow her the chair and they back out of the area. She sits down with a cry of fury and resumes her fierce contest with death. A reserve of power, triggered by the adrenalin, begins to reanimate her. She rises and drags the chair to a small boudoir table and calls out:*]

MRS. GOFORTH: *Chris? Chris?*

BLACKIE: That's her, she's calling for you. Can you stand to go in there?

106

CHRIS: Sure I can—it's a professional duty.

[*As he turns upstage, the* STAGE ASSISTANTS *remove the screen masking the library. He enters that area. One of the* STAGE ASSISTANTS *turns the screen perpendicular to the proscenium so that it represents a wall division between bedroom and library. They retire.*]

Boom! Mrs. Goforth?

MRS. GOFORTH: Oh, you've finally got here. Stay out there, don't come in here right away. The doctor gave me a shot that's made me a little dizzy, I'll call you in—in a minute. . . . [*She staggers up from the chair, knocking it over.*]

CHRIS: Are you all right, Mrs. Goforth? [*He discovers his sack, removes and opens the milk bottle.*]

MRS. GOFORTH: Just a little unsteady after the shot, the doctor said. The bleeding was from a little blood vessel at the back of my throat. But he thinks I ought to lay off the work for a while, just wind up this volume and save the rest for—sequels. . . .

[CHRIS *opens the milk bottle and sips the milk as if it were sacramental wine.*]

Don't you think that's better, since it's such a strain on me?

CHRIS: Yes, I do, I think it's a—[*drinks milk*]—a wise decision. . . . [*He catches some drops of milk that have run down his chin, licks them almost reverently off the palm of his hand.*]

MRS. GOFORTH [*entering the library*]: All that work, the pressure, was burning me up, it was literally burning me up like a house on fire.

CHRIS [*assisting her to the desk chair*]: Yes, we—all live in a house on fire, no fire department to call; no way out, just the upstairs window to look out of while the fire burns the house down with us trapped, locked in it.

107

MRS. GOFORTH: What do you mean by—what windows?

CHRIS [*touching his forehead*]: These upstairs windows, not wide enough to crawl out of, just wide enough to lean out of and look out of, and—look and look and look, till we're almost nothing but looking, nothing, almost, but *vision.* . . .

MRS. GOFORTH: Hmmm.— Yes. It isn't as cool out here as it was in my bedroom and this robe I've put on is too heavy. So come on in. We can talk in my bedroom. [*She retires behind the bedroom screen.*]

MRS. GOFORTH'S VOICE [*from behind her screen*]: Talking between rooms is a strain on the ears and the vocal cords—so come in, now: I'm ready.

[*He crosses to the screens, stops short.*]

CHRIS: Oh. Sorry. [*He turns away from the screens.*] I'll wait till you've—

MRS. GOFORTH'S VOICE: Modesty? *Modesty?* I wouldn't expect you to suffer from modesty, Chris. I never was bothered with silliness of that kind. If you've got a figure that's pleasing to look at, why be selfish with it?

CHRIS: Yes, it *was* a pleasure, Mrs. Goforth.

MRS. GOFORTH'S VOICE: Then why'd you retreat, back away? In my bedroom, in here, I almost never, if ever, wear a stitch of clothes in summer. I like to feel cool air on my bare skin in summer. Don't you like that? Cool air and cool water on the bare skin in summer's the nicest thing about summer. Huh? Don't you think so, too?

CHRIS: I've found my duffel bag. It wandered in here, for some reason.

MRS. GOFORTH'S VOICE: I had it brought there so I could get

108

your passport for the local police. They want a look at the passport of anyone just arrived.

CHRIS: I see.

MRS. GOFORTH'S VOICE: You'll get it back when you go, you know, there's no hurry, is there?

CHRIS: I'm not sure about that. [*Finds passport.*] Anyway, it's already been returned.

MRS. GOFORTH: We've just been getting acquainted. The preliminaries of a friendship, or any kind of relationship, are the most difficult part, and our talk on the terrace was just a—preliminary.

CHRIS [*wryly, so low that she cannot hear*]: Sometimes the preliminaries are rougher than the main bout. [*He is rearranging articles in the rucksack.*]

MRS. GOFORTH: I didn't catch that. What was that?

CHRIS [*to himself*]: I didn't mean you to catch it.

MRS. GOFORTH: Stop mumbling and fussing with that metal stuff in the sack. The fussing drowns out the mumbling. D'ya want me to break another blood vessel in my throat talking to you from here?

CHRIS: Are you dressed now, Mrs. Goforth?

MRS. GOFORTH: Hell, I told you I'm never dressed in my bedroom.

CHRIS: You said "rarely if ever"—not "never." [*He sighs and crosses to the door again.*] You have a beautiful body, Mrs. Goforth. It's a privilege to be permitted to admire it. It makes me think of one of those great fountain figures in Scandinavian countries.

109

MRS. GOFORTH: Yeah, well, baby, a fountain figure is a stone figure and my body isn't a stone figure, although it's been sculpted by several world-famous sculptors, it's still a flesh and blood figure. And don't think it's been easy to keep it the way it still is. I'm going to lie down and rest now on this cool bed. Mmmm, these sheets are so cool—come on in. Why are you standing there paralyzed in that door?

CHRIS: I'm—silent on a peak in—Darien. . . . [*Turns away from the door.*] I came here hoping to be your friend, Mrs. Goforth, but—

MRS. GOFORTH'S VOICE: You said "but" something, but what?

CHRIS: I wouldn't have come here unless I thought I was able to serve some purpose or other, in return for a temporary refuge, a place to rest and work in, where I could get back that sense of reality I've been losing lately, as I tried to explain on the terrace, but— [*He has removed the large mobile under her desk. He climbs on the desk to attach the mobile to the chandelier above it.*] You knew I was hungry but it was "black coffee or else."

MRS. GOFORTH: Is that why you won't come in here?

CHRIS: It would just be embarrasing for us both if I did. [*He jumps off the desk.*]

MRS. GOFORTH: *What's that, what're you doing?*

CHRIS: I hung up a gift I brought you, a mobile called "The Earth Is a Wheel in a Great Big Gambling Casino." And now I think I should leave, I have a long way to go.

MRS. GOFORTH: Just a minute. I'm coming back out there to see this mobile of yours. [*She comes from behind the screen, pulling the regal white robe about her.*] Well, where is it?

CHRIS: Right over your head.

110

[*She looks up, staggering against the desk.*]

MRS. GOFORTH: It doesn't move, doesn't go.

CHRIS: It will, when it's caught by the wind.

[*The mobile begins to turn, casting faint flickers of light.*]
There now, the winds caught it, it's turning. [*He picks up his canvas sack, preparing to leave.*]

MRS. GOFORTH [*picking up the phone, suddenly*]: Kitchen, cucina, cucina!— Cucina? Un momento! [*She thrusts the phone toward* CHRIS.] Tell the cook what you would like for supper.

CHRIS: Anything, Mrs. Goforth.

MRS. GOFORTH [*into the phone*]: O.K.— Cucina? Senta— Pranzo questa sera.— Pastina in brodo, per cominciare. Capish?— Si!— Poi, una grande pesca, si, si, una grandissima pesca, anche— carne freddo, si, si, carne freddo— Roast Beef, Bif, Beeeeeef! [*Gasps, catches her breath.*] Prosciutto, legumi, tutti, tutti legumi Capito? Poi, un' insalata verde. No, Mista! Insalata mista, Mista! They don't know their own language. . . . Poi, dolce, zuppa inglese, frutta, formaggio, tutte formaggio, e vino, vino, bianco e rosso, una bottiglia di Soave e una bottiglia di— [*gasps for breath again.*] Valpolicella. Hanh?— Va bene. . . . [*hangs up.*] This new cook sounds like a—Mau-mau. . . . She'll probably serve us long pig with—shrunk heads on toothpicks stuck in it. . . . [*She tries to laugh, but coughs.*] Now, then, you see, you're not just going to be fed, you're going to be wined and dined in high style tonight on the terrace. But meanwhile, we're going to enjoy a long siesta together in the cool of my bedroom which is full of historical treasures, including myself! [*She crosses to the bedroom doors, beckons him commandingly. He doesn't move.*] Well?!

CHRIS: I'm afraid I came here too late to accept these—invitations.

111

MRS. GOFORTH: Who else has invited you somewhere?

CHRIS: I've passed the point where I wait for invitations, but I think I'll be welcomed by the elderly spinster lady whose mother died in Taormina today.

MRS. GOFORTH: Not if she's heard your nickname. And Sicily's an island. How'll you get there, can you walk on water?

CHRIS: Your discharged secretary gave me a bottle of milk with some ten thousand lire notes attached to it with a— rubber band. So—goodbye, Mrs. Goforth. [*He bends to hoist his rucksack over his shoulder.*]

MRS. GOFORTH: Mr. Flanders, you have the distinction, the dubious distinction, of being the first man that wouldn't come into my bedroom when invited to enter.

CHRIS: I'm sorry.

MRS. GOFORTH: Man bring this up road, huh? [*She has snatched up his book of poems.*]

CHRIS: No, I—

MRS. GOFORTH: What else? Your book of poems, your calling card? Y'must be running short of 'em. Here take it back! [*She hurls it at his feet.*] I haven't read it but I can imagine the contents. *Facile sentiment!* To be good a poem's got to be tough and to write a good, tough poem you've got to cut your teeth on the marrow bone of this world. I think you're still cutting your milk teeth, Mr. Flanders.

CHRIS: I know you better than you know me. I admire you, admire you so much I almost like you, *almost*. I think if that old Greek explorer, Pytheas, hadn't beat you to it by centuries, you would've sailed up through the Gates of Hercules to map out the Western world, and you would have sailed up farther and mapped it out better than he did. No storm could've driven you back or changed your course. Oh, no, you're nobody's fool, but you're a fool, Mrs. Goforth, if you don't know that finally, sooner or later, you need somebody or something to mean God to you, even if it's a cow on the streets of Bombay, or carved rock on the Easter Islands or—

MRS. GOFORTH: You came here to bring me *God,* did you?

CHRIS: I didn't say God, I said someone or something to—

MRS. GOFORTH: I heard what you said, you said *God.* My eyes are out of focus but not my ears! Well, *bring* Him, I'm ready to lay out a red carpet for Him, but how do you bring Him? Whistle? Ring a bell for Him? [*She snatches a bell off her desk and rings it fiercely.*] Huh? How? What? [*She staggers back against the desk, gasping.*]

CHRIS: I've failed, I've disappointed some people in what they wanted or thought they wanted from me, Mrs. Goforth, but sometimes, once in a while, I've given them what they needed even if they didn't know what it was. I brought it up the road to them, and that's how I got the name that's made me unwelcome this summer.

STAGE ASSISTANT ONE: Tell her about the first time!

STAGE ASSISTANTS [*together*]: Tell her, tell her, the first time!

[*They draw back to the wings. Music begins to be heard softly*].

CHRIS: —I was at Mrs. Ferguson's mountain above Palm Springs, the first time. I wasn't used to her world of elegant bitches and dandies. . . . Early one morning I went down the mountain and across the desert on a walking trip to a village in Baja California, where a great Hindu teacher had gathered a group of pupils, disciples, about him. Along the road I passed a rest home that looked like a grand hotel, and just a little farther along, I came to an inlet, an estuary of the ocean, and I stopped

113

for a swim off the beach that was completely deserted. Swam out in the cool water till my head felt cool as the water, then turned and swam back in, but the beach wasn't deserted completely any more. There was a very old gentleman on it. He called "Help!" to me, as if he was in the water drowning, and I was on the shore. I swam in and asked him how I could help him and he said this, he said: "Help me out there! I can't make it alone, I've gone past pain I can bear." I could see it was true. He was elegantly dressed but emaciated, cadaverous. I gave him the help he wanted, I led him out in the water, it wasn't easy. Once he started to panic; I had to hold onto him tight as a lover till he got back his courage and said, "All right." The tide took him as light as a leaf. But just before I did that, and this is the oddest thing, he took out his wallet and thrust all the money in it into my hand. Here take this, he said to me. And I—

MRS. GOFORTH: Took it, did you, you took it?

CHRIS: The sea had no use for his money. The fish in the sea had no use for it, either, so I took it and went on where I was going.

MRS. GOFORTH: How much were you paid for this—service?

CHRIS: It was a very special difficult service. I was well paid for it.

MRS. GOFORTH: Did you tell the old Hindu, the Swami, when you got to his place, that you'd killed an old man on the way and—

CHRIS: I told him that I had helped a dying old man to get through it.

MRS. GOFORTH: What did he say about that?

CHRIS [*reflectively*]: What did he say?— He said, "You've found your vocation," and he smiled. It was a beautiful smile in spite of showing bare gums, and—he held out his hand for the money. The hand was beautiful, too, in spite of being dry skin, pulled tight as a glove, over bones.

MRS. GOFORTH: Did you give him the money?

CHRIS: Yes, they needed the money. I didn't. I gave it to them.

MRS. GOFORTH: I *bet* you did.

CHRIS: I *did.*

MRS. GOFORTH: Did he say thank you for it?

CHRIS: I don't know if he did. You see, they— No, I guess you don't see. They had a belief in believing that too much is said, when feeling, quiet feelings—enough—says more. . . .

And he had a gift for gesture. You couldn't believe how a hand that shriveled and splotched could make such a beautiful gesture of holding out the hand to be helped up from the ground. It made me, so quickly, peaceful. That was important to me, that sudden feeling of quiet, because I'd come there, all the way down there, with the—the spectre of lunacy at my heels all the way— He said: "Stay."— We sat about a fire on the beach that night: Nobody said anything.

MRS. GOFORTH: No message, he didn't have any message?

CHRIS: Yes, that night it was silence, it was the meaning of silence.

MRS. GOFORTH: Silence? Meaning?

CHRIS: Acceptance.

MRS. GOFORTH: What of?

CHRIS: Oh, many things, everything, nearly. Such as how to live and to die in a way that's more dignified than most of us know how to do it. And of how not to be frightened of not knowing what isn't meant to be known, acceptance of not know-

115

ing *anything* but the moment of still existing, until we stop existing—and acceptance of that moment, too.

MRS. GOFORTH: How do you know he wasn't just an old faker?

CHRIS: How do you know that I'm not just a young one?

MRS. GOFORTH: I don't. You *are* what they call you!

CHRIS [*taking hold of her hand*]: As much as *anyone* is what anyone calls him.

MRS. GOFORTH: A butcher is called a butcher, and that's what he is. A baker is called a baker, and he's a baker. A—

CHRIS: Whatever they're called, they're men, and being *men,* they're not known by themselves or anyone else.

MRS. GOFORTH [*presses a button that shrills on the stage*]: Rudy? Rudy!

CHRIS: Your bodyguard's gone, Mrs. Goforth.

[*She goes on pressing the button.*]

He left with the contents of your strongbox, your safe.

MRS. GOFORTH: —I've got on me all my important jewels, and if Rudy's gone, I want you to go, too. Go on to your next appointment. You've tired me, you've done me in. This day has been the most awful day of my life. . . .

CHRIS: I know. That's why you need me here a while longer.

[*He places his arm about her.*]

MRS. GOFORTH: *Don't, don't.* You—*scare* me!

CHRIS: Let me take you into your bedroom, now, and put you to bed, Mrs. Goforth.

MRS. GOFORTH: *No, no,* GO. *Let me* GO!!

[*He releases her and picks up his canvas sack.*]

Hey!

[*He pauses with his back to her.*]

Did somebody tell you I was dying this summer? Yes, isn't that why you came here, because you imagined that I'd be ripe for a soft touch because I'm dying this summer? Come on, for once in your life be honestly frank, be frankly honest with someone! You've been tipped off that old Flora Goforth is about to go forth this summer.

CHRIS: Yes, that's why I came here.

MRS. GOFORTH: Well, I've escorted four husbands to the eternal threshold, and come back alone without them, just with the loot of *three* of them, and, ah, God, it was like I was building a shell of bone round my heart with their goddamn loot, their loot the material for it— It's my turn, now, to go forth, and I've got no choice but to do it. But I'll do it alone. I don't want to be escorted. I want to go forth alone. But you, you counted on touching my heart because you'd heard I was dying, and old dying people are your specialty, your vocation. But you miscalculated wth this one. This milk train doesn't stop here anymore. I'll give you some practical advice. Go back to Naples. Walk along Santa Lucia, the bay-front. Yesterday, there, they smelt the smell of no money, and treated you like a used, discarded used person. It'll be different this time. You'll probably run into some Americans at a sidewalk table along there, a party that's in for some shopping from the islands. If you're lucky, they'll ask you to sit down with them and say, "Won't you have something, Chris?"— Well, *have* something, Chris! and if you play your cards right, they might invite you to go back to an island with them. Your best bet is strangers, I guess. Don't work on the young ones or anybody attractive. They're not ripe to be taken. And not the old ones, either, they've been taken too often. Work on the middle-aged drunks, that's who to work on, Chris, work on them. Sometimes the old milk train still comes to

117

a temporary stop at their crazy station, so concentrate on the middle-aged drunks in Naples.

CHRIS: This isn't the time for such—practical advice. . . .

[*She makes a gasping sound and presses a tissue to her mouth, turning away.*]

MRS. GOFORTH [*facing front*]: —A paper rose . . . [*The tissue is dyed red with blood.*] Before you go, help me into my bedroom, I can't make it alone. . . .

[*He conducts her to the screen between the two rooms as the* STAGE ASSISTANTS *advance from the wings to remove it.*]

—It's full of historical treasures. The chandelier, if the dealer that sold it to me wasn't a liar, used to hang in Versailles, and the bed, if he wasn't lying, was the bed of Countess Walewska, Napoleon's Polish mistress. It's a famous old bed, for a famous old body. . . .

[*The* STAGE ASSISTANTS *remove the screen masking the bed.*]

CHRIS: Yes, it looks like the catafalque of an Empress. [*He lifts her onto the bed, and draws a cover over her.*]

MRS. GOFORTH: *Don't leave me alone till*—

CHRIS: I never leave till the end.

[*She blindly stretches out her jeweled hand. He takes it.*]

MRS. GOFORTH: —*Not so tight, the*—

CHRIS: I know, the rings cut your fingers.

[*He draws a ring off a finger. She gasps. He draws off another. She gasps again.*]

MRS. GOFORTH: Be here, when I wake up.

[*The* STAGE ASSISTANTS *place before her bed the screen with*

118

*the gold-winged griffin on the middle panel. Light dims out
on that area, and is brought up on the turning mobile. Music
seems to come from the turning mobile that casts very delicate
gleams of light on the stage.* BLACKIE *appears on the forestage
as the* STAGE ASSISTANTS *bring out a dinner table and rapidly
set two places. Then they cross to the flagstaff by the right
wings and begin slowly to lower the flag.*]

ONE: Flag-lowering ceremony on the late Mrs. Goforth's
mountain.

TWO: Bugle?

[*A muted bugle is heard from a distance.*]

That's not Taps, that's Reveille.

ONE: It's Reveille always, Taps never, for the gold griffin.

TWO: One more obvious statement is one too many. [*He
snaps his fingers.*] Let's go.

[*They go out with the folded banner.* CHRIS *comes from behind
the bedroom screen, onto the terrace where* BLACKIE *sits coolly
waiting. She rises and pours wine into a medieval goblet as she speaks to* CHRIS.]

BLACKIE: —Is it—is she—?

[CHRIS *nods as he moves out onto the forestage.*]

Was it what they call "peaceful"?

[CHRIS *nods again.*]

With all that fierce life in her?

CHRIS: You always wonder afterwards where it's gone, so far,
so quickly. You feel it must be still around somewhere, in the
air. But there's no sign of it.

119

BLACKIE: Did she say anything to you before she—?

CHRIS: She said to me: "Be here when I wake up." After I'd taken her hand and stripped the rings off her fingers.

BLACKIE: What did you do with—?

CHRIS [*giving her a quick look that might suggest an understandable shrewdness*]: Under her pillow like a Pharaoh's breakfast waiting for the Pharaoh to wake up hungry. . . .

[BLACKIE *comes up beside him on the forestage and offers him the wine goblet. A wave is heard breaking under the mountain.*]

BLACKIE: The sea is saying the name of your next mobile.

CHRIS: *Boom!*

BLACKIE: What does it mean?

CHRIS: It says "Boom" and that's what it means. No translation, no explanation, just "Boom." [*He drinks from the goblet and passes it back to her.*]

THE CURTAIN FALLS SLOWLY.

KINGDOM OF EARTH

(The Seven Descents of Myrtle)

Kingdom of Earth (The Seven Descents of Myrtle) was presented at the Ethel Barrymore Theatre in New York on March 27, 1968 by David Merrick. It was directed by José Quintero; the stage setting and lighting by Jo Mielziner; costumes by Jane Greenwood. The cast, in order of appearance, was as follows:

CHICKEN	HARRY GUARDINO
MYRTLE	ESTELLE PARSONS
LOT	BRIAN BEDFORD

Kingdom of Earth was revived on March 6, 1975, by the McCarter Theatre Company in Princeton, New Jersey, with Michael Kahn as producing director. The production incorporated substantial changes by the author, and it is this, the most recent text, which is included in this volume. Directed by Garland Wright, the set design was by Paul Zalon, the costuming by David James, and the lighting by Marc B. Weiss. The cast was as follows:

CHICKEN	DAVID PENDLETON
MYRTLE	MARILYN CHRIS
LOT	COURTNEY BURR

Place: Rural Mississippi

Time: 1960

ACT ONE

SCENE ONE

At curtain rise, the stage set, uninhabited, has the mood of a blues song whose subject is loneliness. It is the back of a Mississippi Delta farmhouse, a story and a half high, its walls gray against a sky the same color. On either side of it stand growths of cane, half the height of the house, rattling in wind that moans. Continually through these sounds is heard the low, insistent murmur of vast waters in flood or near it.

This back wall of the house, except for a doorway, is represented by a scrim that will lift when the house is entered. Then the interior will be exposed: a kitchen stage right, a mysterious little "parlor" stage left, a narrow, dark hall between them: a flight of stairs to an upper hall and a low, slant-ceilinged bedroom to the right. The stage left side of the upper half-story is never used in the play and is always masked: a difficult set that requires the inventions of a very gifted designer.

A few moments after the curtain rises, a car is heard approaching and stopping close by.

MAN'S VOICE: Hey, Chicken! Chicken!

[*There is a whine of wind. Then the one being called appears from offstage. He is a young man (thirty or thirty-five) in rubber hip boots covered with river slick. He seems a suitable antagonist to a flooding river.*]

We're clearin' out of our place.

CHICKEN: What?

MAN'S VOICE: We're goin' up to Sunset. That's over the crest of the river.

CHICKEN: That's radio talk. I pay no attention to it.

MAN'S VOICE: Sorry we don't have room for you in our car.

CHICKEN: Never mind that. I wouldn't go if I had my own car

125

to go in. [*He is staring straight out as if the voices came from the back of the theatre. Dull lightning flickers about the gray place.*]—So don't worry about it.

MAN'S VOICE [*turned openly malicious*]: But we got word that old man Sikes might dynamite his south bank levee tonight to save his nawth bank levee, least ten foot of water, you know that Chicken.

CHICKEN [*raising his voice*]: They named me Chicken because I set on the roof with the chickens one time this place was flooded.

MAN'S VOICE: Sorry we don't have room fo' *you* in the car. [*The tires catch.*] *Here we go!*

[*The sound of the car and bawling children fade out and we hear the muted warning of the river. The cane stalks make a sad rattling noise in the whining wind. Chicken enters the kitchen and strikes a match; he lights an oil lamp and warms his hands on its chimney as the glass gets hot, the flame making grotesque shadows on his dark face. He is a strange-looking young man but also remarkably good looking with his very light eyes in darker-than-olive skin, and the power and male grace of his body. After his hands are warmed up on the lamp chimney, he crosses with the lamp to the stove but on the way is distracted by a nude girl's body in a calendar picture, tacked directly over a disordered army cot pushed against kitchen wall. He turns the lamp up higher to see the picture more clearly, one hand at the same time falling involuntarily down his body. But he mutters sharply, "Nah!" and then goes on to the stove and cupboard. He starts preparing himself a pot of coffee, from time to time repeating the man's mocking shout, "Sorry we don't have room fo' you in the car." After some moments he abruptly freezes, cocking his head like an animal's at a warning sound. He listens for several beats before the audience can hear what he hears, the sound of an approaching motor. As the sound gets close to the house, he blows out the lamp and leans over it, as if glaring out a dim window in the open wall of the set. Then mutters sharply to himself—*]

126

CHICKEN: *Him!*

[*The motor stops nearby and a woman's voice is heard crying out something. Chicken grunts, astonished. He sets the lamp down quickly and runs to lock the door between the narrow dark hall and the kitchen. Myrtle and Lot appear downstage left, by the back door of the house. Neither is a person that could avoid curious attention. Myrtle is a rather fleshy young woman, amiably loud-voiced. I see her as wearing a pink turtle-neck sweater and tight checkered slacks. Her blonde-dyed hair is tied up in a wet silk scarf, magenta-colored. Her appearance suggests an imitation of a Hollywood glamor girl which doesn't succeed as a good imitation. Lot comes on behind her, bearing with great difficulty two suitcases. He is a frail, delicately—you might say exotically—pretty youth of about twenty—ten years younger than Myrtle, and his frailty makes him look even younger. Myrtle dominates him in an amiable way.*]

[*Lot staggers coughing against the washed-gray wall of the house, dropping his damp cardboard suitcase. He leans panting against the wet frame wall as Myrtle calls to him from out front, above the wind.*]

MYRTLE: Hey, Lot, come awn!

[*Inside the dim kitchen, at a safe distance from the dusty windowpane in the imaginary fourth wall, Chicken is leaning stiffly over to look out and listen, like a crouched animal, muttering barely audibly to himself. After about ten beats, Myrtle stops waiting out front and comes charging back around the side of the house, imitating the howl of the wind.*]

Woooo! Woooo! That wind is penetratin'! Sharp as a butcher's knife!

LOT [*to himself*]: No—breath—left . . .

[*She rushes up to him, an avalanche of motherly concern.*]

MYRTLE: Aw, baby, love!

127

LOT: Shouldn't have tried to carry—luggage . . .

[*He raises his pale, lost eyes to the fading-out sky above Myrtle's look of concern. He bends stiffly, to pick up a suitcase, but Myrtle snatches it from him.*]

MYRTLE: That door is locked.

LOT: No. Just stuck, always sticks in wet weather.

MYRTLE: You come on and stop leanin' against those cold wet boards and let's get into our house.

[*She pulls, the door gives violently, and she almost tumbles off the back steps recovers, laughing, and hauls the suitcase inside, heading straight up the dark, narrow hall, Lot behind her.*]

LOT: Where are you going?

MYRTLE: I want the parlor to be my first impression of my new home. It's stuck, too. [*It gives before her weight.*] *There now!*

LOT: Go in.

MYRTLE: You go in and light the lights in that parlor so I can see it.

LOT [*pressing the switch*]: The lights don't light.

MYRTLE: How come they don't light, baby?

LOT: Sometimes—[*He draws a deep breath.*]—when the river is flooding some places, the electric current that makes the lights light—[*He is talking to her as if she were mentally deficient. He draws another deep breath that wheezes in his throat.*]—is temporarily interrupted, Myrtle.

MYRTLE: How long is temporarily?

LOT: Oh, it comes back on when the—[*deep breath*]—water

128

goes down. These drapes are velvet drapes—neglected lately. [*He opens them as gently as if they had feeling. Fading gray light enters the parlor.*]

MYRTLE:—Well, this is an elegant parlor, an elegant little parlor.

LOT: My mother did all she could to give some quality to the place, but my father—[*deep breath*]—He was a man that liked to sit in a kitchen and wouldn't let Mother build a dining room onto the house. When he died, howling like a wild beast, Mother was free to transform this place or tear it down to the ground, but life was cruel to Mother. It gave her no time to carry out her plans. Outlived my father by shortly less than one year.

MYRTLE:—Sad . . .

LOT:—Yes.—Tragic.

MYRTLE:—Hmmm. A parlor with gold chairs is—like a dream!

LOT: The chandelier is crystal but the pendants are dusty, they've got to be all taken down, one by one, dipped in hot, soapy water. Then rinsed in a bowl of clear water, then dried off with soft tissue paper and hung back up.

[*Chicken grins savagely in the kitchen.*]

Mother and I used to do it, she never allowed the colored girl to touch a thing in this parlor or even come in it. Beautiful things can only be safely cared for by people that know and love them. The day before she died, do you know what she did?

[*Myrtle shakes her head, staring curiously at her exotic young husband.*]

—She removed each crystal pendant from the little brass hook it hung on, passed it down to me, to be soaped and rinsed and dried, and then replaced on its little brass hook.

MYRTLE: Baby, you got a mother complex, as they call it, and I'm gonna make you forget it. You hear me?

129

LOT: You've got a voice that no one in a room with you could help but hear when you speak.

MYRTLE: That's awright. When I speak I want to be heard. Now, baby, this mother complex, I'm gonna get that out of you, Lot, cause I'm not just your wife, I'm also your mother, and I'm not daid, I'm livin'. A-course I don't mean I'm gonna replace her in your heart, but—[*She draws up one of the little gilded chairs close to the one on which he is seated.*]

LOT: Don't sit on Mother's gold chairs. They break too easy.

MYRTLE: You are sittin' on one.

LOT: I'm lighter than you.

MYRTLE: Well! I stand corrected!—Mr. Skin and Bones!—Do I have to stay on my feet in this parlor or can I sit on the sofa?

LOT: Yes, sit on the sofa. [*Slight pause. His head droops forward and his violet-lidded eyes close.*]—The little animal has to make a home of its own . . .

MYRTLE: I didn't catch the remark.

LOT:—What?

MYRTLE: You said something about an animal.

LOT: I'm too tired to know what I'm saying.

MYRTLE: Are you too tired to hear what *I'm* saying?

LOT: What are you saying?

MYRTLE: I'm saying that all my electric equipment is sitting out there under the leaky roof of your car.

LOT:—Oh.—Yes . . .

MYRTLE: Didn' you tell me you had niggers here working fo' you?

LOT: There's a house girl named Clara and her unmarried husband.

MYRTLE: How do you call this unmarried couple of niggers when you want something done?

LOT: You—[*deep breath*]—have to step outside and ring a bell for 'em.

MYRTLE: Where is this bell you ring for 'em?

LOT: The bell is—[*deep breath*]—in the kitchen.

MYRTLE: Well, kitchen, here I come!

[*During the above, Chicken has opened the kitchen door to hear the talk in the parlor. Now he closes and locks it silently.*]

The unmarried nigra couple're gonna step pretty lively fo' Mrs. Lot Ravenstock.

[*She charges to the kitchen door behind which Chicken is lurking. Lot sways and falls off the chair, staggers to the sofa. Myrtle finds the door locked, rattles the knob and calls out—*]

Who is in there? Who is in this kitchen?—Somebody's in there!

[*She presses her ear to the door. Chicken breathes loudly as if he'd been fighting. Myrtle rattles the knob again and a key falls to the floor inside the kitchen. Myrtle is startled and subdued. She returns to the parlor as if a little frightened.*]

—If that's a dawg in there, why don't it bark?

LOT:—Dawg?

MYRTLE: That kitchen door was locked or it was stuck mighty tight. And I swear I heard something breathing right behind it, like a big dawg was in there. Will you wake up an' lissen t'what I tell you?

LOT [*hoarse whisper*]: I thought he was hiding in there.

131

MYRTLE: Who? What?

LOT: —Chicken . . .

MYRTLE: Chicken? Hiding? A chicken, you say, is hiding in the kitchen? What are you tawkin' about!—No chicken breathes that loud that I ever met!

LOT: Myrtle, when I say Chicken I don't mean the kind of chicken with feathers. I mean my half *brother* Chicken who runs this place for me.

MYRTLE: I'll be switched! *This* is a piece of news!

LOT: Keep your voice down, please. I got some things to tell you about the situation on this place.

MYRTLE: —Maybe you should've told me about it before?

LOT: Yes, maybe. But anyhow . . . now . . .

MYRTLE: You are making me nervous. You mean your brother is hiding in that kitchen while we are sitting in here half frozen?

LOT: Cain't you talk quiet?

MYRTLE: Not when I am upset. If he is in there, why don't you call him out?

LOT: He'll come out after awhile. The sight of a woman walking in this house must have give him a little something to think about in that kitchen, is what I figure.

MYRTLE: Well, all I can say is—"*Well!*"

LOT: —That's what I figure.

MYRTLE: And that's why you're shaking all over.

LOT: I'm shaking because I am cold with no fire anywhere in this house except in the kitchen. And it's locked up. With him in it.

132

MYRTLE: This makes about as much sense as a Chinese crossword puzzle to me. Can you explain why this half brother of yours would be hiding in the kitchen when we come home, pretending not to be here or—God knows what?!

LOT: Everything can't be explained to you all at once here, Myrtle. Will you try to remember something? Will you just try to get something in your haid?

MYRTLE: What?

LOT: This place is mine. You are my wife. You are now the lady of the house. Is that understood?

MYRTLE: Then why—?

LOT: Sh! Will you? Please? Keep your voice down to something under a shout?

MYRTLE: But—

LOT: Will you? Will you PLEASE?

MYRTLE: Awright. [*sniffs*] Now I got the shivers, too.—If he's in the kitchen, why don't he come out?

LOT: He won't come out till he's ready. Be patient. Do you like sherry wine?

MYRTLE: I don't think I ever had any.

LOT: Some of Miss Lottie's sherry's still left in this ole cutglass decanter.

MYRTLE [*absently*]: Aw. Good. Good . . .

LOT [*in his thin, breathless voice*]: This is Bohemian glass, these here wineglasses, are.

MYRTLE:—What d'ya know . . .

LOT: Ev'ry afternoon about this time, Miss Lottie would take

133

a glass of this Spanish sherry with a raw egg in it to keep her strength up. It would always revive her, even when she was down to eighty-two pounds, her afternoon sherry and eggs, she called it her sherry flip, would pick her right up and she'd be bright an' lively.

MYRTLE:—Imagine me thinkin' that that was a dawg in there. Yeah, I thought that huffing I heard in there was a big old dawg in the kitchen, locked up in there, I didn't—ha ha!—suspect that it was—ha ha!—your—*brother* . . .

[*He begins to cough; it shakes him like a dead leaf, the cough, and he leans panting against the wall staring at Myrtle with pale stricken eyes. She gathers him close in her arms . . .*]

Why, baby! Precious love!—That's an *awful* cough!—I wonder if you could be comin' down with th' flu?

[*Lot coughs—stops.*

[*Chicken's frozen attitude by the door was released by the sound of Lot's paroxysm of coughing. He crosses to a cupboard, takes out a jug and takes a long, long drink.*]

LOT:—A place with no woman sure does all go to pieces.

MYRTLE: Well, now they's a woman here.

LOT: That's right: we'll make some changes.

MYRTLE: You bet we will. And bright and early tomorrow, the first thing we do after breakfast, we'll, we'll, we'll!—we'll get out that ole stepladder and wash those whatcha-ma-call-ems and make them shine like the chandelier in *Leow's State* on Main Street in Memphis! And we will—oh, we'll do a whole lot of things as soon as this weather clears up. And soon it's going to be summer. You know that, sugar? It's going to be summer real soon and—

LOT: Yeah, it'll be summer, the afternoons'll be long and hot and yellow, the damp'll *dry* out of the walls and—

134

MYRTLE: I'M GONNA MAKE YOU REST! And build you up. You hear me? I'm gonna make you recover your lost strength, baby—you and me are gonna have us a baby, and if it's a boy we're going to call it Lot, and if it's a girl we're gonna name her Lottie.

LOT [*his eyes falling shut*]: If beds could talk what stories they could tell . . .

MYRTLE: Baby, last night don't count. You was too nervous. I'll tell you something I know that might surprise you. A man is twice as nervous as a woman, and you are twice as nervous as a man.

LOT: Do you mean I'm not a man?

MYRTLE: I mean you're superior to a man. [*She hugs him to her and sings—*]

"Cuddle up a little closer, baby mine.
Cuddle up and say you'll be my clinging vine!"

Mmmm, Sugar! Last night you touched the deepest chord in my nature, which is the maternal chord in me. Do you know, do you realize what a beautiful thing you are?

LOT: I realize that I resemble my mother.

MYRTLE: To me you resemble just *you*. The first, the most, the *only* refined man in my life. Skin, eyes, hair any girl would be jealous of. A mouth like a flower. Kiss me!

[*He submits to a kiss.*]

Mmmm, I could kiss you forever!

LOT: I wouldn't be able to breathe.

MYRTLE: You're refined and elegant as this parlor.

LOT: I want you to promise me something. If Chicken asks you, and when he gets drunk he will ask you—

135

MYRTLE: Chicken will ask me nothing that I won't answer in aces and spades.

LOT: There's something you mustn't answer if he asks you.

MYRTLE: What thing is that, baby?

LOT: If I'm a—

MYRTLE: If you're a what?

LOT: Strong lover.—Tell him I satisfy you.

MYRTLE: Oh, now, baby, there'd be no lie about that. Y'know, they's a lot more to this sex business than two people jumpin' up an' down on each other's eggs. You know that, or you *ought* to.

LOT: I'm going to satisfy you when I get my strength back, and meanwhile—make out like I do. Completely. Already. I mean when talking to Chicken.

MYRTLE: Aw, Chicken again, a man that huffs like a dawg an' hides in the kitchen, do you think I'd talk about us to him, about our love with each other? All I want from that man is that he opens the kitchen door so I can go in there and grab hold of that bell and ring the clapper off it for that girl that works here, that Clara. I'll make her step, all right, and step quick, too. The first thing she's gotta do is haul in all that electric equipment settin' in the car, before it gits damp an' rusts on me.

LOT: Myrtle, I told you that when there's danger of flood, the colored help on a place cut out for high ground. Till the danger's over.

MYRTLE: Then what're we doin' on low ground instid of high ground?

LOT: To protect our property from possible flood damage. This is your house, your home. Aren't you concerned with protecting it for us?

136

MYRTLE: My house, my home! I never suspected, how much havin' property of my own could mean to me till all of a sudden I have some. Home, home, land, a little dream of a parlor, elegant as you, refined as you are.

[*During this talk, Chicken has his ear pressed to the kitchen door, fiercely muttering phrases from the talk.*]

LOT:—Chicken calls me a sissy.

MYRTLE: Well, he better not call you no sissy when Myrtle's around. I'll fix his wagon up good, I mean I WILL!

LOT: SHH!—Myrtle, you've got an uncontrollable voice. He's listening to us.—You think you could handle Chicken?

MYRTLE: Want to make a bet on it? I've yet to meet the man that I couldn't handle.

LOT: You ain't met Chicken.

MYRTLE: I'm gonna meet him!—Whin he comes outa that kitchen . . .

LOT: He will, soon, now. It's gettin' dark outside, and I heard him set the jug down on the kitchen table.

MYRTLE: Awright, I'm *ready* for him, anytime he comes out, I'm ready to meet him, and one thing I want to git straight. Who's going to be running this place, me or this Chicken?

LOT: This place is mine. You're my wife.

MYRTLE: That's what I wanted to know. Then I'm in charge here.

LOT: You're taking the place of Miss Lottie. She ran the house and you'll run it.

MYRTLE: Good. Then that's understood.

LOT: It better be understood. Cause Chicken is not my brother, we're just *half* brothers and the place went to me. It's mine.

137

MYRTLE: Did you have diff'rent daddies?

LOT: No, we had diff'rent mothers. *Very* diff'rent mothers!

[*Chicken snorts like a wild horse.*]

He's coming out now!

[*Chicken emerges slowly from the kitchen and starts up the dark narrow hall.*]

MYRTLE: Let's go meet him.

LOT: No. Wait here. Sit tight. And remember that you're the lady of the house.

[*Chicken pauses, listening in the dim hall.*]

MYRTLE: It don't seem natural to me.

[*Lot removes an ivory cigarette holder from a coat pocket, puts a cigarette in it and lights it. His hands are shaky. Myrtle, nervously:*]

—A parlor with gold chairs is like a dream!

LOT:—A woman in the house is like a dream.

[*Chicken is up the stairs.*]

MYRTLE: I, I—thought I heard footsteps.

LOT: Human or animal footsteps?

[*Chicken opens the parlor door.*]

Aw—hello, Chicken. Don't come in the parlor till you take off those muddy boots.

[*Chicken disregards this instruction; he enters the parlor. Myrtle rises nervously but Lot remains seated, smiling icily through a cloud of cigarette smoke.*]

138

CHICKEN: They turn you loose from the hospital?

LOT: I wasn't locked in it. A hospital ain't a jail. I was dismissed.

CHICKEN: Couldn't do nothing more for you?

LOT: I was dismissed as cured.

CHICKEN: I see. And who is this woman?

LOT: You mean who is this lady. This lady is my wife. Myrtle, this is Chicken. Chicken, this is Myrtle.

CHICKEN: Why did you all come back here?

LOT: Wanted to is the reason.

CHICKEN: With this flood in the county?

LOT: That's right. I wanted to see that my mother's things are taken out of the parlor before the downstairs is flooded.

CHICKEN: What good'll that do if the upstairs is flooded, too?

MYRTLE: Oh, my God, the flood won't go *that* high, will it?

CHICKEN: You don't know much about floods.

MYRTLE: All I know is I'm scared to death of deep water.

CHICKEN: Wanta know something? This time tomorrow, both floors of this house will be full of floodwater.

[*Myrtle draws a long, noisy breath of dismay and terror.*]

The river gauge is thirty-two feet of water at Friar's Point, and the crest is still above Memphis. And I just got word from those sons of bitchs, Potters, that ole man Sikes is about to blow up the south end of his levee to save the rest of it, he's planning to dynamite it tonight and you—come home just in time for it.

MYRTLE: Lot, baby, I think we ought to turn right around and drive back.

LOT: No. We're home. We're not gonna leave here. Chicken's just tryin' to scare us. Why don't you leave, Chicken, if you're scared of the flood?

CHICKEN: I ain't about to leave here. You know we got this agreement. Have you forgotten about the agreement we signed between us?

LOT: That was before I got married. Now I am.

CHICKEN [to Myrtle]: Are you his nurse?

MYRTLE: Why, no, I'm Mrs. Lot Ravenstock and have been Mrs. Lot Ravenstock since yesterday mawnin'.

CHICKEN: I known of invalid men to marry their nurses, or anyhow live with 'em like they was married.

MYRTLE: We're married, and I wasn't a nurse. Y'know I don't think I ever seen so little resemblance between two brothers.

CHICKEN: We're *half* brothers.

LOT: Chicken's much darker complected. Don't you notice?

CHICKEN: I work out in the fields and Lot just lays in bed.

LOT [to Chicken]:—I'd like some hot coffee, now.

CHICKEN: Coffee's in the kitchen. [He turns to the kitchen.]

MYRTLE: Git up, Lot. Come along.

LOT: How does he impress you?

MYRTLE: I wouldn't call that man a pleasant surprise.

LOT: Don't let him scare you.

SCENE ONE

MYRTLE: I'm not scared of that man, or any man livin'! No, sir!

CHICKEN [*at the kitchen door*]: Decided y'don't want coffee?

MYRTLE: Be right there.

LOT: If he sees he can bluff an' bully you, that's what he'll do, so remember—we're two against one in this house and the house is ours.

[*They go hand in hand to the kitchen. Chicken sets tin cups on the table.*]

—Myrtle an' I'll have our coffee in china cups.

CHICKEN: The china cups all broke.

LOT: You broke Mother's china cups?

MYRTLE: Lot, baby, china breaks, nobody breaks it on purpose unless there's a fight. This is—I like our kitchen. All but that nakid girl's pitcher on the wall there. I could do without that.

CHICKEN: Jealous of her?

MYRTLE: I don't have to ask if you're a bachelor now.

CHICKEN: Lot an' me are bachelors, both of us.

MYRTLE: You're a bachelor but my baby ain't.

CHICKEN: Your baby's more of a bachelor than me.

MYRTLE: I'm here to prove he ain't.

CHICKEN: Hmmm. I didn't catch your name.

MYRTLE: My maiden name was Myrtle Kane, but now it's legally changed to Mrs. Lot Ravenstock.

141

CHICKEN: How long've you been Lot's nurse?

MYRTLE: I am nobody's nurse. To repeat that statement.

LOT: We've been married two days.

MYRTLE: My girlfriend, Georgia, said I was robbin' the cradle, you know, cradle-snatchin'.

[*No response to her laugh.*]

And I had always boasted that I was too practical-minded for love at first sight, but practicality flew out the window whin this boy come in.—I want you to know it turned my bones to water!

LOT: Chicken, we'll have some coffee.

CHICKEN: Coffee is on the stove. [*He stares steadily at Myrtle.*] So you're in the—nursin' profession?

LOT: Myrtle was in show business.

MYRTLE: Why do you keep askin' if I'm a nurse? Oh, I once did a little of what they call practical nursing, took care of a feeble person till he died on me, out of kindness—sympathy . . . [*She is pouring coffee into three tin cups.*] Is everybody's name in the pot? The coffee's still hot.

CHICKEN: Yeah. Show business, huh?

MYRTLE: I've had all kinds of employment in my life. Respectable employment. [*She laughs genially and gives Chicken a playful little slap on the shoulder.*] Oh, in my life I've taken the sweets with the sours, and it's been smooth as silk in my experience and other times rough as a cob. However, I've kept my haid above water, that I can say for myself, and I've rowed my own boat, too. Never had to depend on another soul. No, sir. Here is my right hand to God if you don't believe me, and nothing, nobody, never has made me bitter. No, sir! What all have I done? I'll tell you.

LOT: Myrtle?

MYRTLE: Huh? What, baby?

LOT: I think it's time to bring in that carload of electric equipment.

MYRTLE: Your brother 'n me'll do that, don't worry about it. Your brother wants to know what all I've done in my life, and I'm gonna tell him. You might find it int'restin', too.

LOT: Yes, I might, If I hadn't already heard it. [*He sinks into a chair and his eyes fall shut. His eyelids are violet. He sways a little as if he might fall from the chair.*]

MYRTLE: I'll just hit the high spots, baby. Whin I was fifteen I worked as operator of a Photomatic machine on the beach at Galveston, Texas. I been—you won't believe this but it's true as I'm standin' here before you!—I been the headless woman in a carnival show. All a fake, done with mirrors! Sat in a chair and pretended to have no haid, it was done with mirrors! But completely convincin'!

LOT: Myrtle, skip to show business.

MYRTLE: Baby, that was show business, my first experience in it and it's where my heart still belongs.

CHICKEN:—What is she talkin' about?

LOT [*as if asleep*]: Myrtle was in show business.

CHICKEN: Hunh.

LOT [*rousing a bit*]: Show him that picture of "The Four Hot Shots from Mobile."

MYRTLE: Oh, that old snap, that ole publicity still, I wonder if I still got it.

LOT: You showed it to me a minute after we met.

MYRTLE: I'll see if I still got it.

143

LOT: You put it back in your handbag.

MYRTLE: Pandora's box!

CHICKEN: Whose box?

[*Myrtle is a bit nervous.*]

Only a lunatic would marry you, and you sure have found the right party.

LOT: Is the black bird of jealousy eating at your heart, Chicken?

MYRTLE: Boys.

CHICKEN: Able to walk or do you have to be carried?

LOT: Sure I can. Without trouble.

[*He gets up and falls to his knees. Chicken laughs.*]

The long trip made me dizzy.

CHICKEN: I bet there's a buzzard circlin' over the house, since you got here.

[*She turns to him with a warm smile, extending the photo to him. Chicken takes it from her and regards it with considerable interest. Consciously or not, he drops one of his large, dusky hands over his crotch, which is emphasized, pushed out, by his hip boots.*]

MYRTLE: Well, there you are, here we are! Here we are outside the Dew Drop Inn—in the live town of Tallahassee, F-L-A! It's in color, you see.

CHICKEN: Yes, I can see color. Where's these hot shots now, gone back to Mobile?

MYRTLE:—You ast me a sad question, where's them girls. You

know somethin'? [*She is sincerely distressed.*] This tall redhead called The Statuesque Beauty.

[*Chicken grunts—but with interest.*]

—Her mutilated corpse was found under a trestle.

[*Chicken grunts again.*]

Some pervert had cut her up with a knife. She was full of vim, vigor, and vitality. The Statuesque Beauty was a continual circus.

CHICKEN: Unh. Circus quit now.

MYRTLE: This one next to her, sweet thing, billed as The Gulf Coast Blaze—a victim of a illegal operation.

CHICKEN: Daid?

MYRTLE [*blowing her nose again*]: Not livin', brother, bless her old sweet soul. And this one next to her, billed as The Texas Explosion, somehow I feel that her end was saddest of all. Devoured a full bottle of sleeping pills one night in a Wichita, Kansas, hotel.

CHICKEN: Suicide, huh?

MYRTLE: Well, brother, you don't devour a full bottle of sleeping pills with much expectation of getting up early tomorrow. Oh, and this one, my God, The Midnight Stawm!—She wint on drugs. Y'see, all of us four girls lived in the same little frame house t' share expenses, y'know, and, well, one night I happened to be passin' down th' hall outside the bedroom of The Midnight Stawm. I smelt a strong smell of incense. I knocked at The Midnight Stawm's door and this strange voice called out "Who's there?" "Me, Myrtle." "Aw, you, come in." So in I wint, and she was sittin' there smokin' this thin cigarette with incense burnin' beside her. "What're you smokin'?" "I'm smokin' grass," she answered, "have a stick with me, Myrtle." But instink tole me not to.

145

LOT: I'm tired, let's go up now.

MYRTLE [*hugging him to her*]: Rest on Myrtle, baby, and lemme finish the story. At that time, in Mobile, I was totally ignorant thin of things like that, but I had a suspicion that something had gone wrong with The Midnight Stawm.

CHICKEN: Aw?

MYRTLE: She'd took the first step to what she finally come to. So we other girls an' me, we talked it over and regretfully hed to ask The Midnight Stawm to give up her room there with us. Painful, very. But we didn't want the house raided. We were clean-livin' girls, as you'd hope to find in show business.—Here is me, The Petite Personality Kid that had all the luck in that outfit, and even her luck come mighty close to petering out once or twice, but strength of character saved me.

CHICKEN: You are The Petite Personality Kid?

MYRTLE: That's how they billed me, brother.

CHICKEN: Built you?

MYRTLE: No, no, billed, not built. It's a term in show business meaning the name by which you're introduced to the public.

CHICKEN: You've been introduced to the public?

MYRTLE: Yes, many times, many places.

[*She returns the snapshot to the patent leather purse.*]

CHICKEN:—How did the public like it? [*He gives her a slow, wolfish grin, his eyes appraising her body.*]—Did they yell "Take it off" or did they yell "Keep it on"?

[*Myrtle laughs heartily but with a note of uncertainty.*]

LOT: Myrtle received an ovation on TV. I saw it, I was there. She has a personality that the public responds to.

MYRTLE: It's my personality that I sell to the public—mainly.

CHICKEN: Yes, I bet. You kick with the right leg, you kick with the left leg, and between your legs you make your living?

MYRTLE:—Some remarks I deliberately don't hear!

LOT: Chicken, now that I'm home, in *my* home, on *my* land, with *my* wife, filthy talk has got to stop around here, I don't care if it means us getting along without you.

CHICKEN: Aw, you want me to go, now.

MYRTLE: Lot baby didn't mean that!

CHICKEN: What did "Lot baby" mean?

MYRTLE: All he means is that we should all talk and act like gentlemen an'—ladies!

LOT: I want to go up to bed while I still have strength to.

CHICKEN: Your nurse'll carry you up.

MYRTLE: Lot, show your brother we're married, let him see the license.

[*Lot produces a paper.*]

CHICKEN: Shit, you can buy those things for two bits in a novelty store to show in a motel where you brought a woman to lay.

MYRTLE: This marriage license is genuine, and if you doubt my word for it, call up the TV station in Memphis where we were married.

LOT: Myrtle and I were married on television yesterday morning.

CHICKEN: That statement makes no more sense than if you told me you licked TB and've got the strength of a mule team.

147

MYRTLE: Want to hear the whole story?

CHICKEN: I like to hear a good joke.

MYRTLE: Brother, this is no joke!

[*Lot coughs.*]

Lie down, baby, and rest your head in my lap while I tell your brother what happened.

[*Lot reclines on the sofa with his head in Myrtle's lap. As she tells her story, she strokes his forehead and hair.*]

My luck had run out, you know luck does that sometimes, it peters out on you no matter how hard you try.

CHICKEN: Make this story short.

MYRTLE: Awright, day before yestiddy I happened to be on the street in Memphis for no particular reason and I seen this long line of people, all wimmen, and I said to myself if that many people are standing in line for something it must be good.

CHICKEN: Uh-huh. Get on with the story.

MYRTLE: Well, I fell in the lineup with these other ladies and suddenly, all at once, this little man come bolting out and hollered, "Ladies, no more admissions today." Everybody went "Awwwwww," disappointed, but I said, "Mister, I been standing here two hours and I want in on this thing, whatever it is!" He gave me a funny look, he must've seen something in me, and he said, "Girlie, you just follow me fast as you can without attracting attention." And you know where I found myself? On a TV stage! And there I was, right smack in the middle of a TV show, and the first I know, d'ya know what I was doin'? I was standin' in front of a mike with cameras and lights on me, telling my story, broadcasting my woes to the world. I started to cry and everyone started to laugh, the studio rocked with 'em laughing.

148

CHICKEN: Come to the point of the story if there is one.

MYRTLE: I sobbed and cried, and to my shock and astonishment a moment later I was led up to and set down on a golden throne and a big gold jeweled crown was set on my haid and the MC shouted to the audience, all applauding, "Hail to the Queen! All hail!" [*She makes a grand gesture.*] "All hail to thee, Queen of the day!"

LOT: Myrtle, condense the story.

MYRTLE [*oblivious*]: WELL!—I'm telling you, brother, I could have dropped through that stage floor to the boiler room in the basement, whin I realized, that accidentally, just out of the blue, that I had been chosen, selected as "The Take-Life-Easy Queen."

CHICKEN: This is a bitch of a story.

MYRTLE: Yais, ain't it! Now the "Hollywood Queen for a Day" is sent to Hollywood, first class on a plane, provided with a sport ensemble for day time and a formal for night, and has her hair styled by the hair stylist for the stars, and she spends eight hours hobnobbing with screen celebrities in famous places. On the other hand, the "Take-Life-Easy Queen" gets a small fortune in electric household equipment. Well, like every girl in show business, and many out of it, too, Hollywood was my dream, but—

LOT: Tell him how we got married on a national hookup.

MYRTLE: That's what I'm working up to.

CHICKEN: You're working up to it slowly.

MYRTLE: Give me patience, you want to know how this happened!

CHICKEN: Not if it takes till midnight.

MYRTLE: I'm leading up to the climax which is the climax of my life. The ceremony was just about finished when somebody touches my arm. I turn around, still in my robe and crown, and

149

there was my precious baby, completely unknown to me then. "Can I have your autograph, please," is what he said to me. In that instant the love bug bit me, cupid's arrow shot a bull's eye in my heart. We made a date. On this date he said the love bug had bit him too, love-at-first-sight for us both. I phoned the TV studio and told 'em what had happened and I was going to git married. "How would you and your husband-to-be like to be married on TV? In a lace bride's gown with a bouquet of lilies?"

LOT: That's the story. We were married on TV.

CHICKEN: You acted out a make-believe marriage to fool the public, huh?

MYRTLE: If it wasn't a genuine marriage it sure fooled us.

LOT: It was a genuine marriage performed by a famous revivalist preacher.

MYRTLE: No more disagreeable talk. [*She snatches up a cowbell on the table.*] Is this the bell you ring fo' th' unmarried colored couple?

[*Chicken turns to give her a slow, blank look.*]

I am goin' out an' ring this bell, and they are gonna bring in my 'lectric equipment before it rusts on me. So many 'lectric appliances we hardly had room enough for 'em in the car. You'll see whin that unmarried couple hauls them in here t' be dried off an' connected.

CHICKEN: Yeah, I'll see. Go out an' ring the bell. Ring it loud and long, they don't hear good from a distance.

[*Myrtle goes out on the back steps and rings the bell while Chicken and Lot stare silently at each other. She rings the bell loud and long but the only response is moaning wind and a dull flicker of lightning.*]

LOT: [*finally speaking*]: Well, I guess I surprised you.

CHICKEN: You got a bigger surprise comin' to you.

150

LOT: What do you mean by that?

CHICKEN: If I said what I mean by it, it wouldn't be as big a surprise to you, would it?

[*Myrtle returns.*]

MYRTLE: I rang an' rang an' got no answer out there.

CHICKEN: Don't let that bother you much. I don't think you all could git it on the roof whin the floodwater fills the house.

LOT: Stop talking about a flood to scare my wife.

MYRTLE: I don't and I can't believe a man would stay in this house if he really thought it was going to be flooded, so I'm not a-tall scared. Now who's going to help me bring in my prizes in the car?

CHICKEN: Your TV husband will do that.

LOT: Chicken will bring it in.

CHICKEN: Oh, no, Chicken won't.

MYRTLE: Thank you both very kindly. I'll bring in what I can carry without much help. [*She goes out and off.*]

LOT: Help her with it. If you still work on the place.

CHICKEN: I will like shit.

LOT: Let's make an effort to forget what's past and work out a—decent—future.

CHICKEN: There is no future for you. You remember that agreement between us, witnessed, signed, notarized, giving the place to me when you take the one-way trip to the kingdom of heaven? I never have that paper out of my wallet in here. [*He taps the pocket of his leather jacket.*]—I was curious to know how long I might have to wait. I got your Memphis doctor on the

151

phone to ask about the condition of your lungs. One's gone, he told me, and the other one's going. Limit: six months. Now passed.

[*Myrtle rushes back into the house with a load of portable electric equipment.*]

MYRTLE: I carried in what I can carry and will get some help to bring the heavy stuff in.

[*She enters; the men ignore her. She sets the electric stuff down, as if she'd forgotten it, observing the tension between the two men. Sad, dull lightning quivers about the house.*]

CHICKEN: Didn't you tell this woman how you bleed?

MYRTLE: Bleed, Lot, baby? Bleed?

CHICKEN: Yeah, Lot baby bleeds. He bleeds like a chicken with its head chopped off. I'm Chicken, he's headless Chicken. Yes, he bleeds, he bleeds. But no, he don't have TB. He just makes a blood donation to Red Cross, only Red Cross is not quick enough to catch it in a—bucket . . .

[*Lot suddenly springs forward, striking fiercely at Chicken. Chicken pushes him almost gently to the floor. Lot crawls groaning to his feet and starts to drag himself up the steep dark narrow steps.*]

MYRTLE: I don't understand! What is it?

CHICKEN [*mimicking her*]: "I don't understand! What is it?"

MYRTLE [*backing up steps*]: You scare me!

CHICKEN: "You scare me!"

MYRTLE [*running up a few more steps*]: I'm going up with Lot!

CHICKEN: "I'm going up with Lot!"

152

[*She draws a gasping breath and scrambles up the narrow steps to the bedroom door that Lot has entered. Myrtle comes up behind him and clings to his arm.*]

MYRTLE: Do you know he mocked every word I said.

LOT [*sadly, reflectively, his eyes searching the dim sky*]: Chicken says my doctor said—I'm dying!

MYRTLE: He mocked everything I said, he just stood there and mocked everything I said!

LOT: Can you imagine that? I'm goin to die!

MYRTLE: Oh, let's go back, let's drive right back to Memphis!

LOT:—We can't, Myrtle.

MYRTLE: Why can't we? Why can't we drive back?

LOT: I'm going to die, that's why . . .

[*He glances at her with a soft, surprised, rueful laugh. The stage dims out.*]

SCENE TWO

The upstairs bedroom is lighted by an oil lamp. Late dusk surrounds the house, the "apple-green dusk" of an evening clearing after rain which has just stopped. Water is heard running busily along tin gutters, down a spout and in a big mossy barrel beside the back door. Bullfrogs and possibly some crickets are making their forlorn and desultory comments, desultory as the forlorn talk in the bedroom where Myrtle is washing out some things at the rosebud-printed washbowl and where Lot is in a rocker facing the audience at an angle; the chair is one of those wicker rockers that they have, or used to have, on verandas of old-fashioned summer hotels in the South, and Lot's fair head, delicataely pretty as a girl's, leans against a souvenir pillow from Biloxi, made of green satin, the same as the counterpane on the brass bed. The aura of its former feminine occupant, Lot's mother, still persists in this bedroom: a lady who liked violets and lace and mother-of-pearl and decorative fringes on things . . . Lot is smoking with his long ivory holder, Myrtle is wringing out some nylons at the curtain rise, and she glances from time to time at her bridegroom as an uneasy scientist might glance at a testtube whose contents had turned an unexpected color . . .

All during this scene between Lot and Myrtle, Chicken is seen in the very dimly lit kitchen carving something into the kitchen table with a switchblade knife—on his face a wolfish grin.

MYRTLE: I wish I knew what was going on back of that long ivory cigarette holder and that Mona Lisa smile.

LOT: I got them both from my mother.

MYRTLE: Yes, well, regardless of where you got 'em, they baffle me. We been up here about two hours, I reckon, and all you've said to me is "I'm dyin', Myrtle." When a couple has been married for twenty or thirty years it's natural for them to fall into long-drawn silences between them because they've talked themselves out, but you and me have been married for less than two days.

154

LOT: Why didn't you say something to me? I would've answered.

MYTRLE: Thanks. That's a comforting piece of news.—I didn't speak till you lit a cigarette because I thought you'd fallen asleep in that rocker.

LOT: No. I was sitting here thinking.

MYRTLE: I was standin' here thinkin', too, while I washed my nylons and undies.

LOT: Tell me your thoughts, Myrtle.

MYRTLE: I'll tell you one of 'em. Do you think you played fair and square with me when you brought me down here without a word of warning about that man, that animal, down there?

LOT: I thought it was better not to mention Chicken.

MYRTLE: Better for who? For you!

LOT: Yes, for me. You might not've come down here, and I couldn't come down here alone.

MYRTLE: Selfishness in your nature isn't a thing to brag of.

LOT: No. I wasn't bragging.

MYRTLE: Every car, truck, wagon, crowds of people on foot headed the opposite way, and you wouldn't turn back! Can you give me a reasonable reason for that?

LOT:—I guess—

MYRTLE: What do you guess?

LOT: I guess I thought in my heart what Chicken told me and wanted to die in this bedroom where I was born. Yes, selfish as hell, but when people are desperate, Myrtle, they only think of themselves.

MYRTLE: Some people. Not all.

LOT: Some people—including me.—Don't hate me for it.

MYRTLE: Whin I love I don't hate.

LOT: You don't have a complex nature.—What time is it, Myrtle?

MYRTLE: My watch don't run. I just wear it now as a bracelet.

LOT: You wound it too tight and broke the springs?

MYRTLE: No, no, baby. Last Fourth of July I wint to a Shriners' picnic on a lake and a couple of drunk Shriners thought it was very funny to throw me in a lake with my watch on, so the works rusted.

LOT: What you should've done to prevent the works from rusting was to take it directly to a jeweler's shop and have the works removed and soaked in oil overnight.

MYRTLE [*sadly*]: I should of done many things in my life which I neglected t'do, and not soaking my watch in oil is not the most important I can think of.

LOT: You mean what you regret is getting married to a—a impotent one-lung sissy who's got one foot in the grave and's about to step in with the other.

MYRTLE: You're putting words in my mouth that I wouldn't speak to anybody I love! [*She has removed her slacks and is getting into a sheer blouse sprinkled with tiny brilliants and a velveteen skirt.*]

LOT: What're you dressing up for?

MYRTLE: I never keep on slacks after dark.

LOT: That outfit you're getting into looks like a costume.

MYRTLE: Baby, all my dresses are made over from costumes.

156

LOT [*slowly, with little pauses for breath*]: This particular one wasn't made over enough to prevent it from still looking like a costume.

MYRTLE: That could be so or not so, but I think it's a sweet little outfit.

LOT: One girl's opinion.

MYRTLE: Yais, an' trusted by her—with your permission.

LOT: I'm not in a position to give or not give permission.

MYRTLE: Lot? Baby? When people are under the weather, it often has the effeck of makin' 'em too critical or sarcastic.

LOT: My mother subscribed to *Vogue* and we both read it. I know the secret of dressing well is to dress in a way that's appropriate to the occasion.

MYRTLE: What occasion is this? Can you tell me?

LOT: It could be the end of the world, but even then—that almost ankle-length imitation velvet skirt might not be appropriate to it.

MYRTLE: This ain't the end of the world, God help me, Jesus, and this skirt is washable velvet.

LOT: There is no such thing as real velvet that's washable, Myrtle.

MYRTLE: Well, I swan, you talk like a dressmaker, baby.

LOT: My mother, Miss Lottie, had a sense of style that a Paris designer might envy.

MYRTLE: If you talk about her much more, you'll turn me against her, Lot.

LOT:—That wouldn't matter. She doesn't exist any more . . .

157

MYRTLE: All this style thet she hed, wasn't it wasted down here?

LOT: No, strangely no. In spite of my father, who had the taste of a hawg, who ate with his hands and wiped them on his trousers, my mother, Miss Lottie, was socially accepted by sev'ral families with standing in Two River County.

MYRTLE: With so much style, accepted instid of refused, why did she marry this hawg?

LOT: That's a question I can no more answer than if you asked me why God made little green apples.

MYRTLE [*opening closet door in the back wall of the bedroom*]: I see, UH-HUH, well, tomorrow, baby, you or me or both of us is gonna clear your mother's clothes outa this closet so I don't have to live out of a suitcase.

LOT:—I'm sorry, but tomorrow—

[*He doesn't complete the sentence. Myrtle's attention is diverted by the loud sound of Chicken pushing his chair back from the kitchen table. He gets up and starts chopping potatoes into a hot skillet, dousing them with grease out of a can on the stove, and tossing into the skillet some strips of bacon. During the bedroom dialogue, he will pick out the fried bacon and eat it, all of it, and wipe his fingers on the seat of his pants. Lot coughs, rackingly. Myrtle feels his forehead.*]

MYRTLE: That's a mean cough you got there, and I don't need a thermometer to tell me you're runnin' a fever, baby. Yes, sir, burnin' up with it!

LOT [*gasping*]: Fever is—the body's protection-reaction—to the enemy in it—any kind of—infection . . .

MYRTLE:—I love you, precious baby, I love you and I'm here to protect and care for you, always! [*She presses her head to his.*]

LOT: Love me but don't smother me with it, Myrtle.

MYRTLE:—What a mean thing to say!

LOT: I didn't mean it that way. I meant I have trouble breathing, and when you crouch over me like that, it makes it harder for me to draw my breath, that's all.

[*He puts another cigarette in the ivory holder. She snatches the holder away from him.*]

—Give that holder back to me!

MYRTLE: The last thing you need is to smoke!

LOT: It makes no difference now!

MYRTLE: It does to me!

LOT: If you don't return my holder, I'll smoke without it, and nobody's going to stop me—at the end of the world . . .

MYRTLE: Here! Take it back and drive a nail in your coffin but don't talk to me about the end of the world, I haven't come to it yet and don't intend to!

LOT: Thank you, Myrtle.

MYRTLE: Never talk that way to your wife that loves you, my precious blond-headed baby.

LOT:—I'm no more blond than you are.—My hair is bleached.

MYRTLE [*shocked*]: Did you say your hair is—bleached?

LOT: As bleached as yours. But I do a better job on my hair than you do on yours because my mother taught me. Ev'ry morning of the world, and if I'm alive tomorrow I'll do it again, I get up, brush my teeth and obey the calls of nature, and the next thing I do, in the hospital or out, is put a wad of cotton on the tip of an orange stick and dip it into a bottle and rub the roots of my hair so it never shows dark, and I don't use peroxide, I use a special formula which my mother invented and passed on to me. She said with blue eyes and fair skin, I'd look best as a blond, the same as she did . . .

159

MYRTLE [*aghast*]: Well, I'll be switched . . . I thought at least I had married a natural blond.

LOT: Don't let it throw you, and don't imagine you have married a fairy.

MYRTLE: Such an idea would never—[*Pause: she leaves the statement in the air.*]

LOT: You've married someone to whom no kind of sex relation was ever as important as fighting sickness and trying with his mother to make, to create, a little elegance in a corner of the earth we lived in that wasn't favorable to it.

MYRTLE:—I—

LOT:—You what?

MYRTLE:—Understand. And I'm going to devote myself to you like a religion, mystery as you are, back of that ivory holder and Mona Lisa smile.

[*Pause. Chicken turns up the lamp in the kitchen and blows on the inscription, grins at it. Then carries the lamp to the back wall of the kitchen and peers at the photo-in-color of a nude girl, tacked to the wall.—After a moment, he crosses into the hall and calls out—*]

CHICKEN: Hey, up there, Myrtle, Mrs. Lot Ravenstock. Ain't you all getting hungry for something besides each other?

MYRTLE: Should I answer that man?

LOT: Answer him if you're hungry.

MYRTLE [*calling down from the upper hall*]: Lot needs feeding and I could eat something, too.

CHICKEN: Come on down, then.

MYRTLE: All right, thank you, I will.

[*Myrtle kisses Lot on the forehead as Chicken returns to the kitchen.*]

Oh, child, you're hot as fire! They say feed a cold and starve a fever, but you got both.

LOT: I'm hungry for nothing.

MYRTLE: You're hungry for love, and you're gonna have supper with it.

LOT: At the same time, with no appetite for either? [*His eyes fall shut.*]

MYRTLE: I oughtn't to go down there after the way he mocked me, but I smell fried potatoes which is something I cain't resist.

LOT: If you didn't smell fried potatoes you'd smell chicken . . .

MYRTLE: What?

LOT: Nothing. Go down in your washable velvet and eat for us both.

MYRTLE: I want to say one thing more before I face that creature in the kitchen. If you don't feel good now, you're gonna feel wonderful later and you believe it. Believe it?

LOT [*with closed eyes and an enigmatic smile*]: Yes, I do, completely.

MYRTLE: Here goes!—To what I don't know . . .

[*She goes down the hall steps as if approaching a jungle.*]

MYRTLE [*entering the kitchen*]: Hi.—Hello.—How are you?

[*He ignores all three salutations.*]

Y'know what I thought I smelt down here?

CHICKEN: Me? Chicken?

MYRTLE: Ha ha, no. I thought I smelt French fries down here.

CHICKEN: There's potatoes down here but there's nothing Frenchy about 'em.

161

MYRTLE: Bacon with 'em?

CHICKEN: You come down too late for the bacon.

MYRTLE: Oh, did I miss out on it?

CHICKEN: You sure missed out on the bacon, but there's some bacon grease in the skillet with the potatoes.

MYRTLE: Bacon grease gives potatoes a wonderful flavor. [*She looks about nervously.*]—Memphis is famous for its French fries.

CHICKEN: 'Sthat what it's famous for?

MYRTLE: Yais.—I worked last winter at a place called the French Fried Heaven.

[*Chicken grunts at this information.*]

—Put on ten pounds.—The way they cooked French fries, they put the potatoes in a *wire basket* and put the wire basket in deep fat.

CHICKEN: The fried potatoes here come out of a skillet.

MYRTLE: Oh, I didn't expeck you t'have a wire basket here.—In the country. I'll, uh, help myself an' then take a plate up to Lot.

[*Chicken grunts.*]

Still hot.

CHICKEN: Who?

MYRTLE: I meant the potatoes.

CHICKEN: Aw. I misunnerstood you.

[*As she fills a plate with potatoes, Chicken turns the lamp up.*]

MYRTLE: Where do you keep the silver?

CHICKEN: You mean knife an' fork?

MYRTLE: Just a fork. I don't need a knife for potatoes.

[*Chicken grunts.*]

—Here's the silver. It needs t'be polished. That colored girl Clara don't make herself very useful, I'll have to talk to her.

CHICKEN [*rising*]: Take this chair, this is a good chair for you.

MYRTLE: I don't want to take your chair. You stay where you are.

CHICKEN: No, you take this chair, I've warmed it up for you, and I'm going back out for another look at the levee.

MYRTLE: Right away?

[*He picks up his hip boots.*]

CHICKEN: I'll stay a while if you want me in here with you.

MYRTLE: This is a perfeck time for us to get better acquainted, don't you think so? [*She avoids his grinning look and sits gingerly down at the kitchen table.*]

CHICKEN: You don' have enough light.

MYRTLE: Yais, enough, I cin see.

CHICKEN [*pushing the oil lamp toward her*]: Don't strain your eyesight an' go blind before time to.

MYRTLE [*noticing the knife with which he'd been carving something onto the table*]:—Is, uh, this, uh, this switchblade knife your knife?

CHICKEN:—Is it yours or Lot's knife?

MYRTLE: I don't, he don't—carry a switchblade knife. [*She tries to laugh; coughs.*]

CHICKEN: Then I reckon it'd be a safe bet that it's mine.

163

MYRTLE: Will you please put it away? I never could stand the sight of a big switchblade knife like that fo' some—reason . . .

CHICKEN: Why's that?

MYRTLE:—It, it—[*shaking her head, tremulously*]—just, just—makes me uncomf'table always.

CHICKEN:—Reminds you of the end of one of the Mobile Hot Shots?

MYRTLE:—Yais.—No.

CHICKEN: Yais and no are two opposite answers. Maybe you mean maybe. [*He laughs and folds the switchblade knife and puts it in his pocket. He moves the plate.*]

MYRTLE: Maybe I ought to fill another plate fo' Lot an' eat with him upstairs. A sick person is lonesome.

CHICKEN: Eat a little with me befo' you go up. I need some company, too.

[*He empties the rest of the potatoes in another plate and starts eating them.*

[*She shoves the lamp toward his seat at the table. He shoves it back toward hers.*]

MYRTLE [*in a strained voice*]: A single boy in the country might amuse hisself by cutting a indecent word and a indecent picture in a kitchen table.

CHICKEN: What brought that up, that subjeck?

MYRTLE: They's no point in me pretendin' I didn't notice these fresh wood-shavings on this table and what's been cut in the wood. I want to say just this. A thing like this's understandable in a, uh, growin' boy in the country but you're past that. You ought to be beyond that. An' you ought to know it's insulting to a clean-livin' woman who is not int'rested or attracted to—indecent things in her life.

CHICKEN: I'm glad you understand that a single man in the country has got to amuse hisself.

MYRTLE: I said a growin' boy in the country, not a—adult—man with a—nawmul—mind.

CHICKEN: Aw. I misunnerstood you. You're not eatin' those good home-fried potatoes. You only like French fried potatoes?

MYRTLE:—I've said what I hed t'say an' now, if you will excuse me, I'll take this plate up to Lot. [*She rises with the plate.*]

CHICKEN: Lemme hold the lamp at the foot of the steps an' watch an' admire your hips as you climb up.

[*She hurries into the hall and he follows with the lamp. She stumbles on the steps and drops the plate.*]

Spilt 'em? On the steps?

MYRTLE: I could go upstairs with them better without your—watching!

[*They face each other a silent moment. Then Chicken laughs and scrapes the spilt potatoes off the steps onto the tin plate.*]

CHICKEN: Here you are. He'll never know you spilt 'em unless you tell him—

MYRTLE: *I'd* know I spilt 'em an' wouldn't dream of—of not infawmin' my husban' exackly of all that wint on down here. Good night!

CHICKEN: Hurry back down again, sister! Enjoyed your company down here!

[*She stumbles rapidly up the steps with the tin plate. As she enters the bedroom, Chicken returns to the kitchen, sets the lamp down by the carving and inscription, and grins savagely at them. Then he blows out the lamp.*]

165

SCENE THREE

MYRTLE: Lot? Are you asleep?

LOT: No. No, I'm awake.

MYRTLE: Can you eat a little?

LOT: No. I don't want food.

MYRTLE: I got to tell you something. Something awful. I am still shaking all over. Feel how cold my hand is. Well. I come down in the kitchen. I said I smelled some bacon. He said I come down too slow. The bacon was gone. But I could have some potatoes. So I hed some potatoes. I had to swallow my pride because I was dyin' of hunger not having nothing to eat since that ham sandwich we hed on the road this mawnin'. Well. I started to try to make some polite conversation. Not that I wanted to talk to that son of a bitch but because I knowed that people living together under one roof have got to make some effort to get along. Well. I noticed a pocket knife and some fresh wood-shavings in the middle of the table. Well. That was peculiar. Then all at once I seen the reason. *That man is a lunatic!* You know what he had done? He had cut out a disgusting picture in the table, in the wood of the table, right in front of my plate, a disgusting word and a disgusting pitcher.

LOT [*mysteriously smiling*]: What was the picture of? A man or a woman?

MYRTLE: Both!

LOT: Both?

MYRTLE: Yes, both.

LOT: Doing what?

MYRTLE: Can't you imagine what? With his dirty mind?

166

[*Lot laughs and coughs.*]

You think it's funny?

LOT: I think everything's funny. In this world. I even think it's funny I'm going to die.

MYRTLE: It may surprise you a little but I'm going to tell you what *I* am planning to do. I'm planning to get on the phone and call to THE POlice.

LOT: You think they'll come?

MYRTLE: I reckon they will when I tell them he's out of his mind and I am your wife and afraid to stay in the house with him over this night!

LOT: Nobody will come. Nobody will answer the phone.

MYRTLE: Why do you say they won't come?

LOT: Have you forgotten this county is half under water, and the crest of the flood is still coming?

MYRTLE: I keep forgetting that fact because it's like a bad dream I don't believe. And anyhow. Decent people have got to be protected, flood or no flood, yes, come hell or high water. I'm going down there and try to phone the police.

LOT: See if you can get hold of his wallet.

MYRTLE: What for?

LOT: He's got a paper in it he made me sign. It leaves the place to him if I should die. I don't know if the paper will still be good or not good if I die with a widow.

MYRTLE:—How could I git this paper?

LOT: How well can you hold liquor?

MYRTLE: I guess that question has a point but I don't see it.

167

LOT: I wondered if you could drink with a man till he passes out but you don't. Chicken's been drinking down there. I've heard him clump the liquor jug on the kitchen table every few minutes or so since we came upstairs, and he was probably drinking a good while before we got here.

MYRTLE: I guess you're drivin' at something, but I don't know what.

LOT: Chicken always has on him, in his wallet, that legal paper that leaves this place to him when I go.

MYRTLE: I don't understand what—

LOT: Let me tell you this without interruption, Myrtle, and try to listen to me. Get Chicken drunk but don't get drunk yourself, and when he passes out, get this legal paper out of his wallet, tear it to bits and pieces and burn 'em up. Then, as my wife, when I die, this place will be yours, go to you.—Valuable property.

MYRTLE: I don't know how to pretend to not drink but—

LOT: This paper in Chicken's wallet—he sleeps on a cot in the kitchen—he keeps this wallet containin' this paper under his pillow like it was sacred to him. Which it is. Sacred.

MYRTLE: It sounds like a risky suggestion, he's such a bull of a man, and—

LOT: Don't you want this place, all your own, when I go?

MYRTLE: Risky. Suppose he—?

LOT: Anything worth having and doing in this world is risky. So go down and use your charms on him and drink, but out of your drink take little sips like a bird while he sloshes down his till he falls on his cot, passed out, and you take out his wallet and out of his wallet take that legal paper and destroy it. Own this place. It would haunt me in my grave and my mother in hers if this place went to Chicken. That paper gone, you'll own

168

a good piece of property, and you can run him off it, marry
again, and be happy.

MYRTLE: How do I know if—?

LOT: Here's your chance to own something.

MYRTLE:—Is this the reason you married me, baby, an' brought
me down here?

LOT: I married and brought you down here to own a place of
your own an' be a lady.

MYRTLE:—Well—I'll give it a try. Hmmm. I wasn't called the
Petite Personality Kid for nothing.

LOT: Hear him? Coming back in the kitchen?

MYRTLE: Yais, down I go, wish me luck. God knows I'm gonna
need it.

LOT: I wish you luck and my mother does, too.

[*Myrtle picks up the oil lamp and starts to the door.*]

Do you have to remove the lamp and leave me in dark?

MYRTLE: Don't I have to light myself down the stairs?

LOT: Go ahead, take it. The moon's out like the bleary eye of
a drunkard.

MYRTLE: 'Sthere anything I can do for you 'fore I go?

LOT: Nothing. Go. Get the paper.

[*She exits from the bedroom with the lamp. The bedroom is
completely dimmed out except for a faint and fitful streak of
moonlight on Lot in the rocker.*]

SCENE FOUR

At the curtain rise, immediately following, Myrtle is descending the stairs with the lamp. Hearing her, Chicken returns to the kitchen table and turns up the lamp.

MYRTLE:—I'm afraid I let my nerves get the better of me. Let's forget it. I, uh, come down to tell you I'm worried sick about Lot. He has trouble drawing his breath.

CHICKEN: It's hard to draw breath without lungs.

MYRTLE: He won't stop smoking. And says it's the end of the world. I simply couldn't stand it a minute longer without a—drink. Have you got some liquor down here?

CHICKEN: They don't sell me bottle liquor in this county but I can git it by the jug from a—ole colored man that brews a pretty good brew.

MYRTLE: Is, uh, that the jug there?

CHICKEN: Yep, and it ain't drained yet. I'll give you a drink—I treat you pretty nice, don't I? For a single man in the country?

MYRTLE: We just—haven't yet got used to each other. And this has been a day an' a night that would make any girl nervous with or without nerves in her.

CHICKEN: I guess you want a stiff drink, a pretty stiff one.

MYRTLE: Oh, uh, for me, just average. You have one with me, let's drink together an' git better acquainted.—Oh. This wash. D'you mind if I hang up some nylons and undies I washed upstairs? And brung down?

CHICKEN: Hang 'em up, they'll dry out nice in the flood.

MYRTLE: Do me a favor and stop reminding me of this—possible flood.

CHICKEN [*sits*]: It's not a possible flood, this flood is certain.

MYRTLE: Let's not—talk about it.

CHICKEN:—Why do you make that whistling noise when you breathe?

MYRTLE: I got that allergy thing—I wint to a Memphis doctor who give me the allergy tests and guess what he found out, he found out I was living with a cat and had a allergy to it. Yes. I had a cat I was real, real fond of, cat named Fluffy. Whew. [*She rises.*] From the way I suffer from my asthma tonight, I'm willing to bet that there's a cat somewhere on this place.

CHICKEN: I got a cat.

MYRTLE: That explains it.

CHICKEN: I brought her in for company tonight.

MYRTLE: Oh, no wonder I am choking with asthma, git that cat out of here, for heaven's sake, please!

CHICKEN: Here, Kitty. [*Lazily he seizes the cat and pulls up a trapdoor near the kitchen table and drops the cat through it. She drops with a howl and a splash below. He drops the trapdoor shut.*]

MYRTLE: Why, that cellar is flooded! I heard a splash!

CHICKEN: You said you wanted her out.

MYRTLE: Out the door, not *drowned!*

[*She raises the trapdoor and cries "Kitty!" He nudges her stooping figure with his knee. She screams and rolls on the floor.*]

Oh, my God, you tried to push me in! You tried to drown me!

CHICKEN: Ha ha ha!

MYRTLE: Oh, my God, my God, you tried to drown me!

CHICKEN: Ha ha ha ha ha ha ha!

LOT [*calling weakly above*]: *Myrtle, Myrtle!*

CHICKEN: Your lover is calling for you.

MYRTLE [*crawling away on the floor*]: Close!—Close that trapdoor!

CHICKEN: Aw, come on, knock it off! Nobody's going to drown you—Myrtle Turtle!

MYRTLE: You wanted to drown me like you drowned that cat!

CHICKEN: That cat ain't drowned. She swum on top of the woodpile.—Same as you'd do if I put you down there with her.

MYRTLE: —I—cain't—swim!

CHICKEN: —Can you do anything?—Outside of bed?

MYRTLE: Chicken, please shut that trapdoor.

[*He kicks it shut.*]

Oh, my heart! How you scared me! I ain't been well since I hed that—operation . . . [*She gasps and rises weakly.*] Please, I—give me a shot of that—whiskey . . .

CHICKEN: Go on. Pour you'self one.

MYRTLE [*breathlessly laughing*]: I'm afraid to git up! I swear to goodness I am!

CHICKEN: Aw, now, knock it off. I was just fooling a little.

MYRTLE [*cautiously crossing to the table*]: Where is—where is a cup? My heart is—still beating!

CHICKEN: Shit, if your heart wasn' beatin' you'd be daid!

MYRTLE: Not like this! It's beatin' like a hammer!

CHICKEN: "My heart beat like a ham-mer!
Your arms—wound around me tight!
And stars—fell on Alabama—last—night!"

MYRTLE:—Do you remember this one?
"Is it true what they say about Dixie?
Is a dream by that stream so sublime?
Do they laugh, do they love
LIKE they say in ev'ry song!!
—If it's true—that's where I—be—long!"

CHICKEN: Ha ha ha ha ha! That one goes back a long way. Yes, siree, Bob, that's a real old-timer!

MYRTLE: And how about this one? Oh, this one is a—

LOT: Myr-tlllllllle!

MYRTLE: Coming, honey, coming in just a minute!—[*fearfully as he approaches the table toward her*]—Oh, this is fun, this— singing—I—love a song-fest, I love a—community—singing! Almost more than anything I can think of.

CHICKEN: Go on and sing! What song?

MYRTLE:—Wait till I—get my drink down! [*She crosses back of the table with whiskey in a tin cup.*]

CHICKEN: Wettin' your whistle, first?

MYRTLE: That's right, wetting my whistle!

CHICKEN: You almost wet something else when I pushed you toward that trapdoor! Huh, Myrtle?—*Ha ha ha ha ha!*

MYRTLE [*faintly and mirthlessly*]: Ha ha ha . . .

CHICKEN: Awright, now, what song was you going to sing for me, next on the program of old-time fav'rites?

MYRTLE: I wish that I had my little ukulele! My—dear ole uke!

173

CHICKEN: How 'bout a guitar, will that do?

MYRTLE [*with an air of delight*]: Oh, hev you got a guitar!

CHICKEN: Yeah. Here. [*He removes guitar from back of closet door and hands it to her.*]

MYRTLE: This is a *man*-size instrument!

CHICKEN: Don't you like a man-size instrument?

MYRTLE: I'm just wondering if I—

CHICKEN: Oh, I bet you can play it!

MYRTLE: We'll find out if I can.

CHICKEN: Sure you can. What's the number? I'll sing with you.

MYRTLE: Here's one I can pick out with a—few—chords . . . [*She is almost too breathless to sing.*]

"*They's a long, long trail a-windin'*
Into the land of my dreams!
Where the nightingale is—"

[*He moves toward the trapdoor. Her voice dies out in panic.*]

CHICKEN: Whacha stop for?

MYRTLE: You was going to sing with me.

CHICKEN: Sing it through once by you'self so I'll get the words.

MYRTLE: You mean you don't know the words to that old number? It's one of those songs that—

CHICKEN: What?

MYRTLE: —Do me a favor, Chicken. Don't stand there by that trapdoor to the cellar. It makes me too nervous to sing. Sit over here by me.

174

CHICKEN: Aw, you ain't nervous, you just think you're nervous.

MYRTLE: I'm nervous enough to scream.

CHICKEN: Don't scream. Sing! Sing some other old song.

MYRTLE: Like, uh—what?

CHICKEN: How about something religious?

MYRTLE: You really want something religious?

CHICKEN: Yeah, yeah, something from church, something out of the hymnbook.

MYRTLE: Funny I—know lots of church songs but—can't think of any right now, ha ha! Ain't that funny? Wait a minute! Wait a minute! One's comin' back to me now. Oh, yes. Oh, yes, I got one, ha ha! I got one now! [*She assumes a rapt, grotesquely stiff smile, throws her head back and croons with half-closed eyes.*] "My feet took a walk in heavenly grass . . ."

CHICKEN: You're gettin' hoarse, Myrtle.

MYRTLE: I thought you was gonna sing with me.

CHICKEN: I don't sing good enough to.

MYRTLE: You got a *good* voice. Ain't I silly? Gaspin' for breath like this!

CHICKEN: It's that cat allergy thing, you got that allergy thing!

MYRTLE: No, no, it's not cats now—

CHICKEN: It's what? What, Myrtle?

MYRTLE: *Nerves!* A nervous condition!

CHICKEN: You're worried about that cat, that's what's your trouble. I think you're a member of that society, that human humane society, maybe the president of it. [*He is pulling on his rubber hipboots.*]

MYRTLE: What's you getting into those rubber boots for?

CHICKEN: I'm going down in the basement to fetch that cat.

MYRTLE: Oh, she's done for, she's gone, now.

CHICKEN: No, she ain't. Come on, let's find that cat. You're worried about her, so let's go down in the basement an' find that cat.

MYRTLE [*backing away from him*]: You—*you* do that—if it's possible for you to do.

[*He jerks the trapdoor open. Myrtle screams and hurls the guitar away as she rushes into the hall and scrambles up the stairs, screaming repeatedly. Chicken howls with laughter; then abruptly leaps into the basement with a splash, calling "Pussy, pussy, pussy?" We hear the cat yowling and Chicken laughing. He leaps back up from the trapdoor, still laughing, with the cat in his hand. He is still laughing and holding the cat as the stage dims out.*]

INTERMISSION

ACT TWO

Immediately following. The bedroom is lighted and, at a much lower level, the back steps of the house where Chicken sits with his cat. The parlor, which won't be used again in the play, is now masked by an opaque transparency—or perhaps has been detached from the set.

Lot remains in the wicker chair, still smoking with his mother's ivory holder and wearing now her white silk wrapper. His "Mona Lisa" smile is more sardonic and the violet shadows about his eyes are deeper.

Myrtle stands, panting, in the doorway.

LOT:—From the singing and other commotions I heard down there, I don't need to ask you if you got the paper.—Did you? No, you didn't.

MYRTLE: You listen here! Enough is enough, and more than enough is too much!

LOT: You didn't get much liquor down him.—Did you?

MYRTLE: That man, that animal down there, could drink a liquor store dry and walk straight to another!

LOT: I thought you told me there wasn't a man on earth that you weren't able to manage. Well. If that statement was accurate, then either Chicken isn't a man or he isn't on earth. And I think he is both.

MYRTLE: Don't be sarcastic with *me.*

LOT: Don't shout so he can hear you. Can you speak without shouting?

MYRTLE: I said don't be sarcastic with me. I'm not in the mood to take it after what I went through in the kitchen with your so-called brother.

LOT: My opposite type.

MYRTLE: Is there a key to this door to lock him out?

LOT: No. I hate and despise him with such a passion that if this place or anything on this place became his property—

MYRTLE: S'pose he comes up here and drags me down?

LOT: Neither mother or me could rest in peace in Old Gray Cemetery.

MYRTLE: I'm not in a cemetery. What about me?

LOT: What about you—

MYRTLE: There's not just you, there's me. The selfish streak in your nature is wide as the river—flooding!

LOT: Have you ever owned much of anything in your life?

MYRTLE: Yais! My self-respeck an' decency as a woman!

LOT: In addition to that, marvelous as it is, would you like to own and possess entirely as your own a place that's worth much more than it gives appearance of being?

MYRTLE:—Worth what?

LOT: Over fifty thousand and could increase well managed. [*long pause*]—Well? Attractive to you or not?

MYRTLE: I've never owned a stone I could call my own.

LOT:—A pitiful confession, but now's your chance if you want it.

[*There is a pause as Myrtle reflects.*]

MYRTLE:—Sugar? Baby? Why don't you get in bed instead of sitting at a window in a light silk wrapper?

LOT: I breathe better sitting up in a chair—and can look at the sky.

MYRTLE: The sky's clouded over.

LOT: Once in a while the moon comes out of those fast-moving clouds, and it—says things to me in the soft voice of my mother . . .

MYRTLE: I wish you would get in bed and let me hold you and love you.

LOT: You don't have to hold me to love me.

MYRTLE: You're shivering. Lemme put something heavier around you like a blanket.

LOT: No, no, don't. I don't want to be smothered.

MYRTLE: I am going and fill a hot-water bottle for you 'an git you in this bed if you like it or not.

LOT: There's not any hot-water bottle.

MYRTLE: I never travel without one. It's in my traveling case.

LOT: I should've known.

MYRTLE: What?

LOT: —Nothing, and not much of that either.

MYRTLE: I am going back down there and get hold of that paper, how I don't know, but somehow, I'm goin' down in my show costume as The Personality Kid. [*She changes quickly into the costume.*]

LOT: I think what attracts you back down there is nothing made of rubber and nothing made of paper, whether you face it or not.

MYRTLE: Your fever's gone to your haid, if you think that.

LOT: I don't just think it, I know it—I won't see daylight again.

MYRTLE: I can pick you up and carry you to the bed and that's what I'm gonna do when I've filled my hot-water bottle.

LOT: Anybody with arms could pick me up—if they wanted to force me against my will.

MYRTLE: Is it against your will to be loved and made well?

LOT: —No.—If you can't make him pass out to get that paper, knock him out with a hammer that's in the drawer of the kitchen table, and *don't come up here again* without that paper. You get that paper and you can pick me up and carry me to the bed with no resistance and I'll—rest in your arms . . .

MYRTLE: I got to take this lamp to get down the stairs in my shaky condition.

LOT: Take it. I get enough light from the sky.

[*She goes back into the hall and starts down the steps. She is halfway down them with the lamp when Chicken slams open the back door and enters the lower hall.*]

MYRTLE [*terrified gasp*]: HAH! [*She drops the oil lamp on the stairs, it goes out*].—I thought—

CHICKEN: Don't strain your brain thinkin'.

MYRTLE: Lot's—Lot's havin' a chill. Terrible. I want to fill up a hot-water bottle for him. Cin I come down?

CHICKEN: Why do you ask to come downstairs in your house?

MYRTLE: I don't possess this house or anything in it except what I brought here with me.

CHICKEN: All that electric equipment to make life easy for you?

[*He laughs and enters the kitchen. Myrtle stops on the steps and speaks tremulously—*]

180

MYRTLE: I know you wuh teasing me with that trapdoor open, but would you please push the table over it now.

CHICKEN: It ain't open now.

MYRTLE: Open or shut, I couldn't be comf'table in the kitchen unless that table was over that trapdoor.

CHICKEN: Why, sure, Mrs. Lot Ravenstock. A hired hand on a place always does what pleases the lady and the bossman. [*He shoves the table further with his foot.*]—How's that now, does that suit you?

MYRTLE [*entering the kitchen*]: Yes, thank you, fine, perfeck. I feel much more easy.

CHICKEN: You're a city lady and I'm a country boy with common habits. I hope you'll excuse me for them.

MYRTLE: I've been teased in my life. I had two older brothers, Jack and Jim, that teased me nearly to death. So you see I'm used to teasing.

CHICKEN: You're walking around like you wuh lookin' fo' something.

MYRTLE: A kettle to boil water in. So I can fill a hot-water bottle. [*She removes the hot-water bottle from the beat-up case and wanders distractedly about the kitchen.*]

CHICKEN: Why don'tcha put the hot-water bottle down while you look for the kettle so you'll have both your hands free?

MYRTLE: Ha!—What's the matter with me? I sure don't seem to have my head on my—!

[*He hands a kettle to her.*]

Thanks. [*She sets the kettle on the stove.*]

CHICKEN:—Is that how you do it?

181

MYRTLE:—Huh?

CHICKEN:—You git the kettle hot first and thin put th' water in it?

MYRTLE: Ha ha! I put that empty kettle on the stove without water in it!

CHICKEN: Gimme th' kettle. I'll git you some water in it from the rain barrel out there. [*He crosses to the door with the kettle and descends to the rain barrel.*]

[*She follows to the door.*]

MYRTLE: They say rain water's the purest water there is.

CHICKEN: Is that what they say? Well, nothin's too pure for Lot.

MYRTLE:—Not that it matters in a hot-water bottle . . .

CHICKEN: Yeah, well . . . [*He hands her the dripping kettle.*]

[*She returns inside. He watches her back as she crosses and gives a slight wolf whistle. She sets the kettle on the stove with a bang that makes her give a startled laugh.*]

What's the joke?

[*She goes on laughing helplessly.*]

Let me in on the joke, it must be a good one.

MYRTLE: I just, just!—*got*—*hysterics!* [*She continues giggling.*]

CHICKEN: They's two ways to stop hysterics in a woman. One way is to give her a slap in the face and the other way is to lay her. Sometimes you got to do both.

MYRTLE: Oh, I'm all right now. I come out of hysterics as quick as I go in them.—How come a handsome man like you is still single?

CHICKEN:—I'm dark-complected.

MYRTLE: What of it?

CHICKEN: They's not been a woman on this place, not since Miss Lottie died, but the colored girl, Clara, and she's took to the hills to get away from the flood.

MYRTLE: You mention this flood like it didn't scare you a bit.

CHICKEN: Floods make the land richer.

MYRTLE: What good does that do if you drown?

CHICKEN: I'm not gonna drown.—Are you?

MYRTLE: Lord God Jesus, I pray to my Savior I won't!

CHICKEN: You'd do better praying to Chicken.

MYRTLE: I'm counting on your protection.

CHICKEN: You better not count on that.

MYRTLE: That's what I'm counting on, Chicken.

CHICKEN: Count on nothing. Set down.

MYRTLE: I prefer to stay on my feet a while if—

CHICKEN: If what?

MYRTLE:—If you don't object.

CHICKEN: Shit, I don't mind if you stand on your head if you want to! But look. I got this old auto cushion I'll put on this here chair and'll make you a nice soft seat. I know a woman don't like a hard seat, does she? Well, here's a real soft cushion for you to sit on while we talk.

MYRTLE:—Thanks! [*She seats herself tensely, on the edge of the auto cushion.*]

183

CHICKEN [*with a slow, wolfish grin*]: Now you got *three* cushions?

MYRTLE:—*Three?*—OH!—*Ha ha!*—Yaiss—three . . .

[*Loud silence in the kitchen.*]

CHICKEN: You feel comf'table?

MYRTLE: Yaiss! Yes, very! Are you?

CHICKEN: I always make myself comfortable as I can.

MYRTLE: Why not? you should!—A man should . . .

CHICKEN:—Should what?

MYRTLE:—Why—uh—make himself as comf'table as he—can . . .

CHICKEN:—How about you? Are you comf'table, too? On those three soft cushions?

MYRTLE: Yes, I told you I was. I'm just a little worried about my husband. I had no idea, I simply had no notion at all that he was in such a bad condition as this. I mean I—I just didn't have any idea . . .

CHICKEN: It's like you bought a used car that turned out to be a lemon.

MYRTLE: Oh, that's not how I look at it. That boy has touched the deepest chord in my nature. I mean I—[*She suddenly sobs.*]

CHICKEN: Quit that. I want to talk to you.

MYRTLE: Yes, talk!

CHICKEN: I guess you know the setup.

MYRTLE [*struggling for composure*]: The what?

CHICKEN: The setup. Do you know it?

184

MYRTLE [*with a weak attempt at levity*]: The only setup I know of is in a dry state they'll serve you a setup for liquor but not the liquor. You got to bring that with you.

CHICKEN:—If I was your lawyer I would advise you not to try to be funny.

MYRTLE: Can't we—joke a little?

CHICKEN: I'd advise you against it. Can you concentrate on the legal setup if I explain it to you, or do you think it's something that don't concern you?

MYRTLE: I'm—anxious to know the—setup. Is the kettle boilin', is that water hot yet?

CHICKEN: Fawgit th' kettle.

MYRTLE: But I told Lot I'd—

CHICKEN: You don't seem t'want to know about the setup.

MYRTLE: Oh, that's not true, I do!

CHICKEN: I'll explain it to you.

MYRTLE: Yais, wonderful, do that! Whatever concerns this place an' my future life on it is impawtent t'me to understand an' t'know.

CHICKEN: Lot an' me are half brothers. Has that sunk into your haid yet?

MYRTLE: Oh, yes, that I do know. It come out in the, the—conversation we hed when we—first met, this—day.

CHICKEN: Daddy got Lot in marriage but not me. You're lookin' at what is called a wood's colt. [*He perches himself on the table and the light is hot on him.*] He married this little blonde-haided woman that worked in a beauty shop in Clarksdale. Are you list'nin' or still too nervous to lissen?

185

MYRTLE: I'm listn'n close. All ears.

CHICKEN: This little lady was named Miss Lottie, so when Lot was bawn, he got the name of Lot. Legal, bawn in marriage. Not a wood's colt. Me—wood's colt. You know what a wood's colt is?

MYRTLE: No, I don't know that I know. All I know is you look—

CHICKEN:—Dark-complected?

MYRTLE: Foreign.—Foreign?

CHICKEN: My son of a bitch of a daddy got me offen a dark-complected woman he lived with in Alabama.—What about it?

MYRTLE: Why—nothing!

[*Slight pause.*]

Ain't you drinkin' no more? This awful night?

CHICKEN: Why're you so anxious for me to drink more?

MYRTLE: I don't like drinking alone. It makes me lonesome.

CHICKEN: I can drink you under this kitchen table, tonight.

MYRTLE: I'd rather stay on my feet with the flood you say's coming.

CHICKEN: You'd rather drown standing up?

MYRTLE: Don't talk about drowning. You wouldn't let that happen.

CHICKEN:—Let's get back to the setup.—Lot's mother, Miss Lottie, she thought she was surely going to bury my daddy. Hell, he was sixty when he married Miss Lottie.

MYRTLE: Is that what you mean by the setup?

186

CHICKEN: Just shut up and listen.—She'd no sooner got married to him than she begun to cheat on him with a good-looking young Greek fellow that had a fruit store in town. Why, ev'ry afternoon, Miss Lottie would say to Daddy, "Daddy, I think I will drive in town to buy some fruit to make us a nice fruit salad." And when she got to the store, the store man would let her in and lock the door, and she'd stay in for two hours and come out with four or five peaches like it had took her them two hours to pick out that small bag of peaches.

MYRTLE: Why didn't you tell your daddy?

CHICKEN: If I had told him, he'd've told her I told him, and she would of got me thrown outa here in minutes!—Well, she did bury my daddy and the place was hers, but she didn't have long to hold it. The Greek sold out his fruit store, quit Miss Lottie, and left.—He just left town but Miss Lottie left the world.

MYRTLE: Daid. Yes. Lot told me.—Tragic.

CHICKEN: Well, she lived long enough to throw me off the place. Called me in her little parlor one day and fired me like a field hand. "Chicken," she said, "I think it's just time for you to clear off this place and make your own way in the world." I said, "Well, gimme what's comin' to me."—What she give me amounted to just about the pay that a field hand gets for a week's work. It got me down the state to Meridian where I worked in a sawmill till . . . And then this happened—Miss Lottie couldn't go on without trips to that fruit store so she quit eating, quit sleeping—quit breathing. And one month after she died, Lot started dying. One lung gone and one going, but trying to run this place. Didn't take long for him to find out he couldn't so I begun to hear from him. He sent for me to come back and operate this place for him, sent for me twice by letter and a third time by wire. First and only wire *I* ever got in my life. "Chicken, come back," was the message, "I will make a deal with you."—Well, I'm no fool.

MYRTLE: No, no, you're no fool.

CHICKEN: I said, "All right, but I'm going to name the deal." I

187

said, "If you want me to run this place for you, well, here's the deal. Whin you are through with TB!—It goes to me . . ."

MYRTLE: TB?

CHICKEN: You ain't paying attention to what I tell you. Not TB. The place, this *place!*

MYRTLE:—Oh!—So that's the setup.

CHICKEN: Yes, ma'am, that is the setup.

MYRTLE: Oh. Uh-huh. I see . . .

CHICKEN: You don't look happy about it!

MYRTLE: Don't I? Well, now, after all, you can't expect me to be overjoyed about it. I mean, after all, I'm human. And—

CHICKEN: And what?

MYRTLE:—Nothin', nothin' but—

CHICKEN: But what?

MYRTLE:—if Lot dies, I'm his widow and—

CHICKEN: That's just the little situation we're tryin' to git straightened out right now in this kitchen before the flood water comes. *I* got a decision to make.

MYRTLE: What decision?

CHICKEN: A big one. A big one for you and me both.—Have you ever climbed on a roof?

MYRTLE: Me? Climbed on a roof? No. Not that I can remember. It don't seem—likely . . . Why? Why do you ask me if I ever climbed on a roof?

CHICKEN: If you can't climb on a roof Lot won't *have* a widow

188

when the flood water comes. Now do you understand why I asked you that question?—Yeah. I can see that you do. So now to go on with what—what's the matter? Why are you getting up?

[*Myrtle has risen stiffly from the chair with a look of slow and dreadful comprehension. Her breathing is audible and rapid.*]

MYRTLE: No, no, no, I'm all right, I'm—*fine*, I'm—all right . . .

CHICKEN: Then why don't you stay in your seat? Ain't that auto cushion comfortable to sit on?

MYRTLE: Sure, it's—fine! [*She remains standing, her eyes wide and bright but not focused.*]

[*He rises deliberately and picks up the auto cushion, examines it and dusts it and puts it back down again.*]

CHICKEN: You women have got a lot of heat in you. That cushion is warm from your body. Why don't you sit down while I finish explaining the setup?

MYRTLE: Oh, it's all clear now. I understand the setup and I want you to know, here is my right hand to God, that everything you told me is okay as far as I am concerned. I got no designs on nothing. You know it's funny how quickly the human mind changes! Ain't it queer how quick it changes? I had my heart set on a quiet, happy married life. Now what I want most in the world is to return to show business!—That's what I'm going to do, I'm going to cut out all fats and sweets and fried foods and get back my shape and go straight back to show business. It keeps you alive. It keeps you trim. It keeps you alert. It's the business for me. Absolutely no other can compare with it for keeping you healthy and active.—Now I think I can fill that hot-water bottle and take it up to that poor child I married . . . —*God please pity us both!*

[*She starts toward the stove. But he seizes her wrist.*]

CHICKEN: I want you to stay sitting here till I've finished talking to you. You going to do that?

MYRTLE: —Why—sure!

CHICKEN: Good. Take a shot of this liquor. It might be good for you.

MYRTLE: Why, thanks! [*The tin cup shakes; she lifts it with both hands to her lips.*]—Thanks . . .

CHICKEN: So I said to my half brother Lot, "I want this place when you're gone. I been on this place all my life. I was here before you come to it, and I want to be here when you go." Is that understood? Is that understood, now, clearly?

MYRTLE: Yes, yes, clearly, clearly . . .

CHICKEN: Good. So. So we put it on paper. Had it drawn up, legal. Now! [*He removes his wallet and unfolds from about it a thick rubber band.*] I got this paper to prove it.

[*She stretches out her hand as he produces the paper from his wallet.*]

Oh, no. Someone's got itchy fingers!—Look but don't touch!— Understand? I never let this paper out of my hands. I guard it with my life and my soul and my body. So now you see.

MYRTLE: Oh, yes, now I see.

CHICKEN: You ain't even looking at it. Look at this paper, will you? [*He shakes it in front of her.*] Does it look legal to you? You see this notary seal and names of witnesses on it? You see Lot's signature on it and my signature on it?

MYRTLE: Yes, yes!

CHICKEN: You want more light so you can see it more clearly? [*He turns up the lamp.*] There now, you can see it clearly!

MYRTLE: —It, it—sure looks—legal.

CHICKEN: —Yeah, but—you never can tell . . .

190

MYRTLE:—What?

CHICKEN: A smart lawyer might find some loopholes in it. Law is a tricky thing. I never would of dreamed that son of a bitch would marry and leave a widow. That changes the situation. Maybe now this agreement will not hold up in a court of law.

MYRTLE: I wouldn't—worry about it.

CHICKEN: Naw, you wouldn't worry about it. Why would you worry about it? You'd git the place, not Chicken!

MYRTLE: I, I, I—don't want this place! What would I do with this place?

CHICKEN: Want it or not you'd git it if bein' his widow makes this paper—not good.

MYRTLE: Chicken, Chicken, look here!

CHICKEN: That's what he figured. Son of a bitch thought he'd screw me by leaving a widow. But one thing he didn't count on was the house being flooded and him and his widow both—

MYRTLE: Oh, now, look here, Chicken!

CHICKEN: Him and his widow both!—Drowned in it!—Unless I haul his widow up on the roof.

MYRTLE: *Chicken, I—can't catch my breath!* I, I, we . . . we . . . [*Myrtle stands gasping like a fish out of water, leaning for support against the table.*]

CHICKEN: Take a good breath. Then talk!

MYRTLE: I'm trying to catch one!—Lot an' me, we—ain't—married!

CHICKEN: You an' Lot ain't married?

MYRTLE: No, a-course not! Are you kiddin'? [*She tries to*

191

laugh.] You didn't *believe* that, did you? Ha ha!—Ha ha . . . —Why, me and that boy are no more married than the man in the moon!

CHICKEN: He showed me a license.

MYRTLE: Yeah, but you said yourself you can buy those things for two bits at a novelty store to git you a hotel room to lay a woman. A joke, can't you take a joke? Ha ha!

CHICKEN: This is no jokin' matter.

MYRTLE: Well, it was just a joke, Chicken, it was all just a joke, ha ha! [*Her laugh is hollow; expires in a gasp.*]

CHICKEN: Yeah. Well. *Maybe.*

MYRTLE: They's no maybe about it. I ought to know I'm not married!

CHICKEN: No?

MYRTLE: No! Look, whin I take that step, a step as serious in my life as marriage would be, I wouldn't take it with a—TB case! You want to know something? You want to know something, Chicken?

CHICKEN: Yeah, I want to know something.

MYRTLE: That poor boy bleaches his hair, not only has TB but bleaches his hair. Look, do you imagine that I'd give up a career in show business to marry a, a, to marry a, to, to, to marry a—

CHICKEN:—What's wrong now?

MYRTLE [*with a grimace*]: Throat's! Stopped!

CHICKEN: Choked on lies! That's what you done, you choked yourself on lies!

MYRTLE: Now, Chicken.

CHICKEN: "Now, Chicken."

MYRTLE: Oh, don't mock me, please!

CHICKEN: I think I better take a new look at that paper. Go up and git me that paper.

MYRTLE: Which, which paper?

CHICKEN: This license you say you got from a novelty store.

MYRTLE: Lot's got it, he's got it! I, I don't have it, Lot's got it!

CHICKEN: Jesus. I never seen anybody in such a condition as you seem to be in.

MYRTLE: I told you about how scared I am of—[*She turns away, gasping as if drowning.*]—water! [*She gasps twice and clutches the chair back.*] Oh, God, Chicken, why don't you take my word? I'm not Lot's widow, I mean I won't be his widow if he dies, 'cause we ain't married.

CHICKEN: Go up and git that paper.

MYRTLE:—Whin?

CHICKEN: Now.

MYRTLE: Lot's water's boiling, the kettle is boiling, I'll fill his hot-water bottle.

CHICKEN: All right. Fill his hot-water bottle and git that paper and bring it down here so I can give it a careful examination.

MYRTLE: Help me. I can't—do—this!

[*She drops the hot-water bottle. Chicken picks it up and fills it by the stove.*]

CHICKEN: Now go up and give him his hot-water bottle and git that marriage license while you're up there.

[She starts upstairs.]

CHICKEN *[to her back]*: Hurry.

MYRTLE: I'm goin' fast as I can, unable to breathe!

CHICKEN: You're breathin'.

[She opens the bedroom door and calls softly.]

MYRTLE: Lot? Lot, baby?

[Light falls on him: he looks like a Far Eastern idol. He doesn't answer except by rocking his wicker chair in the pool of moonlight.]

How are you, now, Lot, baby?

LOT: You know how I am: still breathing. Have you got Chicken drunk yet?

MYRTLE: I don't think he's gonna get drunk, liquor don't seem to affect him.

LOT: Then you won't get the paper and he'll get the place.

MYRTLE: —Well . . .

LOT: You sound resigned to it, Myrtle.

MYRTLE: —If this house is flooded, both floors, could *you* get me up on the roof?

LOT: Aw. Chicken has offered to get you up on the roof.

MYRTLE: You brought me here and put me at his mercy, don't forget that.

LOT: I thought you could handle Chicken.

MYRTLE: You gave me no warning.

CHICKEN [*impatiently, below stairs*]: *Hey! Come on!*

LOT: What's he want? Just your company down there?

MYRTLE: I got your hot-water bottle. Here's your hot-water bottle.

LOT: My chill's gone now. I'm burning up with fever. What I need's an ice pack.

MYRTLE: Honey, you know there ain't no ice in this house.

LOT: What were you doing down there with Chicken.

MYRTLE: I was waitin' for the kettle to boil so I could fill up this hot-water bottle which you don't want no more.

LOT: You know something?

MYRTLE: Huh?

LOT: I think you're a whore.

MYRTLE [*sadly, almost gently*]: Lot, baby, that is the most cruel thing that anybody has ever said to me in my entire life. Here is my right hand to God! After all that I have suffered to stay on the straight and narrow, to be called a whore by my just-married husband.

LOT: I said it looks like I married a prostitute and brought her home for Chicken.

MYRTLE: I know, I know what you said, you don't have to repeat it. The strange thing about this is, *I*, I haven't blamed *you! You* are blaming *me!*

[*The dialogue overlaps.*]

LOT: I married a whore and—

MYRTLE: Here I'm standing, here, full of TB germs because you—

LOT: . . . brought her back here to Chicken—

MYRTLE [*completing her sentence above*]: . . . lied! Lied to me! And have bleached hair and—

LOT: . . . goddam whore an' brought her back here to Chicken for him to lay while I die up here in this rocker, you *common* trash!

MYRTLE: God!—How mean people are!—I'm going downstairs after that.

LOT: Sure, and it makes how many times you gone down them!? To Chicken?

MYRTLE: This time is the last time. I'm not going to come back up. Not till you call me up and apologize to me and maybe not even then. No, not even then—maybe . . . [*She starts out; turns back and roots in his coat pocket: the coat hangs on a hook on the wall.*]

LOT: What are you doing? What did you take from my coat?

MYRTLE: Our marriage license! Your half brother wants to look at it to see if it's real.

[*She starts out again. Lot begins to laugh softly as she closes the door. She pushes it open again and says—*]

—What are you laughing at?

LOT: At life!—I think it's funny.

[*Myrtle closes the door rather softly. Chicken waits in the hall. She descends.*]

SCENE TWO

Myrtle enters the kitchen.

MYRTLE: Here it is, this is it. [*She hands him the license.*] You can see it's no good.

CHICKEN: —It's got signatures on it.

MYRTLE: Sure, they put signatures on 'em to make 'em look real, but—

CHICKEN: This looks like a genuine license to me.

MYRTLE: I give you my right hand to God!—That thing is fake!

CHICKEN: Don't give me your right hand to God. I don't want it and He don't want it neither. Nobody wants your right or left hand to nothing. However, I'll keep this thing. I'll put it with my legal agreement with Lot. [*He folds the license into his wallet and studies her somberly.*] Are you able to write?

MYRTLE: Why, uh—yais!

CHICKEN: I don't mean just your name.

MYRTLE: No! Yais, I mean yais!—I been through four grades of school.

CHICKEN: Take a seat at this table. I'm gonna give you a little test in writing. [*He tears a sheet from a writing tablet; sets it before her with a pen and ink bottle.*] You say you are able to write, and I am able to read. You see this pin an' paper I set befo' you?

MYRTLE: Yais! Perfectly! Plainly!

CHICKEN: Do you write standing up?

MYRTLE: Yais! No, I mean no! [*She scrambles into the chair.*]

CHICKEN: Now take this pin and write out on this paper what I tell you to write.

197

MYRTLE: What do you—?

CHICKEN: Shut up. I'm gonna dictate to you a letter that you will write an' sign, and this letter will be to me.

MYRTLE: Why should I write you a letter when, when—you're right here?

CHICKEN: You'll understand why when you write it and write it out plain enough so anybody can read it.

MYRTLE: —My hand is—

CHICKEN: What?

MYRTLE: Shakin'!

CHICKEN: Control it.

MYRTLE: It's hard to control it with my nerves so unstrung.

CHICKEN: Which hand do you write with, with the left or the right?

MYRTLE: Oh, with the right, I'm right-handed.

CHICKEN: Well, give me that shaky right hand.

MYRTLE: What do you want with my hand?

CHICKEN: Stop it shakin'. [*He takes hold of her hand in both of his.*]

MYRTLE: What big hands you got, Chicken.

CHICKEN: Feel the calluses on 'em? I got those calluses on my hands from a life of hard work on this fuckin' place, worked on it like a nigger and got nothin' for it but bed and board, and the bed was a cot in the kitchen and the board was no better than slops in the trough of a sow. However, things do change, they do gradually change, you just got to wait and be patient till the time comes to strike and then strike hard. [*He is rubbing her hand between his.*] Now it's comin', that time. This place is

198

gonna be mine when the house is flooded an' I won't be unhappy sittin' on the roof of it till the flood goes down.

MYRTLE: No. Me neither. I'll be—pleased and—relieved!

CHICKEN: You mean if you are still in the land of the livin'.

MYRTLE: Don't make my hand shake again.

CHICKEN: I guess you think that I'm hard.

MYRTLE: I don't think a man should be soft.

CHICKEN: You know what life is made out of?

MYRTLE: Evil, I think it's evil.

CHICKEN: I think that life just plain don't care for the weak. Or the soft. I got to be hard. A man and his life both got to be made out of the same hard stuff or one or the other will break. Because life's hard. Man's got to be hard, too. Life, rock. Man, rock. Both rock. Because if they both ain't rock, one breaks. The soft one breaks. And life is never the soft one. Is it? NEVER!—If one is soft the one that is soft will be man. Not life, no, not life ever! Now then. Your hand ain't shakin'.

MYRTLE: No. My hand has stopped shaking because.

CHICKEN:—What?

MYRTLE: I know in my heart that you don't hate Myrtle.

[Pause]

CHICKEN: I hate nobody and I love nobody. Now pick up that pen, hold it steady, and write down what I tell you.

[She picks up the pen, grips it. She wets the pen.]

Ready?

MYRTLE: Ready, my hand is steady.

CHICKEN: I got to be careful how I word this thing, it's too important for me to bugger it up.

MYRTLE: Let's make two copies of it, one for, for—practice and the other—final.

CHICKEN: Won't be necessary. I got it now. Now write down what I tell you in big letters or print. "Me, Mrs. Lot Ravenstock, give up and deny all claims when my husband is dead. Because this place goes to Chicken, all Chicken's, when Lot Ravenstock dies and also if I die too because of river in flood, a natural act of God."

MYRTLE [who has been scribbling frantically]: "All Chicken's when Lot dies."

CHICKEN: Now put in the punctuation and dot all the i's an' cross all the t's an' sign your name plain at the bottom.

MYRTLE: Yais, yais, I did, I already did that, Chicken.

CHICKEN: Give it here. [He takes the paper from her.] Huh. I bet they never give you no spelling or handwriting prize when you went to school. There's still one question, though. You wrote this thing because you're scared of drowning. How do I know you wouldn't back out of it when the flood's over with?

MYRTLE: I swear I wouldn't.

CHICKEN: Well, anyhow it's something, and somethin's better than nothing.

MYRTLE: Chicken, trust my word. I've given you my word and never gone back on my word in all my life.

CHICKEN: I'm not counting on your word, but something else about you.

MYRTLE: What? Else? About me?

CHICKEN: —You're weak.

200

MYRTLE: I've always been weak compared to men, to a man. I think that's natural, don't you?

[*They have been sitting in chairs on opposite sides of the small, square kitchen table, chairs angled toward the audience. Now Chicken rises and crosses close to her.*]

CHICKEN: Look me straight in the eyes and answer a question.

MYRTLE: What? Question?

CHICKEN: Can you kiss and like kissin' a man that's been accused of having some black blood in him?

MYRTLE: No! Yes! It would make no diff'rence to me.

CHICKEN: Let's try it out. Put your arms about me an' give me a kiss on the mouth. Mouth open.

[*She complies nervously, gingerly to this request. During the kiss, he puts a hand on her hips. Releasing her:*]

Well? How did it feel? Disgusting?

MYRTLE: No, not a bit. I was pleased an' relieved that you wanted to kiss me, Chicken.

CHICKEN: That kiss was just a beginning. You know that. Does that please and relieve you?

MYRTLE: I'm a warm-natured woman. You might say passionate, even. A Memphis doctor prescribed me a bottle of pills to keep down the heat of my nature, but those pills are worthless. Have no effect, I'm through with them.—Don't you know I would never back down on that letter you dictated to me? Not if I could, never would!

CHICKEN: No, I reckon you wouldn't. [*He hoists himself onto the kitchen table, directly in front of her, legs spread wide.*]

MYRTLE: Wouldn' you be more comf'table in a chair?

201

CHICKEN: I wouldn' be as close to you—I'm right in front of you now.

MYRTLE: I have to strain my neck to look in your face.

CHICKEN [*with a slow, savage grin*]:—You don't have to look in my face, my face ain't all they is to me, not by a long shot, honey . . .

[*She begins suddenly to cry like a child.*]

Why're you cryin'? You don't have to cry fo' it, it's what you want and it's yours! [*He snatches up the lamp and blows it out.*]

[*The kitchen is blacked out: an opaque scrim falls over its open wall. Light is brought up in the bedroom where Lot sits in the wicker rocker, moonlight on him brightening, fading, and brightening again.*]

LOT: Lamp's gone out in the kitchen and I don't hear a sound.— What I've done is deliver a woman to Chicken, brought home a whore for Chicken that he don't have to pay.—A present from the dying.

[*Fade out. Thunder.*]

SCENE THREE

The kitchen scrim rises as Chicken lights the lamp on the table. He is still perched on the table, and Myrtle is still on a chair so close to the table that she's between his boots, and she looks as if she had undergone an experience of exceptional nature and magnitude.

CHICKEN: Let there be light. That's what they say that God said on the first day of creation. [*There is a slight pause as he fastens the clasp of his belt.*]

MYRTLE: Chicken, I want you to know that—

CHICKEN: What do you want me to know that I don't know?

MYRTLE: That that's the first time I've gone that far with a man, no matter how strongly attracted.

CHICKEN: You mean on the first date?

MYRTLE: I mean practickly never.

CHICKEN: Maybe when instink is powerful enough, then practice is not necessary. But in my opinion, them little white tablets you take to keep your nature down you oughta send back to the Memphis doctor an' demand a refund on whatever they cost you.

MYRTLE: It's possible that the tablets are meant for ordinary attraction but not for terrific attraction.

CHICKEN: Like a levee holds back a river up till a point where the pressure is too strong for it?

MYRTLE: Yes, like that. Exackly. [*She rises from her chair and makes a weak-kneed effort to climb on the table.*]

CHICKEN: What're you doin'?

MYRTLE: Tryin' to climb up beside you an' lean on your shoulder.

CHICKEN: Naw, naw, stay in your chair a while longer. I don't like to touch or be touched by a woman right after havin' such close relations with her.

MYRTLE [*returning to her chair, humbly*]: Are you disgusted with her?

CHICKEN: Just not int'rested in her.

MYRTLE: How long does that feelin' last?

CHICKEN: Sometimes five or tin minutes.

MYRTLE: Minutes cin seem like hours whin the attraction's terrific.

CHICKEN: —I wonder something about you.

MYRTLE [*nervously*]: Wh—what do you wonder?

CHICKEN: If the attraction would still be terrific if I was to tell you the talk an' suspicion about me are based on fact.

MYRTLE: —What, uh, talk an' suspicion?

CHICKEN: That I got colored blood in me.

[*Note: Myrtle has the typical Southern lower-class dread and awe of Negroes.*]

MYRTLE: Oh, I, why, I—I know they's no truth in that.

CHICKEN [*grinning at her savagely*]: How do you know they isn't?

MYRTLE: Lot would of *tole* me.

CHICKEN: I come near to killin' him once fo' sayin' I had colored blood an' Lot hasn't forgotten; he's not so dumb he don't know that if he told you, I'd know.

MYRTLE: Thin why would you tell me that you—

CHICKEN: I thought you oughta know after havin' such close relations.

[*Shaken and awed by the disclosure, she rises from her chair and pulls it back from the table.*]

Why'd you do that, Mrs. Lot Ravenstock?

MYRTLE:—Why'd I do what did I do, I—

CHICKEN: You moved your chair back from the table like a monster was on it. Move your chair back where it was.

MYRTLE: I don't know where it was.

[*Myrtle moves her chair back to approximately its former position.*]

CHICKEN: Then what do you know? Nothin'?

MYRTLE: Was it here?

CHICKEN: About. Now listen to me. My mother had colored blood in her. She wasn't black but she wasn't white neither, and that's why I'm dark-complected with freckled eyes an' live the life of a dawg that nobody owns and owns nothing. Ask any dawg on a road or a street, any dawg, any road, any street, if that ain't th' fuckin' truth which is made me suspicioned around here. So. Are you cryin' again?

MYRTLE:—With, with—nervous—sympathy fo' you.

CHICKEN: Keep it, shove it, forget it. I don't want it. When you want sympathy, then is when you're in trouble. Up to your ass, up to your tits, up to your eyebrows in it, ask any dawg in the street, includin' you'self.

MYRTLE: Please don't talk thet way to me. [*She moves her chair back a little, still sniffling.*]

CHICKEN [*broodingly*]: One night last winter, for instance, I

205

come up to this girl at the Dixie Star, a night-place on the highway. This girl I come up to politely was known as Desperate Dotty because she put out for men right and left and up the center an' down it.

MYRTLE:—No self-respeck?

CHICKEN: No self-respeck an' no white tablets from the quack in Memphis, but I was so horny that night my balls were achin', so I come up to this girl when the man she was with fell outa their booth to th' floor an' laid there belchin' an' snorin'. I spoke to this girl politely. "Hello, how are you, Miss Bows, terrible weather, and so forth." Then lowered my voice an' leaned on the table toward her, an' said, "Miss Bows, this man you're with here t'night cain't do you no good, any dawg on th' road can tell you that, so why not step over his laigs an' sit in a clean booth with me, I got almost a full pint of Four Roses on me."—What did I git fo' this polite invitation?

MYRTLE [*still sniffling*]: I don't, I should, I—

CHICKEN: I'll tell you what I got. She give me a quick, mean look an' said, "Nigger, stay in your place." That's it. That's how it is with me an' wimmen around here. Talk, suspicion, insult. An' when Miss Lottie, Lot's mother, dismissed me off this place, she said to me, "Chicken, I don't want my son to be known as half-brother to a nigra." Wonderful, huh? Yeah, great. I'll tell you what her son does to amuse himself here. He gits in his dead mother's clothes—panties, brassiere, slippers, dress. Ask any dawg in the street!

MYRTLE:—Oh, I—wouldn't ask any dawg, a, a, a—thing like thet, I—

CHICKEN: Comes downstairs lookin' jus' like her an' sits in her parlor, talkin' to himself in the same voice as hers. OK?—Well, I'm back here, now, alone, suspicioned, despised.

MYRTLE:—I, uh—

CHICKEN: Poolhall, I can go to the poolhall, but nobody's

anxious to git me in a game with 'em. Can go to the highway night-place, an' sit by myself, left out of the conversation, talked about in whispers. So what I do, practickly everything, I do by myself, you can ask any dawg that.

MYRTLE: You should, I would—pay no attention, rise above talk an' suspicion you know ain't true.

CHICKEN: I just now told you it was. Oh, but now. You don't wanta believe it after the close relation we had between us, naw, your folks in Mobile wuh so ignorant an' low class they filtered your mind with the idea that you'd be ruined like poisoned by havin' a close relation to someone with colored blood. So? Yais, so. I know.

MYRTLE: I was just, just simply—I was surprised for a—minute, which is over with now.

CHICKEN: You're still holdin' onto th' arms of that chair with your haid leant back like you was about to be electrocuted.

MYRTLE: I been through a good deal t'day, more then some girls go through in their whole lifetimes.

CHICKEN: Like The Four Hot Shots from Mobile?

[He gets off the table and crosses to the back door, which is the only solid enclosure of the set—the rest is created by lighting.]

MYRTLE [rising fearfully]: Where are you goin'?

CHICKEN: The river's louder. I'm goin' to look at the levee.

MYRTLE: What good does it do to look at it?

CHICKEN: I can tell if the levee will hold the crest or not.

MYRTLE: Don't—

[He goes offstage.]

—leave me alone here . . .

[*The bedroom upstairs is lighted by the moon. We see Lot struggling out of the wicker rocker, knocking it over. He staggers to a closet and with his back to the audience, throws off the silk wrapper. He steps quickly into a gauzy white dress and sets on his head a blond wig. He turns again, gasps, staggers to the foot of the brass bed and clings to its bars; slides down them to a kneeling position.*]

LOT:—Will—make it—Miss Lottie! And order them both off the place!

[*The moon is obscured again and the bedroom returns to dark, a scrim descending over its front. During this, Myrtle has stood at the open kitchen door. Now Chicken returns, hip boots covered with wet mud as when we first saw him.*]

MYRTLE: I thought you'd never git back here.

CHICKEN: You thought wrong, missy. [*He sits again on the table.*]

MYRTLE:—Those five or tin minutes are over with, now, ain't they?

CHICKEN: Cain't you see the clock?

MYRTLE: A clock is mechanical but a man is human.

CHICKEN: Sometimes you say a true thing.

MYRTLE: I pride myself on that, and another thing I pride myself on is noticin' an' appreciatin' a man's appearance. Physical. I notice such things about him as a strong figure in fine proportion. Mouth? Full. Teeth? White. Glist'nin'. Why, you look like a man that could hold back the flood of a river!

CHICKEN: No man can hold back a flood but some can live through one.

MYRTLE:—With a—with a woman?

208

CHICKEN: Uh-huh, even with a woman.—How'd you like to stay on here after Lot's gone?

MYRTLE:—Lit's not put it like thet.

CHICKEN: What other way would you put it?

MYRTLE: No, I don't know what other way I could put it. And I know that ev'ry girl in the world has a dream in her heart that's sweeter an' more precious to her than any other.

CHICKEN: What's that dream in her heart?

MYRTLE: That dream is settl'n' down somewhere, sometime, with a man to who she's very strongly attracted.

CHICKEN: Think it over an' I'll think it over, too. You're not a match fo' the pitcher tacked on the wall, but—

MYRTLE: No, no, but I—know!

CHICKEN: Yais, I'd say you know, an' if it's necessary to climb on the roof tonight, I'll git you up the ladder in the hall upstairs with a blanket in case we need more'n each other to keep us warm.

MYRTLE: What'd we eat up there if we had to stay up there long?

CHICKEN: The chickens'll fly up there, and if a helly-copter don't come over to pick us up, we'll drink some warm chicken blood to keep us goin'.

MYRTLE: Oh, I couldn't do that!

CHICKEN: What people have to do they always do.—So ev'rything understood now?

MYRTLE: I think we've come to a perfeck understandin'.

CHICKEN: Good. Let's have a drink on it. [*He pours liquor into two tin cups.*]—Have you ever been what they call saved?

MYRTLE: Why, yais, I have, I have been saved by you.

CHICKEN: What I was speakin' of is *religious* salvation.

[*He removes her importunate hand from his shoulder and re-sumes his seat on the table. The lamp light concentrates on him hotly during the monologue, the expression of his credo that follows, and Myrtle is a shadowy presence.*]

MYRTLE: Oh, *religious* salvation.

CHICKEN: That's right.

MYRTLE: Well, I'm not a steady churchgoer, I wake up so tired on Sundays, y'see, but when I'm perplexed or worried over something, I always appeal to my Savior and, knock on wood, He has never let me down.

[*The bright spotlight is now fixed on Chicken.*]

CHICKEN: Hmm. Uh-huh.—I reckon you'd never guess from me, the way I am now, that I was what they call saved by this preacher Gypsy Smith when he come through here last spring. But I sure in hell was, I was what they call saved, but it didn't last much longer than a cold in the head. Hmmm.

[*Myrtle perches herself beside him on the table and leans against him.*]

The salvation preacher, he claimed that we had to put up a terrible struggle against our lustful body. And I did for a while. Y'know, these preachers all think we got lustful bodies, and that's one thing I know they're right about. Huh?

MYRTLE: Oh, yes. They're right about that.

CHICKEN: They preach about how you should haul down those spiritual gates in your lustful body. Well. Those are two opposite things an' one of 'em's got to be stronger if they're in the same body. One's got to win and one lose. Well, I tried to haul down my spiritual gates for a while but I seemed to be reaching up for something that wasn't in me. You can't haul down your spiritual gates if you don't have any in you. I think that's the case in my case. I was just created without them.

MYRTLE: In my case, I never had that experience, being saved, not even for a short while, but I do say prayers, anyhow, to God and to human beings.

CHICKEN: What do you pray for?

MYRTLE: I pray for protection, and right now I feel like that prayer is going to be answered. Go on talking in that deep voice of yours. I don't just hear it. It, it—it gives me a sensation in my ears and goes all through my body, it it—it *vibrates* in me. I don't even hear the river!

CHICKEN [*sloshing liquor from the jug into their tin cups*]: I'll tell you how I look at life in my life, or in any man's life. There's nothing in the world, in the whole kingdom of earth, that can compare with one thing, and that one thing is what's able to happen between a man and a woman, just that thing, nothing more, is perfect. The rest is crap, all of the rest is almost nothing but crap. Just that one thing's good, and if you never had nothing else but that, no property, no success in the world, but still had *that*, why, then I say this life would still be worth something, and you better believe it. Yes, you could come home to a house like a shack, in blazing heat, and look for water and find not a drop to drink, and look for food and find not a single crumb of it. But if on the bed you seen you a woman waiting, maybe not very young or good-looking even, and she looked up at you and said to you, "Daddy, I want it," why, then I say you got a square deal out of life, and whoever don't think so has just not had the right woman. That's how I look at it, that's how I see it now, in this kingdom of earth.

[*The flight of stairs is lowered and the top of them lighted. Lot appears like an apparition in the pool of cool light at the stair-top. He has put on the gauzy white dress to conjure an image of his mother in summer. As he stands above the stairs he now puts on a translucent, wide "picture hat," the crown of it trimmed with faded flowers. The effect is both bizarre and*

211

beautiful. There is a phrase of music like a muted trumpet playing a blues song. Then Lot starts his descent of the deep stairs. With each step his gasping for breath is louder, but his agony is transfigured by the sexless passion of the transvestite. He has a fixed smile which is almost ecstatic. Chicken leaps off the kitchen table and goes to the position where the kitchen door would be. He seems impressed but not surprised. Myrtle is terrified.]

MYRTLE: Chicken, oh, God, stop him!

CHICKEN: What faw? Naw, naw, let him be in Miss Lottie's parlor.

[At the foot of the stairs, Lot turns blindly upstage, his gasping breath now like a death rattle. Even in death he has the ecstasy of a transvestite. He staggers into the bizarre little parlor as its concealing scrim is lifted and the room is lighted—a delicate rose light. There he stands swaying for a few moments: then sinks into one of the little gold chairs, facing downstage. Myrtle is panicky but not Chicken. He enters the parlor. Lot, in his transfiguration, stares blindly downstage. Perhaps he is even smiling as if on a social occasion. He holds onto his garden hat, holding it by the crown, as if a wind might blow it away. He is swaying back and forth. Chicken's attitude is impassive.]

You're dresed fo' summer t'night.

[Lot is past hearing any remark. He rises from the chair, sways, seems to bow to an applauding audience, then crumples to the floor. Myrtle, in a state of mental shock, has retreated to the kitchen and opened the cupboard as if it were a place of refuge.]

MYRTLE: Potatoes. *[She removes these reassuring items from the cupboard. An egg or two splatters on the floor. She makes a few more rapid, irresolute turns.]* Eggs, bacon, slab of it. New potatoes. Pan?—Pan!—Knife?—Knife! *[She heads for the wall where these utensils are hanging, discovers her arms are full, and rushes back to deposit the foodstuff on the table. Entirely un-*

noticed by her, an egg or two more splatters on the floor. Then she rushes back to remove the utensils from their hooks.] In no condition to—got to! *[She then instructs herself as if she were a pupil in a very primary cooking class. Her words are interspersed with slight, breathless sobs.]* Slice bacon in pan with knife.— Stove?—Burnin'!

[Chicken has stood over the summer gauze apparition of his half-brother without a word or gesture. Now he turns out the chandelier and moves with dark satisfaction down the short hall to the kitchen area. He looks about him appraisingly, a man who has come into possessions, fiercely desired. Myrtle's back is to him, and when he speaks she catches her breath loudly.]

CHICKEN: Makin' supper?

MYRTLE: What I'm doin' I don't know what I'm doin', I—

CHICKEN: You're doin' a sensible thing since it might be sev'ral days before we have a hot meal again.

MYRTLE *[turning to face him]*: Chicken, as Christian people—

CHICKEN: What about Christian people?

MYRTLE: We got to call in a doctor.

CHICKEN: If there was a doctor that hadn't hauled his ass out of Cotton County, there's nothin' he could do here but clean up a mess of aigs you dropt on the floor.

MYRTLE:—Lot is—?

CHICKEN: Isn't.

MYRTLE:—God have mercy on my—

CHICKEN: What?

MYRTLE:—The potatoes will be home-fried.

CHICKEN: That's right. Fried in my home.

[*He stares at her broodingly for a couple of moments as she sucks a cut finger.*]

I don't reckon that, no, I reckon you couldn't.

MYRTLE: Couldn't? What?

CHICKEN: Produce me a son. Produce a child for me, could you? Always wanted a child from an all-white woman.

MYRTLE: The deepest chord in my nature is the—don't that river sound louder? Or am I just more scared to death of it?

CHICKEN: The flood crest is close to here now. [*He starts outside.*]

MYRTLE [*wildly*]: *Don't leave me alone here!*

CHICKEN: I'm goin' out th' door for a minute. Sit down. Peel the home-fried potatoes.—I want to look at my—land. [*He goes out and moves downstage, his face exultant.*]—*Sing it out, frogs an' crickets, Chicken is king!*

[*Myrtle has come out behind him. There is a great booming sound.*]

Up! Quick!

[*He says this as the curtain is descending.*]

END

SMALL CRAFT WARNINGS

TO BILL BARNES:
YOU SAID TO GO ON, AND I WENT.

TOO PERSONAL?*

The greatest danger, professionally, of becoming the subject of so many "write-ups" and personal appearances on TV and lecture platforms is that the materials of your life, which are, in the case of all organic writing, the materials of your work, are sort of telegraphed in to those who see you and to those who read about you. So, when you get to the serious organization of this material into your work, people (meaning audiences and critics—all but the few most tolerant whom you naturally regard as the best) have a sort of *déjà vu* or *déjà entendu* reaction to these materials which you have submitted to the cathartic process of your "sullen craft and art."

You may justifiably wonder why a man of my years in his profession, recognizing this hazard, has yet been willing to expose himself (with a frequency which seems almost symptomatic of clinical exhibitionism) to all of these interviews and the fewer, but equally personal, exposures on platform and "the tube."

I can offer you at least two reasons for this phenomenon. One is probably something with which you will immediately empathize. When one has passed through an extensive period of that excess of privacy which is imposed upon a person drifting almost willfullly out of contact with the world, anticipating that final seclusion of the nonbeing, there comes upon him, when that period wears itself out and he is still alive, an almost insatiable hunger for recognition of the fact that he is, indeed, still alive, both as man and artist. That's reason number one. The other is rather comical, I'm afraid. You get a devastatingly

* This was meant to be submitted to *The New York Times* as a preopening piece, but they chose to interview me instead.—T. W.

bad write-up, and you feel that you are washed up for good. Then some magazine editor gets through to you on that phone in the studio of your tropical retreat, the phone that you never pick up till it's rung so persistently that you assume that your secretary and house guests have been immobilized by nerve gas or something of that nature, and this editor speaks to you as sympathetically as the family doctor to a child stricken with a perforated appendix and tells you that he is as shocked as you were by the tasteless exposé-type of interview which appeared about you in a recent issue of some other mag. And then, of course, you forget about work, and you rage yourself into a slather over the iniquities and duplicities of the "interviewer" referred to. You say, "Why, that creature was so drunk he didn't know what street I lived on, and the guy that set me up for him laced my martini with sodium penathol, and all I remember about this occasion is that my head came off my shoulders and hit the ceiling and I heard myself babbling away like an hysteric and I hadn't the slightest notion that he had a concealed tape recorder with him, and later he offered to play bridge with me that night, and he came over again with the tape recorder in some orifice of his body, I presume, and you know I do not see well and you know I like to hold forth to apparently amiable listeners, and I just assume that when they say 'I am interested only in your work,' that that's what they mean."

Now the editor has you on the hook.

"That's exactly my reaction to the revolting piece and how about letting us do a piece to correct it?"

You grasp at this offer like a drowning rat climbs on to anything that will float it. So you get another write-up. Then after this write-up, which is usually more colorful and better written than the one before, but equally nonserious, if not downright clownish, you feel that it is a life-or-death matter, professionally, with a new play opening somewhere, to correct the hilarious misquotes and exaggerations which embellished the second write-up, and so you go on to others and others. Now at last you have poured out, compulsively and perhaps fatally, all the recent content of your experience which should have been held in reserve for its proper place, which is in the work you're doing every morning (which, in my case, is the writing I do every morning).

Is it or is it not right or wrong for a playwright to put his persona into his work?

My answer is: "What else can he do?"—I mean the very root-necessity of all creative work is to express those things most involved in his experience. Otherwise, is the work, however well executed, not a manufactured, a synthetic thing? I've said, perhaps repeatedly, that I have two major classifications for writing: that which is organic and that which is not. And this opinion still holds.

Now let me attempt to entertain you once more with an anecdote.

Long ago, in the early forties, I attended a very posh party given by the Theatre Guild. I was comfortably and happily seated at a small table with my dear friend Miss Jo Healy, who was receptionist at the Guild in those days, when a lady with eyes that blazed with some nameless frenzy rushed up to me like a guided missile and seized me by the arm and shrieked to me, "You've got to meet Miss Ferber, she's dying to meet you."

Now in those days I was at least pliable, and so I permitted myself to be hauled over to a large table at which were seated a number of Diamond T trucks disguised as ladies.

"Oh, Miss Ferber," shrieked my unknown pilot, "this is Tennessee Williams."

Miss Ferber gazed slowly up and delivered this annihilating one-liner:

"The best I can manage is a mild 'Yippee.' "

"Madam," I said, "I can't even manage that."

Now everyone knows, who is cognizant of the world of letters, that Miss Edna Ferber was a creature of mammoth

219

productivity and success. She was good at doing her thing; her novel and picture sales are fairly astronomical, I would guess.

I bring her up because she represents to me the classic, the archetypal, example of a writer whose work is impersonal, at least upon any recognizable level. I cannot see her in the oil fields of Texas with Rock Hudson and the late James Dean. Nor can I see her in any of her other impressive epics. I see her only as a lady who chose to put down a writer who was then young and vulnerable with such a gratuitously malicious one-liner. I mean without provocation, since I had literally been dragged to the steps of her throne.

So far I have spoken only in defense of the personal kind of writing. Now I assure you that I know it can be overdone. It is the responsibility of the writer to put his experience as a being into work that refines it and elevates it and that makes of it an essence that a wide audience can somehow manage to feel in themselves: "This is true."

In all human experience, there are parallels which permit common understanding in the telling and hearing, and it is the frightening responsibility of an artist to make what is directly or allusively close to his own being communicable and under-standable, however disturbingly, to the hearts and minds of all whom he addresses.

T.W.
March 26, 1972

Small Craft Warnings was presented at the Truck and Warehouse Theatre in New York on April 2, 1972, by Ecco Productions, Robert Currie, Mario De Maria, William Orton. It was directed by Richard Altman; the stage setting and costumes were by Fred Voelpel, lighting by John Gleason; production stage manager, Robert Currie. The cast was as follows:

VIOLET	CHERRY DAVIS
DOC	DAVID HOOKS
MONK	GENE FANNING
BILL McCORKLE	BRAD SULLIVAN
LEONA DAWSON	HELENA CARROLL
STEVE	WILLIAM HICKEY
QUENTIN	ALAN MIXON
BOBBY	DAVID HUFFMAN
TONY, THE COP	JOHN DAVID KEES

SKETCH OF STAGE SETTING FOR THE NEW YORK PRODUCTION BY FRED VOELPEL

Act I: A bar along the Southern California Coast

Act II: An hour or two later

The curtain rises. The sound of ocean wind is heard. The stage is lighted at a very low level.

The scene is a somewhat nonrealistic evocation of a bar on the beach-front in one of those coastal towns between Los Angeles and San Diego. It attracts a group of regular patrons who are nearly all so well known to each other that it is like a community club, and most of these regulars spend the whole evening there. Ideally, the walls of the bar, on all three sides, should have the effect of fog rolling in from the ocean. A blue neon outside the door says: "Monk's Place." The bar runs diagonally from upstage to down; over it is suspended a large varnished sailfish, whose gaping bill and goggle-eyes give it a constant look of amazement. There are about three tables, with red-checked tablecloths. Stage right there is a juke box, and in the wall at right are doors to the ladies' and gents' lavatories. A flight of stairs ascends to the bar-owner's living quarters. The stairs should be masked above the first few steps.

The bar interior is dimly, evenly lit at rise. At some time in the course of the play, when a character disengages himself from the group to speak as if to himself, the light in the bar should dim, and a special spot should illuminate each actor as he speaks.

Monk is behind the bar serving Doc. Monk, the bar-owner, and Doc, who lost his license for heavy drinking but still practices more or less clandestinely, are middle-aged.

At a downstage table sits Violet, at her feet a battered suitcase fastened with a rope. Her eyes are too large for her face, and they are usually moist: her appearance suggests a derelict kind of existence; still, she has about her a pale, bizarre sort of beauty. As Leona Dawson later puts it, she's like a water plant.

MONK [*to Doc*]: Notice? [*He nods his head.*] Over there?

[*Doc emerges from introspection to glance the way indicated by Monk. They both gaze at Violet.*]

VIOLET [*singing a bit, self-conscious under their scrutiny*]: The wheel of fortune
Keeps turning around . . .
[*She can't remember past this.*]

DOC [*voice filtered through booze*]: Oh, yes, she's a noticeable thing. She has a sort of not-quite-with-it appearance. Amorphous, that's the word. Something more like a possibility than a completed creature.

MONK: What I mean is the *suitcase. With* her.

DOC: Oh, yes, the suitcase. Does she think she's in the waiting room of a depot?

MONK: I think she thinks she's moved in here.

DOC: Oh. That's a possible problem for you there.

MONK: You're Goddam right. I'm running a tavern that's licensed to dispense spirits, not a pad for vagrants. You see, they see those stairs. They know I live up there.

DOC: Yep, they see those stairs to the living quarters above, and it hits them dimly that you might need the solace of their companionship up there some nights when they find it convenient to offer it to you, and I don't need to tell you that this solace of companionship is not the least expensive item on the shelves of the fucking supermarket a man of my age has to spend what's left of his life in. Oh, that solace, that comfort of companionship is on the shelves of the market even for me, but I tell you, the price is inflated on it. I had me one last summer. Remember that plump little Chicano woman used to come in here with me some nights last summer? A little wet-leg woman, nice boobs on her and a national monument for an ass? Well, she came to me for medical attention.

[*Monk laughs heartily at this.*

[*Bill enters the bar; he comes up to it with an overrelaxed amiability like a loser putting up a bold front: by definition, a "stud"—but what are definitions?*

[*Monk mechanically produces Bill's can of Miller's but doesn't open it for him.*]

She had worms, diet of rotten beef tacos, I reckon, or tamales or something. I diagnosed it correctly. I gave her the little bottle and the wooden spoon and I said to her, "Bring me in a sample of your stool for lab analysis." She didn't know what I meant. Language barrier. I finally said, "Señorita, bring a little piece of your shit in the bottle tomorrow." [*He and Monk laugh heartily.*]

[*Bill is worried over the fact his beer can is not opened and served.*]

VIOLET: Hey, Bill . . .

DOC: Some beginning of some romance. Dewormed the lady and laid her in place of payment. Jesus, what a love story. I had her all summer, but in September she met a good-looking young pimp who made her critical of me. She called me a dirty old man, so I let her go.

BILL: Hey, Monk. About that beer.

MONK [*ignoring Bill*]: I don't remember you coming in here with a woman.

DOC: We always sat at a back table arguing over the fair expense of her ass.

BILL: Jesus, Monk, how big a tab has Leona run up here!? For Chrissake! [*He leans across the bar and snatches the can of*

Miller's from Monk's hand. Monk had ignored him only half deliberately and is annoyed by the grab.]

MONK: Look, I don't run Leona's tab through a computer, since I know she's good for it. If you want the can opened, give it back here. [*He opens the can.*] Now if it was your tab, not hers, I'd worry, but since it's hers, not yours, I don't. OK? No offense, no complaint, just . . .

VIOLET: Bill?

BILL: I could tell you some things.

MONK: Why don't you tell 'em to Violet, she's called you three times.

BILL [*glancing at her*]: Hi, Vi.

VIOLET: I had an awful experience today with Mr. Menzies at the amusement arcade. [*Sobbing sound*] Oh, I don't know what to do. Min broke in. Last night. Menzies said I . . . Come over here so I can tell you. Oh, and bring me a beer and a pepperoni, I'm famished. Lonesome and famished.

BILL: You want me to solve both those situations for you?

VIOLET: Yes, please.

BILL [*to Monk*]: Another Miller's and a coupla Slim Jims.

MONK: Yep, I got that message. Have you left Leona?

VIOLET: Bill, where's Leona?

BILL: Crying into a stew in her Goddam trailer.

[*Monk opens another beer, and Bill ambles over to Violet with the pepperonis and beer and the smile he meets the world with. It is a hustler's smile, the smile of a professional stud— now aging a bit but still with considerable memorabilia of his young charm.*]

VIOLET: Thanks, Bill . . .

[*Monk is toying with a radio which is over the bar.*]

RADIO VOICE: Heavy seas from Point Conception south to the Mexican border, fog continuing till tomorrow noon, extreme caution should be observed on all highways along this section of the coastline.

MONK [*ironically, turning off radio*]: Small craft warnings, Doc.

DOC: That's right, Monk, and you're running a place of refuge for vulnerable human vessels, and . . .

VIOLET: [*closer to Bill*]: Have you left Leona? For good?

BILL: Just till she gets her knickers out of that twist. She had this brother, a faggot that played the fiddle in church, and whenever she's drunk, she starts to cry up a storm about this little fag that she admitted was arrested for loitering in the Greyhound bus station men's room, and if I say, "Well, he was asking for it," she throws something at me.

VIOLET [*leaning amorously toward him*]: A man like you.

BILL: A man like me?

VIOLET: A bull of a man like you. You got arms on you big as the sides of a ham. [*She strokes his bare arm.*]

BILL: That ain't all I got big.

VIOLET: You mean what I think?

BILL: If you can't see you can feel.

[*She reaches under the table, and it is obvious that she is feeling him.*]

A man likes appreciation. Now I got a letter this week from a female guv'ment employee in Sacramento who's a Reagan supporter.

229

VIOLET: Huh?

BILL: Shit. She ain't seen me since '65 but remembers me clearly and wants me back on her aquabed with her, and if you've slept in an aquabed it don't matter who's in it with you.

[*The door bursts open. Leona enters like a small bull making his charge into the ring. Leona, a large, ungainly woman, is wearing white clam-digger slacks and a woolly pink sweater. On her head of dyed corkscrew curls is a sailor's hat which she occasionally whips off her head to slap something with— the bar, a tabletop, somebody's back—to emphasize a point. There are abrupt changes of position at the downstage table at her entrance, but she notices only Bill there.*]

LEONA: YOUUUUU . . . MOTHER! I was talkin' to you from the stove and you weren't there!

[*Bill chuckles and winks.*]

Three hours I spent shopping for and preparing a . . . memorial dinner while you watched TV.

BILL: Stew and veg.

LEONA [*lyrically, as a pop-poem*]: Lamb stew with garden fresh vegetables from the Farmer's Market, seasoned with bay leaves, and rosemary and thyme.

BILL: Stew.

LEONA: I'd set up a little banquet table in that trailer tonight, my grandmother's silver and Irish lace tablecloth, my crystal candlesticks with the vine leaves filigreed on 'em in silver which I'd polished, all spit-polished for this memorial dinner, set the candles on either side of my single rose vase containing a single talisman rose just opened, a table like a photo from *House and Garden*. I talk from the stove to no one. I open the fridge to get out the jellied bouillon, madrilene, topped with . . . "Okayyyy,

230

ready." I come in and I'm received by the TV set and the trailer
door hanging open, and in the confusion I knock over and break
my cut-glass decanter of Burgundy, imported.

BILL: I went out for a bottle. You'd kilt a fifth of Imp. She
was crying in the stew to save on salt.

LEONA: Without word or a note on the table. You went!
Why? For what?

VIOLET: Leona, Bill's not happy tonight, so let him be.

LEONA: Two people's not happy and one of 'em with *reason!*
Is that your suitcase with you? Are you thrown out, evicted? A
lady of the street? Oh, my God, here's a good one I heard at the
shop today about a pair of street-ladies in Dublin. One enters
a pub, elegant but pissed, and she says to the barman, "Two
gins for two ladies." He observes her condition and says,
"Where is the other lady?" "The other lady," she says, "is in
the gutter, resting." [*Only she is amused by the story.*] Oh, well,
I thought it was funny. [*Leona sits at table with Violet and Bill.*]
Violet, dear, will you look at your nails?

VIOLET: I know, the enamel's chipping.

LEONA: Yes! Exposing the dirt.

[*Violet drops her hands under the table.*]

Oh, my God, forget it, forget the whole enchilada. Not worth
a thought.

[*No response.*]

Excuse me a moment. I'm going to press one button three times
on that multiselector, and Violet, here's an orange stick for your
nails . . . Don't be depressed. A sure cure for depression is the ax.

VIOLET: I'm not depressed.

LEONA [*laughing*]: Then you must not be conscious. [*She
crosses to the juke box.*] I hope nobody objects to the number

231

I play. It's going to be played here repeatedly tonight, appreciated or not. [*She bends over the juke box to find the desired number, which she herself contributed to the "Classicals" on the box.*] Róck? No! Popular? No! Classicals—yes! Number? Number? Which?

VIOLET: Tell her I'm not depressed.

[*Violet's hand has dropped under the table. It is apparent that she is reaching for Bill.*]

BILL: She's depressed . . . and depressing. [*Leans back luxuriously in chair. A look to Leona. He speaks with emphasis, rather than volume.*] . . . Not bad, huh? A definite . . . personal . . . asset?

[*Monk turns up radio. Gets static.*]

LEONA: Do you have to turn that on when I'm . . .

[*At this precise moment she is caught by the change in attitudes at the downstage table. Her eyes widen; her hands clench; she takes a couple of paces toward the table and crouches a bit to peer under it. Then quick as a shot:*]

YOUUU . . . CUNT!

[*She charges.*

[*Violet screams and springs up, overturning her chair.*]

MONK: Hold her!

[*Bill's massive frame obstructs Leona, not only her motion but her view of Violet. Bill is holding her by both shoulders, grinning into her face.*

[*The following lines overlap.*]

LEONA: OFF HANDS!

MONK: Nope, nope, nope, nope, nope!

232

LEONA: McCorkle, DON' YOU . . . !

MONK: Keep her at that table!

[*During this Monk has crossed from behind the bar.*

[*Violet has turned about dizzily, then fled into the ladies'.*

[*Leona stamps on Bill's foot. He yells, falls back an instant, releasing her. As she rushes forward, he gives her a hard slap on the butt; she turns to give him battle, and is caught from behind by Monk. She kicks at Monk's shin, and gives Bill a wallop in the face with her cap.*]

BILL [*rubbing his eyes*]: Goddam, she . . .

MONK: I'm havin' no violence here! Never! None! From no one!

[*A sudden hush falls: a sudden moment of stillness in a corrida.*]

LEONA [*incredulously, profoundly, hurtly, right into Bill's face*]: YOU! Let *her!* In front of ME? . . . in PUBLIC! . . . In a BAR!

BILL: What the fuck of it! You hit me right in the eyes with . . .

LEONA [*makes a big-theater turn and shouts*]: Where IS she? Where's she gone? [*Receiving no answer—there is still no sound from Violet's place of refuge—she suddenly rushes for the stairs.*]

MONK: Nobody's up my stairs! Come down those . . .

[*Violet's lamentation begins.*]

LEONA: Aw! She's gone to the LADIES'! Change the name on that door.

MONK: I'm operating a place for gents and ladies. [*He is panting a bit.*]

233

LEONA: Gents and . . . what?

MONK: Ladies.

LEONA: Aw, now, Monk. I thought you run a clean place but don't come on with . . . her? Lady? Him? Gent? [*She points toward the ladies' room and then toward Bill.*] There's limits to . . .

MONK: Yes. Stay away from . . .

[*Leona had started toward the ladies'. Monk blocks her. She throws her head back and utters an apocalyptic outcry. It's like the outcry of all human protest.*]

No more disturbance of . . .

LEONA [*drawing herself up heroically as she confronts Monk almost nose-to-nose*]: LET ME SET YOU STRAIGHT ABOUT WHAT'S A LADY! A lady's a woman, with respect for herself and for relations of others! HER? IN THERE? WAILING? RESPECT FOR? . . . She's got no respect for herself and that is the single respect in which she's correct to! No one could blame her for that! [*She has resumed her pacing and slapping at things with sailor's cap.*] What could she possibly find to respect in herself? She lives like an animal in a room with no bath that's directly over the amusement arcade at the foot of the pier, yeah, right over the billiards, the pinball games, and the bowling alleys at the amusement arcade, it's bang, bang, bang, loud as a TV western all day and all night, and then bang, bang again at eight A.M. It would drive a sane person crazy but she couldn't care less. She don't have a closet, she didn't have a bureau so she hangs her dresses on a piece of rope that hangs across a corner between two nails, and her other possessions she keeps on the floor in boxes.

BILL: What business is it of yours?

LEONA: None, not a Goddam bit! When she was sick? I went there to bring her a chicken. I asked her, where is your silver?

She didn't have any silver, not a fork, spoon, or knife, hell, not even a plate, but she ate the chicken, aw, yeah, she ate the chicken like a dog would eat it, she picked it up in her paws and gnawed at it just like a dog. Who came to see if she was living or dead? ME! ONLY! I got her a bureau, I got her a knife, fork, and spoon, I got her china, I got her a change of bed linen for her broken-down cot, and ev'ry day after work I come by that Goddam rathole with a bottle of hot beef bouillon or a chicken or meatloaf to see what she needed and bring it, and then one time I come by there to see what she needed and bring it. The bitch wasn't there. I thought my God she's died or they put her away. I run downstairs, and I heard her screaming with joy in the amusement arcade. She was having herself a ball with a shipload of drunk sailor boys; she hardly had time to speak to me.

BILL: Maybe she'd gotten sick of you. That's a possible reason.

LEONA: It's a possible reason I was sick of her, too, but I'd thought that the bitch was dying of malnutrition, and I thought she was human, and a human life is worth saving or what the shit *is* worth saving. But is she human? She's just a parasite creature, not even made out of flesh but out of wet biscuit dough, she always looks like the bones are dissolving in her.

BILL [*banging his beer bottle on the table*]: DO YOU THINK I BELONG TO YOU? I BELONG TO MYSELF, I JUST BELONG TO MYSELF.

LEONA: Aw, you pitiful piece of . . . worthless . . . conceit! [*She addresses the bar.*] . . . Never done a lick of work in his life . . . He has a name for his thing. He calls it Junior. He says he takes care of Junior and Junior takes care of him. How long is that gonna last? How long does he figure Junior is going to continue to provide for him, huh? HUH! . . . Forever or *less* than forever? . . . Thinks the sun rises and sets between his legs and that's the reason I put him in my trailer, feed him, give him beer-money, pretend I don't notice there's five or ten bucks less in my pocketbook in the morning than my pocketbook had in it when I fell to sleep, night before.

BILL: Go out on the beach and tell that to the sea gulls, they'd be more int'rested in it.

VIOLET [*shrilly, from the ladies' room*]: Help me, help me, somebody, somebody call the po-liiiiice!

LEONA: Is she howling out the ladies' room window?

VIOLET: How long do I have to stay in here before you get the police?

LEONA: If that fink is howling out the ladies' room window, I m going out back and throw a brick in at her.

MONK: Leona, now cool it, Leona.

LEONA: I'll pay the damage, I'll pay the hospital expenses.

MONK: Leona, why don't you play your violin number on the box and settle down at a table and . . .

LEONA: When I been insulted by someone, I don't settle down at a table, or nowhere, NOWHERE!

[*Violet sobs and wails as Steve comes into the bar. Steve is wearing a floral-patterned sports shirt under a tan jacket and the greasy white trousers of a short-order cook.*]

STEVE: Is that Violet in there?

LEONA: Who else do you think would be howling out the ladies' room window but her, and you better keep out of this, this is between her and me.

STEVE: What happened? Did you hit Violet?

LEONA: You're Goddam right I busted that filthy bitch in the kisser, and when she comes out of the ladies', if she ever comes out, I'm gonna bust her in the kisser again, and kiss my ass, I'm just the one that can do it! MONK! DRINK! BOURBON SWEET!

MONK: Leona, you're on a mean drunk, and I don't serve liquor to no one on a mean drunk.

LEONA: Well, you can kiss it, too, you monkey-faced mother. [*She slaps the bar top with her sailor hat.*]

STEVE: Hey, did you hit Violet?

[*Bill laughs at this anticlimactic question.*]

LEONA: Have you gone deaf, have you got wax in your ears, can't you hear her howling in there? Did I hit Violet? The answer is yes, and I'm not through with her yet. [*Leona approaches the door of the ladies' room.*] COME ON OUT OF THERE, VIOLET, OR I'LL BREAK IN THE DOOR! [*She bangs her fist on the door, then slaps it contemptuously with her cap, and resumes her pacing.*]

[*Bill keeps grinning and chuckling.*]

STEVE: Why did she hit Violet?

LEONA: Why don't you ask *me* why?

STEVE: Why did you hit Violet?

LEONA: I hit Violet because she acted indecent with that son of a bitch I been supporting for six months in my trailer.

STEVE: What do you mean "indecent"?

LEONA: Jesus, don't you know her habits? Are you unconscious ev'ry night in this bar and in her rathole over the amusement arcade? I mean she acted indecent with her dirty paws under the table. I came in here tonight and saw her hands on the table. The red enamel had nearly all chipped off the nails and the fingernails, black, I mean *black*, like she'd spend every day for

237

a month without washing her hands after making mud-pies with filthy motherless kids, and I thought to myself, it's awful, the degradation a woman can sink down into without respect for herself, so I said to her, Violet, will you look at your hands, will you look at your fingernails, Violet?

STEVE: Is that why you hit Violet?

LEONA: Goddam it, NO! Will you listen? I told her to look at her nails and she said, oh, the enamel is peeling, I know. I mean the dirtiness of the nails was not a thing she could notice, just the chipped red enamel.

STEVE: Is that why you hit Violet?

LEONA: Shit, will you shut up till I tell you why I hit her? I wouldn't hit her just for being unclean, unsanitary. I wouldn't hit her for nothing that affected just her. And now, if you'll pay attention, I'm going to tell you exactly why I did hit her. I got up from the table to play "Souvenir."

STEVE: What is she talking about? What are you talking about?

LEONA: When I come back to the table her hands had disappeared off it. I thought to myself, I'm sorry, I made her ashamed of her hands and she's hiding them now.

STEVE: Is that why you hit Violet?

LEONA: Why do you come in a bar when you're already drunk? No! Listen! It wasn't embarrassment over her filthy nails that had made her take her hands off the table top, it was her old habit, as filthy as her nails. The reason her pitiful hands had disappeared off the table was because under the table she was acting indecent with her hands in the lap of that ape that moved himself into my trailer and tonight will move himself out as fast as he moved himself in. And now do you know why

238

I hit her? If you had balls, which it doesn't look like you do, you would've hit her yourself instead of making me do it.

STEVE: I wasn't there when it happened, but that's the reason you hit her?

LEONA: Yeah, now the reason has got through the fog in your head, which is thick as the fog on the beach.

[*Violet wails from the ladies' room.*]

STEVE: I'm not married to Violet, I never was or will be. I just wanted to know who hit her and why you hit her.

LEONA [*slapping at him with her cap*]: Annhh!

STEVE: Don't slap at me with that cap. What do I have to do with what she done or she does?

LEONA: No responsibility? No affection? No pity? You stand there hearing her wailing in the ladies' and deny there's any connection between you? Well, now I feel sorry for her. I regret that I hit her. She can come back out now and I won't hit her again. I see her life, the awfulness of her hands reaching out under a table, automatically creeping under a table into the lap of anything with a thing that she can catch hold of. Let her out of the ladies', I'll never hit her again. I feel too much pity for her, but I'm going out for a minute to breathe some clean air and to get me a drink where a barman's willing to serve me, and then I'll come back to pay up whatever I owe here and say good-bye to the sailfish, hooked and shellacked and strung up like a flag over . . . over . . . lesser, much lesser . . . creatures that never, ever sailed an inch in their . . . lives . . .

[*The pauses at the end of this speech are due to a shift of her attention toward a young man and a boy who have entered the bar. Her eyes have followed them as they walked past her to a table in the front.*]

[*She continues speaking, but now as if to herself.*]

. . . When I leave here tonight, none of you will ever see me again. I'm going to stop by the shop, let myself in with my passkey and collect my own equipment, which is enough to open a shop of my own, write a good-bye note to Flo, she isn't a bad old bitch, I doubled her trade since I been there, she's going to miss me, poor Flo, then leave my passkey and cut back to my trailer and pack like lightning and move on to . . .

BILL: . . . Where?

LEONA: Where I go next. You won't know, but you'll know I went fast.

[*Now she forgets her stated intention of going out of the bar and crosses to the table taken by the young man and the boy.*

[*The boy, Bobby, wears faded jeans and a sweatshirt on the back of which is lettered "Iowa to Mexico." The young man, Quentin, is dressed effetely in a yachting jacket, maroon linen slacks, and a silk neck-scarf. Despite this costume, he has a quality of sexlessness, not effeminacy. Some years ago, he must have been remarkably handsome. Now his face seems to have been burned thin by a fever that is not of the flesh.*]

LEONA: [*suddenly very amiable*]: Hi, boys!

QUENTIN: Oh. Hello. Good Evening.

BOBBY [*with shy friendliness*]: Hello.

[*Bill is grinning and chuckling. Violet's weeping in the ladies' room no longer seems to interest anyone in the bar.*]

LEONA [*to Bobby*]: How's the corn growing out there where the tall corn grows?

BOBBY: Oh, it's still growing tall.

LEONA: Good for the corn. What town or city are you from in Iowa?

BOBBY: Goldenfield. It's close to Dubuque.

LEONA: Dubuque, no shoot? I could recite the telephone book of Dubuque, but excuse me a minute, I want to play a selection on the number selector, and I'll come right back to discuss Dubuque with you. Huh? [*She moves as if totally pacified to the juke box and removes some coins from a pocket. They fall to the floor. She starts to bend over to pick them up, then decides not to bother, gives them a slight kick, gets a dollar bill out of a pocket, calling out:*] Monk, gimme change for a buck. [*Leona crosses to Monk at bar, waving a dollar bill.*]

QUENTIN: Barman? . . . Barman? . . . What's necessary to get the barman's attention here, I wonder.

[*Leona crosses back to juke box, stage right. Bobby hands Leona the change he's picked up off the floor. She looks for a number on the juke box.*]

MONK: I heard you. You've come in the wrong place. You're looking for the Jungle Bar, half a mile up the beach.

QUENTIN: Does that mean you'd rather not serve us?

MONK: Let me see the kid's draft card.

BOBBY: I just want a Coke.

QUENTIN: He wants a plain Coca-Cola, I'd like a vodka and tonic.

[*Leona lights up the juke box with a coin and selects a violin number, "Souvenir." A look of ineffable sweetness appears on her face, at the first note of music.*]

BILL: Y' can't insult 'em, there's no way to bring 'em down except to beat 'em and roll 'em.

[*The bar starts to dim, and a special spot comes up on Bill. The violin music on the juke box plays softly under.*]

241

I noticed him stop at the door before he come in. He was about to go right back out when he caught sight of me. Then he decided to stay. A piss-elegant one like that is asking for it. After a while, say about fifteen minutes, I'll go in the gents' and he'll follow me in there for a look at Junior. Then I'll have him hooked. He'll ask me to meet him outside by his car or at the White Castle. It'll be a short wait and I don't think I'll have t'do more than scare him a little. I don't like beating 'em up. They can't help the way they are. Who can? Not me. Left home at fifteen, and like Leona says, I've never done a lick of work in my life and I never plan to, not as long as Junior keeps batting on the home team, but my time with Leona's run out. She means to pull out of here and I mean to stay . . .

[*The bar is relighted. Leona is still at the juke box. She is leaning against the juke box, listening intently to the music.*]

MONK [*rapping at the ladies'*]: Violet, you can come out, now, she's playing that violin number.

[*Bill and Steve laugh. The bar starts to dim, and a special spot comes up on Steve. The violin number still plays under.*]

STEVE: I guess Violet's a pig, all right, and I ought to be ashamed to go around with her. But a man unmarried, forty-seven years old, employed as a short-order cook at a salary he can barely get by on alone, he can't be choosy. Nope, he has to be satisfied with the Goddam scraps in this world, and Violet's one of those scraps. She's a pitiful scrap, but . . . [*He shrugs sadly and lifts the beer bottle to his mouth.*] . . . something's better than nothing and I had nothing before I took up with her. She gave me a clap once and tried to tell me I got it off a toilet seat. I asked the doctor, is it possible to get a clap off a public toilet seat, and he said, yes, you can get it that way but you don't. [*He grins sadly and drinks again, wobbling slightly.*] . . . Oh, my life, my miserable, cheap life! It's like a bone thrown to a dog! I'm the dog, she's the bone. Hell, I know her habits,

242

She's always down there in that amusement arcade when I go to pick her up, she's down there as close as she can get to some Navy kid, playing a pinball game, and one hand is out of sight. Hustling? I reckon that's it. I know I don't provide for her, just buy her a few beers here, and a hot dog on the way home. But, Bill, why's he let her mess around with him? One night he was braggin' about the size of his tool, he said all he had to do to make a living was wear tight pants on the street. Life! . . . Throw it to a dog. I'm not a dog, I don't want it. I think I'll sit at the bar and pay no attention to her when she comes out . . .

[*The light in the bar comes up to normal level as the spot fades out. After a moment, Violet comes out of the ladies' room slowly, with a piteous expression. She is dabbing her nostrils with a bit of toilet tissue. Her lips are pursed in sorrow so that she is like travesty of a female saint under torture. She gasps and draws back a little at the sight of Leona; then, discreetly sobbing, she edges onto a bar stool, and Monk gives her a beer. Steve glares at her. She avoids looking at him. Bill grins and chuckles at his table. Leona ignores the fact that Violet has emerged from her retreat. She goes on pacing the bar, but is enthralled by the music.*]

LEONA: My God, what an instrument, it's like a thing in your heart, it's a thing that's sad but better than being happy, in a . . . crazy drunk way . . .

VIOLET: [*piteously*]: I don't know if I can drink, I feel sick at my stomach.

LEONA: Aw, shit, Violet. Who do you think you're kidding? You'll drink whatever is put in the reach of your paws. [*She slaps herself on the thigh with the sailor cap and laughs.*]

VIOLET: I do feel sick at my stomach.

LEONA: You're lucky you're sick at your stomach because your stomach can vomit, but when you're sick at your heart, that's

243

when it's awful, because your heart can't vomit the memories of your lifetime. I wish my heart could vomit, I wish my heart could throw up the heartbreaks of my lifetime, my days in a beauty shop and my nights in a trailer. It wouldn't surprise me at all if I drove up to Sausalito alone this night. With no one . . .

[*She glances at Bill, who grins and chuckles. Violet sobs piteously again. Leona gives Violet a fairly hard slap on the shoulders with her sailor's cap. Violet cries out in affected terror.*]

Shuddup, I'm not gonna hit you. Steve, take her off that bar stool and put her at a table, she's on a crying jag and it makes me sick.

STEVE [*to Violet*]: Come off it, Violet. Sit over here at a table, before you fall off the bar stool.

LEONA: She hasn't got a mark on her, not a mark, but she acts like I'd nearly kilt her, and turns to a weeping willow. But as for that ape that I put up in my trailer, I took him in because a life in a trailer, going from place to place any way the wind blows you, gets to be lonely, sometimes. But that's a mistake I'll not make again . . . knock wood! [*Knocks table top.*]

STEVE [*wishing to smooth troubled waters*]: Know what that means, to knock wood? It means to touch the wood of the true cross, Leona. [*He peers gravely and nearsightedly into Leona's face.*]

LEONA: Yeh, for luck, you need it.

MONK [*to Violet at bar*]: That's mine! Here's yours. [*She has reached out for Monk's drink.*]

STEVE: Violet, get off that stool and sit at a table.

LEONA: You got to move her. She's got to be moved.

ACT I

[*Steve accepts this necessity. He supports Violet's frail, liquid figure to a table upstage, but her long, thin arm snakes out to remove Monk's drink from the bar top as she goes.*]

[*The phone rings, and Monk lifts it.*]

MONK: Monk's Place . . . Doc, it's for you.

DOC [*crossing to the end of the bar*]: Thanks, Monk.

MONK: The old Doc's worked up a pretty good practice for a man in retirement.

LEONA: Retirement your ass, he was kicked out of the medical profession for performing operations when he was so loaded he couldn't tell the appendix from the gizzard.

MONK: Leona, go sit at your table.

LEONA: You want responsibility for a human life, do you?

MONK: Bill, I think she's ready to go home now.

LEONA: I'll go home when I'm ready and I'll do it alone.

BILL: I seen a circus with a polar bear in it that rode a three-wheel bicycle. That's what you make me think of tonight.

LEONA: You want to know something, McCorkle? I could beat the shit out of you.

BILL: Set down somewhere and shut up.

LEONA: I got a suggestion for you. Take this cab fare. . . [*She throws a handful of silver on the table.*] . . . And go get your stuff out of my trailer. Clear it all out, because when I go home tonight and find any stuff of yours there, I'll pitch it out of the trailer and bolt the door on you. I'm just in the right mood to do it.

BILL: Don't break my heart.

245

LEONA: What heart? We been in my trailer together for six months and you contributed nothing.

BILL: Shit, for six months I satisfied you in your trailer!

LEONA: You never satisfied nothing but my mother complex. Never mind, forget it, it's forgotten. Just do this. Take this quarter and punch number K-6 three times on the juke box.

BILL: Nobody wants to hear that violin number again.

LEONA: I do, I'm somebody. My brother, my young brother, played it as good if not better than Heifetz on that box. Y'know, I look at you and I ask myself a question. How does it feel to've never had anything beautiful in your life and not even know you've missed it? [*She crosses toward the juke box.*] Walking home with you some night, I've said, Bill, look at the sky, will you look at that sky? You never looked up, just grunted. In your life you've had no experiation . . . experience! Appreciation! . . . of the beauty of God in the sky, so what is your life but a bottle of, can of, glass of . . . one, two, three! [*She has punched the violin selection three times.*]

MONK: The Doc's still on the phone.

LEONA: "Souvenir" is a soft number.

[*The violin number starts to play again on the juke box.*]

DOC [*returning to the bar*]: I've got to deliver a baby. Shot of brandy.

LEONA [*returning to Bill's table*]: It wouldn't be sad if you didn't know what you missed by coming into this world and going out of it some day without ever having a sense of, experience of and memory of, a beautiful thing in your life such as I have in mine when I remember the violin of and the face of my young brother . . .

BILL: You told me your brother was a fruit.

LEONA: I told you privately something you're repeating in public with words as cheap as yourself. My brother who played this number had pernicious anemia from the age of thirteen and any fool knows a disease, a condition, like that would make any boy too weak to go with a woman, but he was so full of love he had to give it to someone like his music. And in my work, my profession as a beautician, I never seen skin or hair or eyes that could touch my brother's. His hair was a natural blond as soft as silk and his eyes were two pieces of heaven in a human face, and he played on the violin like he was making love to it. I cry! I cry! . . . No, I don't, I *don't* cry! . . . I'm proud that I've had something beautiful to remember as long as I live in my lifetime . . .

[*Violet sniffles softly.*]

When they passed around the plate for the offering at church, they'd have him play in the choir stall and he played and he looked like an angel, standing under the light through the stained glass window. Um-hummm. [*Her expression is rapt.*] . . . And people, even the tightwads, would drop paper money in the plates when he played. Yes, always before the service, I'd give him a shampoo-rinse so that his silky hair, the silkiest hair I've ever known on a human head in my lifetime as a beautician, would look like an angel's halo, touched with heavenly light. Why, people cried like I'm crying and the preacher was still choked up when he delivered the sermon. "Angels of Light," that was it, the number he played that Easter . . . [*She sings a phrase of the song.*] Emotions of people can be worse than people but sometimes better than people, yes, superior to them, and Haley had that gift of making people's emotions uplifted, superior to them! But he got weaker and weaker and thinner and thinner till one Sunday he collapsed in the choir stall, and after that he failed fast, just faded out of this world. Anemia— pernicious . . .

VIOLET [*sobbing*]: Anemia, that's what I've got!

LEONA: Don't compare yourself to him, how dare you compare yourself to him. He was too beautiful to live and so he died. Otherwise we'd be living together in my trailer. I'd train him to be a beautician, to bring out the homeliness in . . . I mean the, I mean the . . . [*She is confused for a moment. She lurches into a bar stool and knocks it over.*] I mean I'd train my young brother to lay his hands on the heads of the homely and lonely and bring some beauty out in them, at least for one night or one day or at least for an hour. We'd have our own shop, maybe two of 'em, and I wouldn't give you . . . [*She directs herself to Bill.*] . . . the time of the day, the time of the night, the time of the morning or afternoon, the sight of you never would have entered my sight to make me feel pity for you, no, noooo! [*She bends over Bill's table, resting her spread palms on it, to talk directly into his face.*] The companionship and the violin of my brother would be all I had any need for in my lifetime till my death-time! Remember this, Bill, if your brain can remember. Everyone needs! One beautiful thing! In the course of a lifetime! To save the heart from colluption!

BILL: What is "colluption," fat lady?

LEONA: *CORRUPTION!* . . . Without one beautiful thing in the course of a lifetime, it's all a death-time. A woman turns to a slob that lives with a slob, and life is disgusting to her and she's disgusting to life, and I'm just the one to . . .

BILL [*cutting in*]: If you'd rather live with a fruit . . .

LEONA: *Don't say it! Don't say it!* [*She seizes hold of a chair and raises it mightily over her head. Violet screams. Leona hurls the chair to the floor.*] Shit, he's not worth the price of a broken chair! [*Suddenly she bursts into laughter that is prodigious as her anger or even more, it's like an unleashed element of nature. Several patrons of the bar, involuntarily, laugh with her. Abruptly as it started, the laughter stops short. There is total silence except for the ocean sound outside.*]

VIOLET: Steve, love, get me a hot dog with chili and onion, huh? Or maybe a Whopper.

STEVE: Oh, now you want a Whopper, a king-size burger, now, huh? Always got your hand out for something.

VIOLET: That's a cruel injustice. [*Sobs.*]

STEVE: Stop it!

VIOLET: I'm in paiii-in!

LEONA: Look at her, not a mark on her, but says she's in pain and wants a hot dog with everything on it, and I heard on TV that the Food Administration found insect and rodent parts in some hot dogs sold lately. [*She has been stalking the bar.*] Let her have him for supper! [*Indicates Bill.*]

DOC [*rising from his bar stool*]: Well, I better be going. Somebody's about to be born at Treasure Island.

LEONA: That's my trailer court where I keep my trailer. A baby's about to be born there?

BILL: Naw, not a baby, a full-grown adult's about to be born there, and that's why the Doc had t'brace himself with a coupla shots of brandy.

DOC [*turning about on his bar stool, glass in hand*]: You can't make jokes about birth and you can't make jokes about death. They're miracles, holy miracles, both, yes, that's what both of them are, even though, now, they're usually surrounded by . . . expedients that seem to take away the dignity of them. Birth? Rubber gloves, boiled water, forceps, surgical shears. And death? . . . The wheeze of an oxygen tank, the jab of a hypodermic needle to put out the panic light in the dying-out eyes, tubes in the arms and the kidneys, absorbent cotton inserted in the rectum to hold back the bowels discharged when the . . . the *being* stops. [*During this speech the bar dims, and a special*

249

spot comes up on Doc.] . . . It's hard to see back of this cloud of . . . irreverent . . . paraphernalia. But behind them both are the holy mysteries of . . . birth and . . . death . . . They're dark as the face of a black man, yes, that's right, a Negro, yes. I've always figured that God is a black man with no light on his face, He moves in the dark like a black man, a Negro miner in the pit of a lightless coal mine, obscured completely by the . . . irrelevancies and irreverencies of public worship . . . standing to sing, kneeling to pray, sitting to hear the banalities of a preacher . . . Monk, did I give you my . . . ?

[*As light comes up in bar, the spot fades out.*]

MONK: Bag? Yeah, here. [*Monk hands a medical kit across the bar.*]

LEONA: I want to know, is nobody going to stop him from going out, in his condition, to deliver a baby? I want to know quick, or I'll stop him myself!

DOC: Thanks. And I'll have a shot of brandy to wash down a Benzedrine tablet to steady my hands.

LEONA: NOBODY, HUH?

DOC: Tonight, as I drove down Canyon Road, I noticed a clear bright star in the sky, and it was right over that trailer court, Treasure Island, where I'm going to deliver a baby. So now I know: I'm going to deliver a new Messiah tonight.

LEONA: The hell you are, you criminal, murdering quack, leggo of that bag!

[*Leona rushes Doc and snatches his bag. She starts toward the door but is blocked by one of the men; starts in another direction and is blocked again. She is then warily approached from three or four sides by Monk, Doc, Bill, and Steve as trainers approaching an angry "big cat."*]

[*All ad-lib during this, and in the lines that follow, Monk, Leona, and Doc speak almost simultaneously, while Steve keeps up a continual placating repetition of "Violet says" and "Have a beer with us, Leona."*]

[*The effect should almost suggest a quartet in opera: several voices blended but each pursuing its separate plaint.*]

MONK: Don't let her out with . . .

DOC: My bag! The instruments in that bag . . .

MONK: Steve, Bill, hold her, I can't with my . . .

DOC: Are worth and insured for . . . over two thousand! If you damage the contents of that bag . . . I'll sue you for their value and for slander!

[*Leona sits on Doc's bag at center table.*]

LEONA: I'll surrender this bag to you in a courtroom only!

DOC: Very expensive, very, very expensive.

STEVE: Look, she's sitting on Doc's bag. Violet says she's, Leona, Violet wants to, listen, listen, listen Leona, set down and have a beer with us! Violet says she . . .

VIOLET: Not at this table, no, no, I'm scared of Leona, she . . .

STEVE: Violet, shuddup. Leona? Violet's offered you to a . . . drink! Have a drink with us, Leona.

LEONA: I'll stay sitting on it till some action is taken to stop this man from illegal . . .

[*Bill squirts a mouthful of beer at her, and she immediately leaps up to strike at him fiercely with the sailor's cap. In that instant Monk seizes the bag from the chair and tosses it to Doc, who rushes out the door with it.*]

All of you are responsible! . . . If he murders a baby tonight and the baby's mother! Is life worth nothing in here? I'm going out. I am going to make a phone call.

[*Bill makes a move to stop her.*]

Don't you *dare* to! Try to!

MONK: Who're you going to call?

STEVE: Who's she going to call?

LEONA [*to Monk*]: That's my business, strictly. I'm not gonna use your phone. [*She charges out the door, and the door is again left open on the sound of surf.*]

MONK: What's she up to?

STEVE: What's she up to, Bill?

BILL [*grinning and shrugging*]: I know what she's up to. She's gonna call the office at Treasure Island and tell 'em the Doc's comin' out there to deliver a baby.

MONK: Well, stop her, go stop her!

STEVE: Yeh, you better stop her.

BILL [*indifferently*]: She's disappeared in the fog.

MONK: She can get the Doc into serious trouble, and his condition's no better than mine is . . .

BILL: Shit, they know her too well to pay any attention to her call.

MONK: I hate to eighty-six anyone out of my place; I never have done that in the six years I've run it, but I swear to God, I . . . have to avoid . . . disturbance.

VIOLET [*plaintively*]: Last week she gave me a perm and a rinse for nothing, and then tonight she turns on me, threatens to kill me.

BILL: Aw, she blows hot and cold, dependin' on whichever way her liquor hits her.

VIOLET: She's got two natures in her. Sometimes she couldn't be nicer. A minute later she . . .

MONK [*at the telephone*]: Shut up a minute. Treasure Island? This is Monk speaking from Monk's Place . . . Yeah. Now. If you get a phone call out there from Leona Dawson, you know her, she's got a trailer out there, don't listen to her; she's on a crazy mean drunk, out to make trouble for a capable doctor who's been called by someone out there, an emergency call. So I thought I'd warn you, thank you. [*Monk hangs up the telephone.*]

[*Violet comes downstage, and the light is focused on her.*]

VIOLET: It's perfectly true that I have a room over the amusement arcade facing the pier. But it wasn't like Leona describes it. It took me a while to get it in shipshape condition because I was not a well girl when I moved in there, but I got it clean and attractive. It wasn't luxurious but it was clean and attractive and had an atmosphere to it. I don't see anything wrong with living upstairs from the amusement arcade, facing the pier. I don't have a bath or a toilet but I keep myself clean with a sponge bath at the washbasin and use the toilet in the amusement arcade. Anyhow it was a temporary arrangement, that's all it was, a temporary arrangement . . .

[*Leona returns to the bar. Bill rises quickly and walks over to the bar.*]

LEONA: One, two, button my shoe, three, four, shut the door, five, six, pick up sticks . . . [*No one speaks.*] . . . Silence, absolute silence. Am I being ostracized? [*She goes to the table of Quentin and Bobby.*] Well, boys, what went wrong?

QUENTIN: I'm afraid I don't know what you mean.

LEONA: Sure you know what I mean. You're not talking to each other, you don't even look at each other. There's some kind of tension between you. What is it? Is it guilt feelings? Embarrassment with guilt feelings?

BOBBY: I still don't know what you mean, but, uh . . .

LEONA: "But, uh" what?

QUENTIN: Don't you think you're being a little presumptuous?

LEONA: Naw, I know the gay scene. I learned it from my kid brother. He came out early, younger than this boy here. I know the gay scene and I know the language of it and I know how full it is of sickness and sadness; it's so full of sadness and sickness, I could almost be glad that my little brother died before he had time to be infected with all that sadness and sickness in the heart of a gay boy. This kid from Iowa, here, reminds me a little of how my brother was, and you, you remind me of how he might have become if he'd lived.

QUENTIN: Yes, you should be relieved he's dead, then.

[*She flops awkwardly into a chair at the table.*]

QUENTIN [*testily*]: Excuse me, won't you sit down?

LEONA: D'ya think I'm still standing up?

QUENTIN: Perhaps we took your table.

LEONA: I don't have any table. I'm moving about tonight like an animal in a zoo because tonight is the night of the death-day of my brother and . . . Look, the barman won't serve me, he thinks I'm on a mean drunk, so do me a favor, order a double bourbon and pretend it's for you. Do that, I'll love you for it, and of course I'll pay you for it.

QUENTIN [*calling out*]: Barman? I'd like a double bourbon.

MONK: If it's for the lady, I can't serve you.

ACT I

[*Bill laughs heartily at the next table.*]

QUENTIN: It isn't for the lady, it's for me.

LEONA: How do you like that shit? [*She shrugs.*] Now what went wrong between you before you come in here, you can tell me and maybe I can advise you. I'm practically what they call a faggot's moll.

QUENTIN: Oh. Are you?

LEONA: Yes, I am. I always locate at least one gay bar in whatever city I'm in. I live in a home on wheels, I live in a trailer, so I been quite a few places. And have a few more to go. Now nobody's listening to us, they're involved in their own situations. What went wrong?

QUENTIN: Nothing, exactly. I just made a mistake, and he did, too.

LEONA: Oh. Mistakes. How did you make these mistakes? Nobody's listening, tell me.

QUENTIN: I passed him riding his bicycle up Canyon Road and I stopped my car and reversed it till I was right by his bike and I . . . spoke to him.

LEONA: What did you say to him?

BOBBY: Do you have to talk about it?

QUENTIN: Why not? I said: "Did you really ride that bike all the way from Iowa to the Pacific Coast," and he grinned and said, yes, he'd done that. And I said: "You must be tired?" and he said he was and I said: "Put your bike in the back seat of my car and come home with me for dinner."

LEONA: What went wrong? At dinner? You didn't *give* him the dinner?

QUENTIN: No, I gave him drinks, first, because I thought that after he'd had dinner, he might say: "Thank you, good night."

255

BOBBY: Let's shut up about that. I had dinner after.

LEONA: After what?

QUENTIN: After . . .

BOBBY: I guess to you people who live here it's just an old thing you're used to, I mean the ocean out there, the Pacific, it's not an *experience* to you any more like it is to me. You say it's the Pacific, but me, I say THE PACIFIC!

QUENTIN: Well, everything is in "caps" at your age, Bobby.

LEONA [*to Quentin*]: Do you work for the movies?

QUENTIN: Naturally, what else?

LEONA: Act in them, you're an actor?

QUENTIN: No. Script writer.

LEONA [*vaguely*]: Aw, you write movies, huh?

QUENTIN: Mostly rewrite. Adapt. Oh, I had a bit of a setback when they found me too literate for my first assignment . . . converting an epic into a vehicle for the producer's doxy, a grammar school dropout. But the industry is using me now to make blue movies bluer with . . . you know, touches of special . . . erotica . . . lovely.

[*Leona laughs.*]

LEONA: Name?

QUENTIN: Quentin . . . Miss? [*He rises.*]

LEONA: Leona. Dawson. And he's?

QUENTIN: Bobby.

LEONA: Bobby, come back to the party. I want you back here, love. Resume your seat. [*Resting a hand on the boy's stiff shoulder*] . . . You're a literary gent with the suede shit-kickers and a brass-button blazer and a . . . [*Flicks his scarf.*]

BILL [*leering from bar*]: Ask him if he's got change for a three-dollar bill.

QUENTIN: Yes, if you have the bill.

LEONA: Ignore the peasants. I don't think that monkey-faced mother will serve us that bourbon . . . I never left his bar without leaving a dollar tip on the table, and this is what thanks I get for it, just because it's the death-day of my brother and I showed a little human emotion about it. Now what's the trouble between you and this kid from Iowa where the tall corn blows, I mean grows?

QUENTIN: I only go for straight trade. But this boy . . . look at him! Would you guess he was gay? . . . I didn't, I thought he was straight. But I had an unpleasant surprise when he responded to my hand on his knee by putting his hand on mine.

BOBBY: I don't dig the word "*gay*." To me they mean nothing, those words.

LEONA: Aw, you've got plenty of time to learn the meanings of words and cynical attitudes. Why he's got eyes like my brother's! Have you paid him?

QUENTIN: For disappointment?

LEONA: Don't be a mean-minded mother. Give him a five, a ten. If you picked up what you don't want, it's your mistake and pay for it.

BOBBY: I don't want money from him. I thought he was nice, I liked him.

LEONA: Your mistake, too. [*She turns to Quentin.*] Gimme your wallet.

[*Quentin hands her his wallet.*]

BOBBY: He's disappointed. I don't want anything from him.

257

LEONA: Don't be a fool. Fools aren't respected, you fool. [*She removes a bill from the wallet and stuffs it in the pocket of Bobby's shirt. Bobby starts to return it.*] OK, I'll hold it for you till he cuts out of here to make another pickup and remind me to give it back to you when he goes. He wants to pay you, it's part of his sad routine. It's like doing penance . . . penitence.

BILL [*loudly*]: Monk, where's the head?

MONK: None of that here, Bill.

QUENTIN [*with a twist of a smile toward Bill*]: Pity.

LEONA [*turning to Quentin*]: Do you like being alone except for vicious pickups? The kind you go for? If I understood you correctly? . . . Christ, you have terrible eyes, the expression in them! What are you looking at?

QUENTIN: The fish over the bar . . .

LEONA: You're changing the subject.

QUENTIN: No, I'm not, not a bit . . . Now suppose some night I woke up and I found that fantastic fish . . . what is it?

LEONA: Sailfish. What about it?

QUENTIN: Suppose I woke up some midnight and found that peculiar thing swimming around in my bedroom? Up the Canyon?

LEONA: In a fish bowl? Aquarium?

QUENTIN: No, not in a bowl or aquarium: free, unconfined.

LEONA: Impossible.

QUENTIN: Granted. It's impossible. But suppose it occurred just the same, as so many impossible things *do* occur just the same. Suppose I woke up and discovered it there, swimming round and round in the darkness over my bed, with a faint phosphorescent glow in its big goggle-eyes and its gorgeously iridescent fins and tail making a swishing sound as it circles around and about and around and about right over my head in my bed.

LEONA: Hah!

QUENTIN: Now suppose this admittedly preposterous thing did occur. What do you think I would say?

LEONA: To the fish?

QUENTIN: To myself and the fish.

LEONA: . . . I'll be raped by an ape if I can imagine what a person would say in a situation like that.

QUENTIN: I'll tell you what I would say, I would say: "Oh, well . . ."

LEONA: . . . Just "Oh, well"?

QUENTIN: "Oh, well" is all I would say before I went back to sleep.

LEONA: What I would say is: "Get the hell out of here, you goggle-eyed monstrosity of a mother," that's what I'd say to it.

MONK: Leona, let's lighten it up.

QUENTIN: You don't see the point of my story?

LEONA: Nope.

QUENTIN [to Bobby]: Do you see the point of my story?

[Bobby shakes his head.]

Well, maybe I don't either.

LEONA: Then why'd you tell it?

QUENTIN: What is the thing that you mustn't lose in this world before you're ready to leave it? The one thing you mustn't lose ever?

LEONA: . . . Love?

[*Quentin laughs.*]

BOBBY: Interest?

QUENTIN: That's closer, much closer. Yes, that's almost it. The word that I had in mind is surprise, though. The capacity for being surprised. I've lost the capacity for being surprised, so completely lost it, that if I woke up in my bedroom late some night and saw that fantastic fish swimming right over my head, I wouldn't be really surprised.

LEONA: You mean you'd think you were dreaming?

QUENTIN: Oh, no. Wide awake. But not really surprised. [*The special spot concentrates on him. The bar dims, but an eerie glow should remain on the sailfish over the bar.*] There's a coarseness, a deadening coarseness, in the experience of most homosexuals. The experiences are quick, and hard, and brutal, and the pattern of them is practically unchanging. Their act of love is like the jabbing of a hypodermic needle to which they're addicted but which is more and more empty of real interest and surprise. This lack of variation and surprise in their . . . "love life" . . . [*He smiles harshly.*] . . . spreads into other areas of . . . "sensibility?" [*He smiles again.*] . . . Yes, once, quite a long while ago, I was often startled by the sense of being alive, of being *myself, living!* Present on earth, in the flesh, yes, for some completely mysterious reason, a single, separate, intensely conscious being, *myself: living!* . . . Whenever I would feel this . . . *feeling*, this . . . shock of . . . what? . . . self-realization? . . . I would be stunned, I would be thunderstruck by it. And by the existence of everything that exists, I'd be lightning-struck with astonishment . . . it would do more than astound me, it would give me a feeling of panic, the sudden sense of . . . I suppose it was like an epileptic seizure, except that I didn't fall to the ground in convulsions; no, I'd be more apt to try to lose myself in a crowd on a street until the seizure was finished . . . They were dangerous seizures. One time I drove into the mountains and smashed the car into a tree, and I'm not sure if I *meant* to do that, or . . . In a forest you'll sometimes see a giant tree, several hundred years old, that's scarred, that's blazed by lightning, and the wound is almost obscured by the obstinately still living and growing bark. I wonder if such a tree has learned the same lesson that I have, not to feel astonishment any more but just go on, continue for two or three hundred years more? . . . This boy I picked up tonight, the kid from the tall corn country, still has the capacity for being surprised by what he sees, hears and feels in this kingdom of earth. All the way up the canyon to my place, he kept saying, *I can't believe it, I'm here, I've come to the Pacific, the world's greatest ocean!* . . . as if nobody, Magellan or Balboa or even the Indians had ever seen it before him; yes, like he'd discovered this ocean, the largest on earth, and so now, because he'd found it himself, it existed, now, for the first time, never before . . . And this excitement of his reminded me of my having lost the ability to say: "My God!" instead of just: "Oh, well." I've asked all the questions, shouted them at deaf heaven, till I was hoarse in the voice box and blue in the face, and gotten no answer, not the whisper of one, nothing at all, you see, but the sun coming up each morning and going down that night, and the galaxies of the night sky trooping onstage like chorines, robot chorines: one, two, three, kick, one two, three, kick . . . Repeat any question too often and what do you get, what's given? . . . A big carved rock by the desert, a . . . monumental symbol of worn-out passion and bewilderment in you, a stupid stone paralyzed sphinx that knows no answers that you don't but comes on like the oracle of all time, waiting on her belly to give out some outcries of universal wisdom, and if she woke up some midnight at the edge of the desert and saw that fantastic fish swimming over her head . . . y'know what she'd say, too? She'd say: "Oh, well" . . . and go back to sleep for another five thousand years. [*He turns back; and the bar is relighted. He returns to the table*

261

and adjusts his neck-scarf as he speaks to Bobby.] . . . Your bicycle's still in my car. Shall I put it on the sidewalk?

BOBBY: I'll go get it.

QUENTIN: No. You will find it here, by the door. [*Desires no further exposure to Bobby.*]

LEONA [*to Bobby*]: Stay here awhile . . . Set down. He wants to escape.

BOBBY: From me? [*Meaning "Why?"*]

LEONA [*visibly enchanted by Bobby, whom she associates with her lost brother*]: Maybe more from himself. Stay here awhile.

BOBBY: . . . It's . . . late for the road. [*But he may resume his seat here.*]

LEONA: On a bike, yeh, too late, with the dreaded fog people out. Y'know, I got a suggestion. It's sudden but it's terrific. [*She leans across the table, urgently.*] Put your bike in my trailer. It's got two bunks.

BOBBY: Thank you but . . .

LEONA: It wouldn't cost you nothing and we'd be company for each other. My trailer's not ordinary, it's a Fonda deluxe, stereo with two speakers, color TV with an eight-inch screen, touchamatic, and baby, you don't look well fed. I'm a hell of a cook, could qualify as a pro in that line, too.

BILL [*to Steve*]: What a desperate pitch. I was the wrong sex. She wants a fruit in her stinkin' trailer.

LEONA: Nothing stunk in my trailer but what's out now . . . He can't understand a person wanting to give protection to another, it's past his little reception. [*To Bobby*] Why're you staring out into space with visibility zero?

262

BOBBY [*slowly, with a growing ardor*]: I've got a lot of important things to think over alone, new things. I feel new vibes, vibrations, I've got to sort out alone.

LEONA: Mexico's a dangerous country for you, and there's lonely stretches of road . . . [*She's thinking of herself, too.*]

BOBBY [*firmly but warmly to her*]: Yes . . . I need that, now.

LEONA: Baby, are you scared I'd put the make on you?

[*Bill grunts contemptuously but with the knowledge that he is now truly evicted.*]

I don't, like they say, come on heavy . . . never, not with . . . [*She lightly touches Bobby's hand on the table.*] This is my touch! Is it *heavy?*

[*Bobby rises. Quentin is seen dimly, setting the bicycle at the door.*]

BOBBY: That man didn't come on heavy. [*Looking out at Quentin.*] His hand on my knee was just a human touch and it seemed natural to me to return it.

LEONA: Baby, his hand had . . . ambitions . . . And, oh, my God, you've got the skin and hair of my brother and even almost the eyes!

BILL: Can he play the fiddle?

BOBBY: In Goldenfield, Iowa, there was a man like that, ran a flower shop with a back room, decorated Chinese, with incense and naked pictures, which he invited boys into. I heard about it. Well, things like that aren't tolerated for long in towns like Goldenfield. There's suspicion and talk and then public outrage and action, and he had to leave so quick he didn't clear out the shop. [*The bar lights have faded out, and the special spot illuminates Bobby.*] A bunch of us entered one night. The drying-up flowers rattled in the wind and the wind-chimes tinkled and the . . . naked pictures were just . . . pathetic, y'know. Except for a sketch of Michelangelo's David. I don't think anyone noticed me snatch it off the wall and stuff it into my pocket. Dreams . . . images . . . nights . . . On the plains of Nebraska I passed a night with a group of runaway kids my age and it got cold after sunset. A lovely wild young girl invited me under a blanket with just a smile, and then a boy, me between, and both of them kept saying "love," one of 'em in one ear and one in the other, till I didn't know which was which "love" in which ear or which . . . touch . . . The plain was high and the night air . . . exhilarating and the touches not heavy . . . The man with the hangup has set my bike by the door. [*Extends his hand to Leona. The bar is relighted.*] It's been a pleasure to meet a lady like you. Oh, I've got a lot of new adventures, experiences, to think over alone on my speed iron. I think I'll drive all night, I don't feel tired. [*Bobby smiles as he opens the door and nods good-bye to Monk's Place.*]

LEONA: Hey, Iowa to Mexico, the money . . . here's the money! [*She rushes to the door, but Bobby is gone with his bicycle.*]

BILL: He don't want a lousy five bucks, he wants everything in the wallet. He'll roll the faggot and hop back on his bike looking sweet and innocent as her brother fiddling in church.

[*Leona rushes out, calling.*]

STEVE: The Coast is overrun with 'em, they come running out here like animals out of a brushfire.

MONK [*as he goes to each table, collecting the empty cans and bottles, emptying ash trays on a large serving tray*]: I've got no moral objections to them as a part of humanity, but I don't encourage them here. One comes in, others follow. First thing you know you're operating what they call a gay bar and it sounds like a bird cage, they're standing three deep at the bar and lining up at the men's room. Business is terrific for a few months. Then in comes the law. The place is raided, the boys hauled off in the wagon, and your place is padlocked. And then a cop or gangster pays you a social visit, big smile, all buddy-buddy. You had a good thing going, a real swinging place, he tells you, but you needed protection. He offers you protection and you buy it. The place is reopened and business is terrific a few months more. And then? It's raided again, and the next time it's reopened, you pay out of your nose, your ears, and your ass. Who wants it? I don't want it. I want a small steady place that I can handle alone, that brings in a small, steady profit. No buddy-buddy association with gangsters and the police. I want to know the people that come in my place so well I can serve them their brand of liquor or beer before they name it, soon as they come in the door. And all their personal problems, I want to know that, too.

[*Violet begins to hum softly, swaying to and fro like a water plant.*

[*When Monk finishes cleaning off the tables, he returns behind the bar. The bar lights dim, and his special spot comes up.*]

I'm fond of, I've got an affection for, a sincere interest in my regular customers here. They send me post cards from wherever they go and tell me what's new in their lives and I am interested in it. Just last month one of them I hadn't seen in about five years, he died in Mexico City and I was notified of the death and that he'd willed me all he owned in the world, his personal effects and a two-hundred-fifty-dollar savings account in a bank. A thing like that is beautiful as music. These things, these people, take the place of a family in my life. I love to come down those steps from my room to open the place for the evening, and when I've closed for the night, I love climbing back up those steps with my can of Ballantine's ale, and the stories, the jokes, the confidences and confessions I've heard that night,

SMALL CRAFT WARNINGS

it makes me feel not alone . . . I've had heart attacks, and I'd be a liar to say they didn't scare me and don't still scare me. I'll die some night up those steps, I'll die in the night alone, and I hope it don't wake me up, that I just slip away, quietly.

[*Leona has returned. The light in the bar comes up but remains at a low level.*]

LEONA: . . . Is there a steam engine in here? Did somebody drive in here on a steam engine while I was out?

MONK [*returning from his meditation*]: . . . Did what?

LEONA: I hear something going huff-huff like an old locomotive pulling into a station. [*She is referring to a sound like a panting dog. It comes from Bill at the unlighted table where Violet is seated between him and Steve.*] . . . Oh, well, my home is on wheels . . . Bourbon sweet, Monk.

MONK: Leona, you don't need another.

LEONA: Monk, it's after midnight, my brother's death-day is over, I'll be all right, don't worry. [*She goes to the bar.*] . . . It was selfish of me to wish he was still alive.

[*A pin-spot of light picks up Violet's tear-stained and tranced face at the otherwise dark table.*]

. . . She's got some form of religion in her hands . . .

CURTAIN

An hour later. "Group singing" is in progress at the table stage right. Leona is not participating. She is sitting moodily at the bar facing front.

VIOLET: "I don't want to set the world on fii-yuh."

STEVE: "I don't want to set the world on fii-yuh."

VIOLET: I like old numbers best. Here's an oldie that I learned from my mother. [*She rises and assumes a sentimental look.*]
"Lay me where sweet flowers blos-som,
Where the dainty lily blows
Where the pinks and violets min-gle,
Lay me underneath the rose."

LEONA: Shit. Y'don't need a rose to lay her, you could lay her under a cactus and she wouldn't notice the diff-rence.

[*Bill crosses to the bar for a beer.*]

I guess you don't think I'm serious about it, hitting the highway tonight.

[*Bill shrugs and crosses to a downstage table.*]

Well, I am, I'm serious about it. [*She sits at his table.*] An experienced expert beautician can always get work anywhere.

BILL: Your own appearance is a bad advertisement for your line of work.

LEONA: I don't care how I look as long as I'm clean and decent . . . and *self-supporting*. When I haul into a new town, I just look through the yellow pages of the telephone directory and pick out a beauty shop that's close to my trailer camp. I go to the shop and offer to work a couple of days for nothing, and after that couple of days I'm in like Flynn, and on my own terms, which is fifty per cent of charges for all I do, and my tips,

267

of course, too. They like my work and they like my personality, my approach to customers. I keep them laughing.

BILL: You keep me laughing, too.

LEONA: . . . Of course, there's things about you I'll remember with pleasure, such as waking up sometimes in the night and looking over the edge of the upper bunk to see you asleep in the lower. [*Bill leaves the table. She raises her voice to address the bar-at-large.*] Yeah, he slept in the lower 'cause when he'd passed out or nearly, it would of taken a derrick to haul him into the upper bunk. So I gave him the lower bunk and took the upper myself.

BILL: As if you never pass out. Is that the idea you're selling?

LEONA: When I pass out I wake up in a chair or on the floor, oh, no, the floor was good enough for me in your opinion, and sometimes you stepped on me even, yeah, like I was a rug or a bug, because your nature is selfish. You think because you've lived off one woman after another woman after eight or ten women you're something superior, special. Well, you're special but not superior, baby. I'm going to worry about you after I've gone and I'm sure as hell leaving tonight, fog or no fog on the highway, but I'll worry about you because you refuse to grow up and that's a mistake that you make, because you can only refuse to grow up for a limited period in your lifetime and get by with it . . . I *loved* you! . . . I'm not going to cry. It's only being so tired that makes me cry.

[*Violet starts weeping for her.*]

VIOLET: Bill, get up and tell Leona good-bye. She's a lonely girl without a soul in the world.

LEONA: I've got the world in the world, and McCorkle don't have to make the effort to get himself or any part of him up, it's easier to stay down. And as for being lonely, listen, ducks,

268

that applies to every mother's son and daughter of us alive, we were given warning of that before we were born almost, and yet . . . When I come to a new place, it takes me two or three weeks, that's all it takes me, to find somebody to live with in my home on wheels and to find a night spot to hang out in. Those first two or three weeks are rough, sometimes I wish I'd stayed where I was before, but I know from experience that I'll find somebody and locate a night spot to booze in, and get acquainted with . . . friends . . . [*The light has focused on her. She moves downstage with her hands in her pockets, her face and voice very grave as if she were less confident that things will be as she says.*] And then, all at once, something wonderful happens. All the past disappointments in people I left behind me, just disappear, evaporate from my mind, and I just remember the good things, such as their sleeping faces, and . . . Life! Life! I never just said, "Oh, well," I've always said "Life!" to life, like a song to God, too, because I've lived in my lifetime and not been afraid of . . . changes . . . [*She goes back to the bar.*] . . . However, y'see, I've got this pride in my nature. When I live with a person I love and care for in my life, I expect his respect, and when I see I've lost it, I GO, GO! . . . So a home on wheels is the only right home for me.

[*Violets starts toward Leona.*]

What is she doing here?

[*Violet has weaved to the bar.*]

Hey! What are *you* doing here?

VIOLET: You're the best friend I ever had, the best friend I . . . [*She sways and sobs like a* religieuse *in the grip of a vision.*]

LEONA: What's that, what're you saying?

[*Violet sobs.*]

She can't talk. What was she saying?

269

VIOLET: . . . BEST . . . !

LEONA: WHAT?

VIOLET: . . . *Friend!*

LEONA: I'd go further than that, I'd be willing to bet I'm the *only* friend that you've had, and the next time you come down sick nobody will bring you nothing, no chicken, no hot beef bouillon, no chinaware, no silver, and no interest and concern about your condition, and you'll die in your rattrap with no human voice, just bang, bang, bang from the bowling alley and billiards. And when you die you should feel a relief from the conditions you lived in. Now I'm leaving you two suffering, bleeding hearts together, I'm going to sit at the bar. I had a Italian boy friend that taught me a saying, *"Meglior solo que mal accompanota,"* which means that you're better alone than in the company of a bad companion.

[*She starts to the bar, as Doc enters.*]

Back already, huh? It didn't take you much time to deliver the baby. Or did you bury the baby? Or did you bury the mother? Or did you bury them both, the mother and baby?

DOC [*to Monk*]: Can you shut up this woman?

LEONA: Nobody can shut up this woman. Quack, quack, quack, Doctor Duck, quack, quack, quack, quack, quack!

DOC: I'M A LICENSED PHYSICIAN!

LEONA: SHOW *me your license. I'll shut up when I see it!*

DOC: A doctor's license to practice isn't the size of a drunken driver's license, you don't put it in a wallet, you hang it on the wall of your office.

LEONA: Here is your office! Which wall is your license hung on? Beside the sailfish or where? Where is your license to practice hung up, in the gents', with other filthy scribbles?!

270

MONK: Leona, you said your brother's death-day was over and I thought you meant you were . . .

LEONA: THOUGHT I MEANT I WAS *WHAT?*

MONK: You were ready to cool it. BILL! . . . Take Leona home, now.

LEONA: Christ, do you think I'd let him come near me?! Or near my trailer?! Tonight?! [*She slaps the bar several times with her sailor cap, turning to the right and left as if to ward off assailants, her great bosom heaving, a jungle-look in her eyes.*]

VIOLET: Steve, if we don't go now the King-burger stand will shut on us, and I've had nothing but liquids on my stomach all day. So I need a Whopper tonight.

[*Bill laughs.*]

STEVE: You'll get a hot dog with chili and everything on the way home. Get me . . . get me . . . get me. Grab and grope. You disgrace me! . . . your habits.

VIOLET: You're underdeveloped and you blame me.

LEONA [*looking out*]: Yes . . . [*She slaps something with her cap.*] *Yes!*

VIOLET: What did she mean by that? Another sarcastic crack?

LEONA: When I say "yes" it is not sarcacstic . . . It means a decision to act.

MONK: The place is closing so will everybody get themselves together now, please.

VIOLET: I do have to have something solid. Too much liquids and not enough solids in the system upsets the whole system. Ask the Doc if it don't. Doc don't it upset the system, liquids without solids? All day long?

271

[*Doc has been sunk in profoundly dark and private reflections. He emerges momentarily to reply to Violet's direct question.*]

DOC: If that's a professional question to a doctor whose office is here . . . [*A certain ferocity is boiling in him and directed mostly at himself.*] My fee is . . . another brandy. [*He turns away with a short, disgusted laugh.*]

MONK: Something wrong, Doc?

[*Violet has crossed to Bill, as a child seeking protection.*]

DOC: Why, no, what could be wrong? But a need to put more liquid in my system . . .

LEONA [*convulsively turning about*]: Yes . . . *yes!* [*This no longer relates to anything but her private decision.*]

BILL [*to himself*]: I'm not about to spend the night on the beach . . .

VIOLET: [*leaning toward Bill*]: I am not neither, so why don't we check in somewhere? Us, two, together?

STEVE: I heard that.

LEONA: Yes . . . *yes!*

MONK: I said the place is closing.

VIOLET: Let's go together, us three, and talk things over at the King-burger stand.

STEVE: Being a cook I know the quality of those giant hamburgers called Whoppers, and they're fit only for dog food.

VIOLET: I think we better leave, now. [*Extends her delicate hands to both men.*] Steve? Bill? [*They all rise unsteadily and prepare to leave.*] Bill, you know I feel so protected now. [*Violet, Steve, and Bill start out.*]

272

LEONA [*stomping the floor with a powerful foot*]: Y' WANT YOUR ASS IN A SLING? BEFORE YOU'RE LAID UNDER THAT ROSE?

VIOLET [*shepherded past Leona by Steve and Bill*]: If we don't see you again, good luck wherever you're going.

[*They go out the door.*]

LEONA [*rushing after them*]: That's what she wants, she wants her ass in a sling!

[*She rushes out the door. A moment or two later, as Monk looks out, and above the boom of the surf, Violet's histrionically shrill outcries are heard. This is followed by an off-stage quarrel between Leona and a night watchman on the beach. Their overlapping, ad-lib dialogue continues in varying intensity as background to the business on stage: "If you don't settle down and come along peaceful-like, I'm going to call the wagon! . . ." "Do that, I just dare you to do it— go on, I just dare you to call the wagon! I want to ride in a wagon—it's got wheels, hasn't it—I'll ride any Goddam thing on wheels! . . ." "Oh, no—listen, lady, what's your name anyhow? . . ." "I'm just the one to do it! . . . I tell you my name? I'm going to tell you my name? What's your name? I want your name! Oh boy, do I want your name! . . ." "Listen, please, come on, now, let's take this thing easy . . ." "I've been drinking in this bar, and it's not the first time you . . ." "Let's go! You raise hell every night! . . ." "Every night! This isn't the first time—I've been meaning to report you! Yes, I'm going to report you! Yes, how's that for a switch? . . ." "I'm just trying to do my duty! . . ." "I live in a home on wheels, and every night you try to molest me when I come home! . . ." "No! You're wrong—you're always in there drinking and raising hell and . . ." "Yeah, but you let criminals go free, right? . . ." "No, I don't! . . ." "People can't walk in the street, murdering, robbing, thieving, and all I do is*

*have a few Goddam drinks, just because it's my brother's
death-day, so I was showing a little human emotion—take
your hands off me!* . . ." "Come on now!* . . ." "Don't you put
your hands on a lady like me!* . . ." "No, I'm not!* . . ." "I'm
a Goddam lady! That's what I am, and you just lay off!* . . ."
"I've had enough of this!* . . ." "Every night I come out here,
you're looking for free drinks, that's what's the matter with
you!* . . ." "I've never had a drink in my life, lady!* . . ."
"You never had a drink in your life!* . . ." "No, I haven't, I've
. . ." "Show me your identification, that's what I want to
see!* . . ." "I'm just trying to do my duty . . ." "Look here,
old man . . ." "I don't know why I have to put up with an old
dame like you this way . . ." "Oh!—Oh!—Why you Goddam
son of a!* . . ." "Now!* . . ." "Don't you talk to me like that
. . ." "I'm not talking to you, I'm telling you to come over
here and let me get you to the telephone here!* . . ." "You've
been harassing that man Monk!* . . ." "I'm not harassing anybody!* . . ." "You're not harassing anybody? . . ." "You come
over to this Monk's Place every night and raise hell, the whole
damn bunch of you, and a poor man like me trying to earn
a few dollars and make a living for his old woman and . . ."
"Let me see your identification! What precint are you from?
. . ." "Oh, yeah . . ." "Go on, I want that identification, and
I want that uniform off you, and that badge . . ." "You won't
do anything of the sort!* . . ." "Oh, yeah . . ." "Yes, I'm doing
my job, what I'm doing is legal!* . . ." "I happen to have more
influence up at that station than you . . . Goddam pig!* . . ."
"I haven't done nothing to you, I'm just trying to do my job
. . ." "Do your job? . . ." "Yes, and you're giving me a lot of
hard time!* . . ." "There's raping and thieving and criminals
and robbers walking the streets, breaking store fronts, breaking into every bar . . ." "Well, that's not my—listen, lady!
I'm just the night watchman around this beach here. I'm just
on the beach nights, I don't have anything to do with what's
going on somewhere else in the city, just on this beach!* . . ."*

274

"*You don't know what's going on on the beach . . .*" "*I know what's going on on the beach, and it's you and that crowd drinking every night, raising hell! . . .*" "*We're not raising hell every night! . . .*" "*If I was your husband, golly, I—I—by God I would take care of you, I wouldn't put up with your likes, you and that crowd drinking every night! . . .*" "*I like that uniform you've got on you, and I'm gonna have it! . . .*" "*Why do you have to pick on a little man like me for? . . .*" "*I've seen you sneaking around, Peeping Tom, that's what you are! . . .*" "*No, that's not so! . . .*" "*I've seen you sneaking around looking in ladies' windows . . .*" "*That's not true! I'm just trying to do my duty! I keep telling you . . .*" "*Yeah, peeping in windows . . .*" "*No! . . .*" "*Watching people undress . . .*" "*No! You . . *" "*I've seen you, you lascivious old man! . . .*" "*I've seen you taking these young men over to your trailer court and making studs out of them! . . .*" "*Yeah!—Yeah!— Yeah! Men, that's what I take to my trailer! I wouldn't take a palsied old man like you! . . .*" "*You know damn well I wasn't trying to get you to . . . ! I was trying to get you to this telephone box, where I was going to! . . .*" "*You will not be able to, old man! . . .*" "*Listen, Miss, I asked you to give me your identification! You give me your identification so I can tell who you are! . . .*" "*I want your identification! I've seen you, I've seen you sneaking around the trailer court, I've seen you looking in windows . . .*" "*Oh, that's a lie! I never did a thing like that in all my life, I go to church. I'm a good Christian man! . . .*" "*Oh yeah! Yeah! Yeah! . . .*" "*I could take you in if I were younger, I wouldn't have to call the highway patrol, but I'm going to do that right now! . . .*" "*Listen, Holy Willie! I've seen your likes in church before! I wouldn't trust you with a . . .*" "*A little church wouldn't do you any harm neither! . . .*" "*Old man . . . Yeah! Yeah! . . .*" "*I've seen you with those young studs! . . .*" "*Doesn't that make you excited? . . .*" "*No, by God, it doesn't! . . .*" "*Is that your problem? . . .*" "*No, I don't have none! You're the one with*

275

*the hang-ups and problems—you are a problem! You hang out
here all night in that damn Monk's Place! . . ." "I've got my
own man, I don't have to worry about any other man, I got
my own man in my trailer! . . ." "Anyone want to spend the
night with you, he must be a pig then, he must be some kind
of pig living with you! . . ." "Fat old bag of wind, don't you
talk to me! . . ." "Look, I'm tired of talking to you, by God,
I've put up with you all I'm going to! I told you I was going
to call the highway patrol! . . ." "I've seen the way you look
at me when you . . ." "That's a lie!—I never . . ." "Yeah!
Yeah! . . ." "I—I . . ." "I've seen you skulking around in the
dark, looking in windows! . . ." "I don't need your kind! I've
got a good woman at home, and she takes care of me, she
takes good care of me! If I can get this job done and you'll
just settle down and be quiet, we wouldn't have all this noise!
. . ." "Does your wife know about the girls you go out with?
. . ." "You're trying to incriminate me! . . ." "Does she know
about that? . . ." "I know what you're trying to do . . ." "I've
seen you . . ." "Trying to get me in trouble! Trying to get
me to lose my job here! . . ." "I know what you holy boys are
like! . . ." "Why don't you go back in there and raise some
more hell with those young studs? . . ." "I ain't doing that
neither . . ." "If you'd be quiet! . . ." "Stop harassing! . . ."
"I ain't harassing nothing! . . ." "Every time you want a drink,
yes? . . ." "I don't, I don't . . ."]*

MONK [*to Doc*]: Goddam, she's left her suitcase.

DOC [*musing darkly*]: . . . Done what?

MONK: She's left that bag in here, which means she's coming
back.

DOC: Aw, yeah, a guarantee of it, she's going to provide you
with the solace of her companionship up those stairs to the living quarters. [*He faces out from the bar.*] Y'know, that narrow
flight of stairs is like the uterine passage to life, and I'd say that

strange, that amorphous-looking creature is expecting to enter the world up the uterine passage to your living quarters above. [*He rises, chuckling darkly.*] Is the toilet repaired in the gents' room?

MONK [*listening to noises outside*]: Yeh, plumber fixed it today.

[*Doc sighs and lumbers heavily the way pointed by the chalk-white hand signed "GENTS" off stage right.*

[*Monk crosses to the door to assess the disturbance outside. Bill rushes into the bar.*]

BILL: For Chrissake, get an ambulance with a strait jacket for her.

MONK: You mean you can't hold her, you stupid prick?

BILL: No man can hold that woman when she goes ape. Gimme a dime, I'm gonna call the Star of the Sea psycho ward.

MONK: Don't put a hand on that phone.

[*Violet now rushes in the door. She continues her histrionic outcries.*]

VIOLET: They're callin' the wagon for her, she's like a wild thing out there, lock the door, don't let her at me. Hide me, help me! Please! [*She rushes toward the stairs.*]

MONK: Stay down those stairs, pick up your luggage, I'll . . . I'll . . . call a taxi for you.

VIOLET: Steve done nothin' to . . . nothin' . . . Just run!

[*Altercation rises outside. Violet rushes into the ladies'. Monk closes the door and bolts it. Doc returns from the gents', putting on his jacket. His pant cuffs are wet.*]

DOC: The toilet still overflows.

277

[*Steve calls at the locked door.*]

STEVE: Vi'let? Monk?

[*Monk admits him. Steve enters with a confused look about, two dripping hot dogs in his hand.*]

STEVE: Vi'let, is Vi'let, did Vi'let get back in here?

MONK: Yeh, she's back in the ladies'. [*Monk closes door.*]

STEVE [*shuffling rapidly to the ladies'*]: Vi'let? Vi'let? Hear me?

MONK: No. She don't.

STEVE: Vi'let, the King-burger's closed. So I couldn't get a Whopper . . . I got you two dogs, with chili and sauerkraut. You can come out now, Leona's getting arrested. Violet screamed for help to a cop that hates and hassles me ev'ry time I go home.

MONK: Those dogs you're holding are dripping on the floor.

DOC: Committing a nuisance . . .

STEVE: Vi'let, the dogs'll turn cold, the chili's dripping off 'em. You can't stay all night in a toilet, Vi'let.

VIOLET [*from the ladies'*]: I can, I will, go away.

STEVE: She says she's gonna stay all night in a toilet. Wow . . . I mean . . . wow. [*Starts eating one of the hot dogs with a slurping sound.*]

MONK: If she's called the law here I want her to shut up in there.

STEVE: Vi'let, shut up in there. Come out for your dog.

VIOLET: Take your dog away and leave me alone. You give me no protection and no support a'tall.

[*Doc utters a laugh that is dark with an ultimate recognition of human absurdity and his own self-loathing.*]

MONK: [*touching his chest*]: . . . Doc? . . . Have a nightcap with me.

DOC: Thanks, Monk, I could use one.

MONK [*leaning back in chair and tapping his upper abdomen*]: Angina or gastritis, prob'ly both.

DOC: In that location, it's gas.

MONK: What happened at Treasure Island?

DOC [*sipping his "shot"*]: Tell you when I . . . get this . . . down.

BILL: Time . . . runs out with one and you go to another. Got a call from a woman guv'ment employee in Sacramento. She's got a co-op in a high-rise condominium, lives so high on the hog with payoffs an' all she can't see ground beneath her.

MONK: Why're you shouting, at who?

BILL: Nobody's ever thrown McCorkle out.

MONK: Unusual and not expected things can happen.

[*Leona is heard from off stage: "Okay, you make your phone call, and I'll make mine."*]

So, Doc, how'd it go at the trailer camp?

[*He and Doc are seated in profile at the downstage table. Steve and Bill are silhouetted at the edge of the lighted area.*]

DOC: The birth of the baby was at least three months premature, so it was born dead, of course, and just beginning to look like a human baby . . . The man living with the woman in the trailer said, "Don't let her see it, get it out of the trailer." I agreed with the man that she shouldn't see it, so I put this fetus in a shoe box . . . [*He speaks with difficulty, as if compelled to.*] The trailer was right by the beach, the tide was coming in with heavy surf, so I put the shoe box . . . and contents . . . where the tide would take it.

MONK: . . . Are you sure that was legal?

DOC: Christ, no, it wasn't legal . . . I'd barely set the box down when the man came out shouting for me. The woman had started to hemorrhage. When I went back in the trailer, she was bleeding to death. The man hollered at me, "Do something, can't you do something for her!"

MONK: . . . Could you?

DOC: . . . I could have told the man to call an ambulance for her, but I thought of the probable consequences to me, and while I thought about that, the woman died. She was a small woman, but not small enough to fit in a shoe box, so I . . . I gave the man a fifty-dollar bill that I'd received today for performing an abortion. I gave it to him in return for his promise not to remember my name . . . [*He reaches for the bottle. His hand shakes so that he can't refill his shot-glass. Monk fills it for him.*] . . . You see, I can't make out certificates of death, since I have no legal right any more to practice medicine, Monk.

MONK: . . . In the light of what happened, there's something I'd better tell you, Doc. Soon as you left here to deliver that baby, Leona ran out of the bar to make a phone call to the office at Treasure Island, warning them that you were on your way out there to deliver a baby. So, Doc, you may be in trouble . . . If you stay here . . .

DOC: I'll take a Benzedrine tablet and pack and . . .

MONK: Hit the road before morning.

DOC: I'll hit the road tonight.

MONK: Don't let it hit you. [*Stands to shake.*] G'bye, Doc. Keep in touch.

DOC: G'bye, Monk. Thanks for all and the warning.

MONK: Take care, Doc.

STEVE: Yeh, Doc, you got to take care. Bye, Doc.

BILL: No sweat, Doc, g'bye.

[*Doc exits.*]

MONK: That old son of a bitch's paid his dues . . .

[*Altercation rises outside once more: "I'm gonna slap the cuffs on you! . . ." "That does it, let go of me, you fink, you pig!" Approach of a squad car siren is heard at a distance.*]

Yep, coming the law!

BILL: I don't want in on this.

STEVE: Not me neither.

[*They rush out. Squad car screeches to a stop. Leona appears at the door, shouting and pounding.*]

LEONA: MONK! THE PADDY WAGON IS SINGING MY SONG!

[*Monk lets her in and locks the door.*]

MONK: Go upstairs. Can you make it?

[*She clambers up the steps, slips, nearly falls.*

[*Policeman knocks at the door. Monk admits him.*]

Hi, Tony.

TONY: Hi, Monk. What's this about a fight going on here, Monk?

281

MONK: Fight? Not here. It's been very peaceful tonight. The bar is closed. I'm sitting here having a nightcap with . . .

TONY: Who's that bawling back there?

MONK: [*pouring a drink for Tony*]: Some dame disappointed in love, the usual thing. Try this and if it suits you, take the bottle.

TONY [*He drinks.*]: . . . O.K. Good.

MONK: Take the bottle. Drop in more often. I miss you.

TONY: Thanks, g'night. [*He goes out.*]

MONK: Coast is clear, Leona. [*As Monk puts another bottle on the table, Leona comes awkwardly back down the stairs.*]

LEONA: Monk? Thanks, Monk. [*She and Monk sit at the table. Violet comes out of the ladies' room.*]

VIOLET: Steve? . . . Bill? [*She sees Leona at the table and starts to retreat.*]

LEONA: Aw, hell, Violet. Come over and sit down with us, we're having a nightcap, all of us, my brother's death-day is over.

VIOLET: Why does everyone hate me? [*She sits at the table: drinks are poured from the bottle. Violet hitches her chair close to Monk's. In a few moments she will deliberately drop a matchbook under the table, bend to retrieve it, and the hand on Monk's side will not return to the table surface.*]

LEONA: Nobody hates you, Violet. It would be a compliment to you if they did.

VIOLET: I'd hate to think that I'd come between you and Bill.

LEONA: Don't torture yourself with an awful thought like that. Two people living together is something you don't understand,

and since you don't understand it you don't respect it, but, Violet, this being our last conversation, I want to advise something to you. I think you need medical help in the mental department and I think this because you remind me of a . . . of a . . . of a plant of some kind . . .

VIOLET: Because my name is Violet?

LEONA: No, I wasn't thinking of violets, I was thinking of water plants, yeah, plants that don't grow in the ground but float on water. With you everything is such a . . . such a . . . well, you know what I mean, don't you?

VIOLET: Temporary arrangement?

LEONA: Yes, you could put it that way. Do you know how you got into that place upstairs from the amusement arcade?

VIOLET: . . . How?

LEONA: Yes, *how* or *why* or *when?*

VIOLET: . . . Why, I . . . [*She obviously is uncertain on all three points.*]

LEONA: Take your time. And *think.* How, why, when?

VIOLET: Why, I was . . . in L.A., and . . .

LEONA: Are you sure you were in L.A.? Are you sure about even that? Or is everything foggy to you, is your mind in a cloud?

VIOLET: Yes, I was . . .

LEONA: I said take your time, don't push it. Can you come out of the fog?

MONK: Leona, take it easy, we all know Violet's got problems.

LEONA: Her problems are mental problems and I want her to face them, now, in our last conversation. Violet? Can you

283

come out of the fog and tell us how, when, and why you're living out of a suitcase upstairs from the amusement arcade, can you just . . .

MONK: [*cutting in*]: She's left the amusement arcade, she left it tonight, she came here with her suitcase.

LEONA: Yeah, she's a water plant, with roots in water, drifting the way it takes her.

[*Violet weeps.*]

And she cries too easy, the water works are back on. I'll give her some music to cry to before I go back to my home on wheels and get it cracking up the Old Spanish Trail. [*She rises from the table.*]

MONK: Not tonight, Leona. You have to sleep off your liquor before you get on the highway in this fog.

LEONA: That's what you think, not what I think, Monk. My time's run out in this place. [*She has walked to the juke box and started the violin piece.*] . . . How, when, and why, and her only answer is tears. Couldn't say how, couldn't say when, couldn't say why. And I don't think she's sure where she was before she come here, any more sure than she is where she'll go when she leaves here. She don't dare remember and she don't dare look forward, neither. Her mind floats on a cloud and her body floats on water. And her dirty fingernail hands reach out to hold onto something she hopes can hold her together. [*She starts back toward the table, stops; the bar dims and light is focused on her.*] . . . Oh, my God, she's at it again, she got a hand under the table. [*Leona laughs sadly.*] Well, I guess she can't help it. It's sad, though. It's a pitiful thing to have to reach under a table to find some reason to live. You know, she's worshipping her idea of God Almighty in her personal church. Why the hell should I care she done it to a nowhere person that I put up in my trailer for a few months?

I wish that kid from I-oh-a with eyes like my lost brother had been willing to travel with me, but I guess I scared him. What I think I'll do is turn back to a faggot's moll when I haul up to Sausalito or San Francisco. You always find one in the gay bars that needs a big sister with him, to camp with and laugh and cry with, and I hope I'll find one soon . . . it scares me to be alone in my home on wheels built for two . . . [*She turns as the bar is lighted and goes back to the table.*] Monk, HEY, MONK! What's my tab here t'night?

MONK: Forget it, don't think about it, go home and sleep, Leona. [*He and Violet appear to be in a state of trance together.*]

LEONA: I'm not going to sleep and I never leave debts behind me. This twenty ought to do it. [*She places a bill on the table.*]

MONK: Uh-huh, sure, keep in touch . . .

LEONA: Tell Bill he'll find his effects in the trailer-court office, and when he's hustled himself a new meal ticket, he'd better try and respect her, at least in public . . . . Well . . . [*She extends her hand slightly. Monk and Violet are sitting with closed eyes.*]

. . . I guess I've already gone.

VIOLET: G'bye, Leona.

MONK: G'bye . . .

LEONA: "Meglior solo," huh, ducks? [*Leona lets herself out of the bar.*]

MONK: . . . G'bye, Leona.

VIOLET: . . . Monk?

MONK: [*correctly suspecting her intent*]: You want your suitcase, it's . . .

VIOLET: I don't mean my suitcase, nothing valuable's in it but my . . . undies and . . .

MONK: Then what've you got in mind?

VIOLET: . . . In *what?*

MONK: Sorry. No offense meant. But there's taverns licensed for rooms, and taverns licensed for liquor and food and liquor, and I am a tavern only licensed for . . .

VIOLET: [*overlapping with a tone and gesture of such ultimate supplication that it would break the heart of a stone*]: I just meant . . . let's go upstairs. Huh? Monk? [*Monk stares at her reflectively for a while, considering all the potential complications of her taking up semi- or permanent residence up there.*] Why're you looking at me that way? I just want a temporary, a night, a . . .

MONK: . . . Yeah, go on up and make yourself at home. Take a shower up there while I lock up the bar.

VIOLET: God love you, Monk, like me. [*She crosses, with a touch of "labyrinthitis," to the stairs and mounts two steps.*] Monk! . . . I'm scared of these stairs, they're almost steep as a ladder. I better take off my slippers. Take my slippers off for me. [*There is a tone in her voice that implies she has already "moved in" . . . She holds out one leg from the steps, then the other. Monk removes her slippers and she goes on up, calling down to him:*] Bring up some beer, sweetheart.

MONK: Yeh, I'll bring some beer up. Don't forget your shower. [*Alone in the bar, Monk crosses downstage.*] I'm going to stay down here till I hear that shower running, I am not going up there till she's took a shower. [*He sniffs the ratty slipper.*] Dirty, worn-out slipper still being worn, sour-smelling with sweat from being worn too long, but still set by the bed to be worn again the next day, walked on here and there on—pointless—errands till the sole's worn through, and even then not thrown away, just padded with cardboard till the cardboard's worn through and still not thrown away, still put on to walk on till it's . . . past all repair . . . [*He has been, during this, turning out lamps in the bar.*] Hey, Violet, will you for Chrissake take a . . . [*This shouted appeal breaks off with a disgusted laugh. He drops the slipper, then grins sadly.*] She probably thinks she'd dissolve in water. I shouldn't of let her stay here. Well, I won't touch her, I'll have no contact with her, maybe I won't even go up there tonight. [*He crosses to open the door. We hear the boom of the ocean outside.*] I always leave the door open for a few minutes to clear the smoke and liquor smell out of the place, the human odors, and to hear the ocean. Y'know, it sounds different this late than it does with the crowd on the beach-front. It has a private sound to it, a sound that's just for itself and for me. [*Monk switches off the blue neon sign. It goes dark outside. He closes door.*]

[*Sound of water running above. He slowly looks toward the sound.*]

That ain't rain.

[*Tired from the hectic night, maybe feeling a stitch of pain in his heart (but he's used to that), Monk starts to the stairs. In the spill of light beneath them, he glances up with a slow smile, wry, but not bitter. A smile that's old too early, but it grows a bit warmer as he starts up the stairs.*]

CURTAIN

NOTES AFTER THE SECOND
INVITED AUDIENCE:
(And a Troubled Sleep.)

The play has drifted out of focus: I was almost inclined to think, "My God, this is a play about groping!"

The production of this play, and I think the play itself, deserves something better than that. The designer, the lighting and sound men, have caught perfectly the mood, the poetry, the ambience of the play.

But unfortunately in performance that lyricism—which is, as always, what I must chiefly rely upon as a playwright—is not being fully explored and utilized. At this moment, I must make a number of exceptions which will be made privately: I would say, however, to all the cast that at last night's performance the only parts that were totally and beautifully realized were those of "Doc," "Steve," "Quentin," and "Bobby."

We have now arrived at a point where we must approach this undertaking with the same seriousness—and I do not mean ponderousness but the opposite of ponderousness—that I had buried somewhere in me, beneath the liquor and the drugs that made my life a death-time in the late sixties; a sort of lyric appeal to my remnant of life to somehow redeem and save me —not from life's end, which can't be revealed through any court of appeals, but from a sinking into shadow and eclipse of so much of everything that had made my life meaningful to me.

I am sorry to return to a self-concerned note. Believe me, my concern is now much broader than self-concern, and in this particular instance, the case of this play and its players and its producers and its artists—which all of you certainly are (I doubt that you can believe how much I care for each of you as a person, and with the truest and purest kind of caring)—I would set down as an axiom that a playwright should never direct his work unassisted by someone who shares his concept but is better able to implement it through discipline.

The word "discipline" is not a pretty word to bring up at this point, and yet it must be. I am too old a hand at the abuse of self-discipline to fail to recognize a failure of self-discipline when I see it so nakedly on a stage before audiences.

The clinical name for this failure to discipline the self to achieve its goal is "the impulse toward self-destruction," which is the opposite and dark side of the will to create and to flower.

Self-transcendence, as well as self-discipline, is now in order. Each of us must put aside as best we can his and her personal stake in this adventure, this play, in order to serve its true creation as a whole. Ensemble and entity must take precedence, now, over that Mae West line to her manager, "How did the lady come on tonight?"—the wonderful bitch did not expect to receive a negative response, and she never got one, but it's a pity he didn't catch her act in the "Breckinridge" comeback. Or speak up about it.

Now to specifics about *Small Craft Warnings:*

I know that our designer, Fred Voelpel, will move that sailfish about a foot and a half out from the wall of the bar and have it suspended over the bar directly, with always just a bit of a light on its astonished expression. This will not upstage but will just provide a muted but persistent key to the tender irony which is the keynote to the still-possible success of this play.

Right now what troubles me most—in the way of specific staging and writing—is that, as physical climaxes to both acts, we have such closely corresponding chase-scenes of Violet by Leona. Of course this could be solved by returning to the opening of *Confessional** and starting the play with Violet wailing in the ladies' room and Leona pacing about in the middle of a

---

* Included in *Dragon Country* (New Directions, New York, 1970).

tirade. This would eliminate one chase scene. However, it would also eliminate the establishment of place, situation, and identification of characters. And, incidentally, it would finally persuade me that I am no longer able to write a Goddam thing for the American theatre.

The other option—which I hope we can take—is to sharply differentiate the second chase scene from the first. I love the return of Steve and Bill, but I don't like the total absence of a "rhubarb" on the beach until the squad car siren is heard. I think something better than this can somehow be managed for us. I think that Leona has been in furious altercation with a cop or watchman on the beach-front all this time, and the sound of it should "bleed under" like the lights "bleed under" Doc's big monologue. But let us be aware it is going on out there, although —for the uses of a really not literal or naturalistic play—it is faded under the monologue till that has scored for us and is then brought up again a few beats preceding Leona's rush back into the bar, because the beach cop has finally had to call the wagon for her.

For a while, let Leona ad-lib the altercation outside at a level set by the director—and meanwhile, I will write it. Let's say, for the moment, it goes something like this:

LEONA: Okay, do that! I just dare you to do that! Call the wagon! I'm willing to ride in a wagon! It's got wheels, I'll ride in any Goddam thing on wheels, I'm just the one to do it! Okay? Want to call the wagon out here for me? What are you waiting for? Me to go? Oh, no, I'm not going yet. Take your hand off my arm, you fuckin' pig! Don't put your hand on the arm of a lady! [*Sound of a slap: then Bill rushes back in to make his phone call.*]

I think that there can be an interior of bar "hold" for this loud outside altercation between Leona and the beach cop right after Monk calls Doc over to the table: he can do this before

Bill and Steve enter. And there can be a dramatic tension in Doc's unreadiness to tell of the disasters at Treasure Island for the time that Leona's off-stage rhubarb with the beach cop is heard. At the end of the Doc's story and just after his exit, Leona's voice can be heard again, continuing her rhubarb with the beach cop: "All right, I'm waiting, I am standing here waiting till that wagon gets here"—then the siren begins:

LEONA: That does it, let go of me, you fink, you pig!" [*Having struggled free of the beach cop's clasp on her arm, she now charges back into the bar, crying out:*] MONK! THE PADDY-WAGON IS SINGING MY SONG!

And let us please have "singing," not "playing."

Other specifics:

I think I've already gotten across to you the necessity of building up those elements in the play not concerned with the groin and the groping so that the audiences will recognize that this is not a sordid piece of writing. Now I think—with the exception of "Steve"—everybody in the cast—except "Monk" and "Doc"—is giving us a Bowery drunk bit, and that's not where the play's at. We don't want to sit out there looking at "vulnerable human vessels" that can touch us with their individual hearts, each at a time of crisis that compels it to cry out.

Finally, unless there's a sudden upsurge of energies and of selective focus, I think we need a later opening than is now scheduled.* I have always opposed an Easter Sunday opening for very personal but understandable reasons. Now I oppose it for reasons that seem almost desperately practical. The play strikes me as inviting disaster unless it is given time to pull itself together from its present state—and I gravely doubt that four more days are enough. It seems to me that the book has to be studied till there is no longer any groping after lines. Till mugging is not substituted for the delivery of the right ones.

* Sunday, April 2, 1972.

I have always suspected that actors regard playwrights as hostile beings, and this has always made me shy around them. I hope you prove me wrong, since we are all sitting together in this small craft and have been warned by two audiences that the sea is very rough.

However, at this moment I prefer the *Marseillaise* to "extreme unction."

Corággio!

T. W.

SMALL CRAFT WARNINGS:
GENESIS AND EVOLUTION

A well-received production in the summer of 1971 at Bar Harbor, Maine, of Tennessee Williams's *Confessional* prompted him to expand and reshape this earlier short play into the longer work, *Small Craft Warnings*. The following excerpts are selected from the playwright's correspondence with Bill Barnes (his agent), William Hunt (who was responsible for the Maine performances), and Robert Currie, Mario De Maria, and William Orton (the producers of *Small Craft Warnings*).

Key West, October 17, 1971

Dear Bill:

I'm writing you on my secretary's self-designed stationary. He's making a similar batch for me with my name in smaller type and without the cabalistic inscriptions on the left margin.

I am enclosing a revised draft of the curtain-raiser of *Two Plays*, the project for off-Broadway this season. Would you please get it typed up for me. . . .

It reads slow but I feel it would play well and that the end would be touching, and it seems very "now."

When I come back up in early December for Dotson's benefit thing at the Episcopal Cathedral, could a reading of the two plays be arranged for possible backers? With gifted actors reading? I feel it's so important, psychologically, for me to stay active in the theatre and just staying active is sufficient for my purposes, I don't need more than the assurance that I am not prematurely counted out as an active playwright. —Like swimming and love, it's all that keeps me going.

Yours fondly,
10.
Tenn.

P.S. The above *cri de coeur* is obsoleted by our phone talk and the news about *Confessional*. I have read that one over: it is all well written, I think, the main problem being too much writing. But a truly good production could bring it to life so sharply that the overwriting would be generally excused, if anything I do is still excused by the press. . . .

Key West, October 25, 1971

Dear Mr. Hunt:

My new agent, Bill Barnes at IFA, called me a couple of nights ago to say that you were interested in an off-Broadway production of *Confessional*—which I hope is true. It's very important to me to stay active in the theatre, I only feel half alive when I'm not.

I recall receiving from you last summer in Chicago some photos and résumés of actors for a Maine production of this play but the Chicago situation was so frantic that I could give no attention to anything else. I would certainly be interested in knowing how the production worked out. It's a very demanding play with all of those long "arias" and the heavy content: but when I read it over, the writing seemed good and some of the characters, notably "Violet" and "Leona," struck me as quite touching and funny. In any case, it might prove an interesting enterprise for off-Broadway this season.

Would you let me hear from you about it? I am taking an apartment in New Orleans for two or three months but do not yet have an address there. I will be here in Key West till this coming Sunday. After that I'll be briefly at the Hotel Royal Orleans while apartment-hunting and for a week end in Houston to see the Alley Theatre production of *Camino Real*. If you feel like traveling, I would be happy to have you as a guest in the New Orleans apartment when I have one, or we might even get together at the Houston gig. . . .

> With due apologies, cordially,
> Tennessee

New Orleans, November 1, 1971

Dear Bill Hunt:

Many thanks for sending me the notices. They are about the best I've received in ten years and clearly indicate that you did an excellent job on the play. The promise of some action in the New York theatre gives me a much-needed boost of morale. . . . I would gather from the notices that the play was well and carefully cast in Maine. Perhaps my favorite part in *Confessional* is that of "Violet". . . .

It is possible that I will get to New York late this month as Barnes wants me to tape a TV interview there: that would give us a chance to meet personally and discuss all aspects of the project and get it moving.

Barnes feels that the second scene of the play is too short: which may be, but it strikes me as the most natural point of division. I am not satisfied with the final bit, "Monk's" monologue about the slipper. I like the speech but it seems to give the play an unnecessarily bleak curtain. I wondered if he could not cross to the open door and stand there inhaling the ocean air deeply for the curtain: the waves booming as the set disappears in mist. Sometimes a bit of business like that can offer a sort of catharsis without words.

If I am not able to get to New York, it would be great if you could visit me here in New Orleans. I am taking an apartment tomorrow which is said to have an attractive guest room. (No good—still looking.)

It is four a.m. and I am tired after my flight from Key West: but happy over the way things are shaping up.

With warmest regards,
Tennessee

New Orleans, December 13, 1971

Dear Billy:

. . . I have no intentions of not participating in the making of this production. As I said . . . last night, "You know that I am going to be reviewed more than the play and that is how it has been for the last ten years." It is wrong and a scandal but that is how it has been and will be, perhaps more than ever. I want each one of those male roles to be cast as well as they can possibly be cast: THE PLAY NEEDS IT." —So far, in the male roles I am totally satisfied only with "The Boy." I think we can get superior actors for all the other men in the play. Since this play is so much talk and character, stock players, even if the best stock players, will not suffice. . . .

Please don't fear that I am going to come on like gang-busters. I am a reticent man. But I have too much at stake in the show—morally, I mean. . . . We can and we gotta get better!

Right on! With love,
10.

New Orleans, December 21, 1971

Dear Bill:

Here is a batch of rewrites in varying degrees of completion. You all will notice that my intent is to focus the play more on Helena. And to provide more action, to balance the monologues. I have also suggested an alternative title.

... I feel very fortunate to have these three young producers and I do not want to jeopardize the production by extended contract negotiations. I think the producers' contract—unless it demands my immediate decapitation—ought to be signed at once so they can move. ...

I am not into money-making gimmicks but artistic advantages. I think Bill, Bob, and Mario will assure them for us. The size of the cast is formidable: the actors have to be fine ones:—everything possible should be done to enhance the play's chance of production and survival, I mean from the producers' and backers' POV ...

So much for business. ...

Yours,
10.

New Orleans, January 1, 1972

Dear Bill:

By the end of this week we'll be in Key West where I'll stay in our other *pied-à-terre* till I hear from you. It's turned cold here, I need a couple of week's sun to prepare me for what I *still* hope will bring me back to New York. ...

But I'm not a man who can live on prospects continually deferred. You know, one side of the three—or is it four?—

dimensional continum that we live in is that relentless thing called time, and I feel it running out on me, so when things remain in a state of nebulous prospects, well, my feet get itchy. Isn't it plausible to suppose that if the off-Broadway gig was really going to occur, if the money was really there, wouldn't there be a house set for it by this time, and wouldn't "the full steam ahead" be a palpable if not visual force? . . .

Please let me know what progress or regression or total collapse has occurred before I leave here this week end: I've got to know to make plans.

With warmest regards,
Tennessee

Key West, January 20, 1971

Dear Bill:

I get strong vibes over the phone and I sensed that nobody wants me to change a thing in the play. OK, I won't. But just let it end with the transposition, "Monk," at the open door, letting the human odors out of the place and breathing the ocean.

I feel about this play that it can't do any harm, even if it fails to do good to anyone but Helena. And since I love that girl, I will settle for that. . . .

After some reflection—I think "The Truck & Warehouse Theatre"* has a lovely sound to it. Could it be interpreted as a metaphor for posterity . . .

With affection,
Tennessee

* *Small Craft Warnings* opened at The Truck and Warehouse Theatre in New York on April 2, 1972.

New York, April 24, 1972

Dear Mario, Bob, and Bill:

Knowing from long experience that the sight of the play-wright is temporarily odious to actors and producers of a play in trouble, I have had the discretion to stay away from the scene of my (probably) last New York production.

However I want to repeat that I've never had producers with whom it was happier for me to work, nor a cast . . . that I felt more affection toward. . . .

I am delivering to Billy Barnes today some last rewrites—one which I think might be particularly helpful: a dialogue between "Doc" and "Monk" which—with good timing and style of delivery—would keep the stage alive during the off-stage bru-haha which isn't or wasn't quite happening the last time I saw the show.

Please read it over a couple of times before you dismiss it. It makes of those stairs to the living quarter above a very organic thing.

Thank you for a very lovely production.

Fondest best wishes to all,
Tennessee

Lafayette (Indiana), April 27, 1972

Dear Mario: Bill: Bob:

There are several things besides my return to New York and further saturation interviews and talk-shows that can be done to improve the situation at the T. & W.

I know it's no use suggesting that the show be transferred to

299

a theatre further uptown or in a section less associated in the public mind with the hazards of the ghetto. The set could probably not be fitted onto another off-B'dway stage.

The gig which I completed here last night was something for the books. We had to play to a banquet hall with two wings—it reminded me of the old Penn Station in N. Y. Still, it held. And we got a standing ovation.

I leave this afternoon for Minneapolis (University of Minnesota) where I shall do my fan dance with falling feathers and a kangaroo partner. So life goes on and on when your heart belongs to show biz.

With love as ever,
10.

Key West, May 10, 1972

Dear Bill:

When I get a really good night's sleep I usually hit a good day at work. I am sending you a really good piece of writing for the top of SCW. Of course I don't know if it is still running but if it is, this new beginning could really send it off to a good start. Why don't we let it be known that the play is still being worked on and improved so that there will be fresh interest in it? . . .

I hope you will see why I am characterizing and building up "Doc" so much. He has to be a major character, full dimension, at the end of the play.*

Love,
Tenn.

* Tennessee Williams made his acting debut on June 6, 1972, playing the role of "Doc" for the first five performances at The New Theatre, in New York, where the production had relocated.

THE TWO-CHARACTER PLAY

"A garden enclosed is my sister . . ."

Song of Solomon, 4:12

The Two-Character Play opened at the Quaigh Theatre in New York on August 14, 1975, produced by William H. Lieberson (artistic director) and Martin Ewenstein (production coordinator), directed by Bill Lentsch, with Barbara Murphy as production stage manager and Debbie Tanklow as stage manager. The lighting and stage design were by Greg Husinko, the costumes by Isabelle Harris. The cast included Robert Stattel as Felice and Maryellen Flynn as Clare.

In the course of its evolution, several earlier versions of *The Two-Character Play* have been produced, the texts of which differ considerably from the one included in this volume. The first of them was offered at the Hampstead Theatre Club, London, on December 12, 1967, with Mary Ure and Peter Wyngarde, and James Rosse-Evans directing. The next, under the title *Out Cry*, was presented in Chicago on July 8, 1971, at the Ivanhoe Theatre. It was produced and directed by George Keathley, with Donald Madden and Eileen Herlie in the principal roles. Reworked, the play opened at the Lyceum Theatre in New York on March 1, 1973, produced by David Merrick Arts Foundation and Kennedy Center Productions, Inc., and directed by Peter Glenville. The lighting and stage design were by Jo Mielziner, the costumes by Sandy Cole, with Alan Hall as stage manager. The players were Michael York and Cara Duff-MacCormick.

SYNOPSIS OF SCENES

Before and after the performance: an evening in an unspecified locality.

During the performance: a nice afternoon in a deep Southern town called New Bethesda.

ACT ONE

Before the performance.

The whole stage is used as the setting for the play, but at the front, in a widely angled V-shape, are two transparent, flat pieces of scenery which contain the incomplete interior of a living room in Southern summer. The stage-right flat contains a door, the other a large window looking out upon an untended patch of yard or garden dominated by a thick growth of tall sunflowers.

The furnishings of the interior are Victorian, including an old upright piano, and various tokens of the vocation of an astrologer, who apparently gave "readings" in this room. Perhaps the wallpaper is ornamented with signs of the Zodiac, the solar twelve-petaled lotus, and so on. (The designer should consult an astrologer about these tokens, which should give the interior an air of mystery. He might also find helpful a book called Esoteric Astrology*).*

About the stage enclosing this incomplete interior are scattered unassembled pieces of scenery for other plays than the play-within-a-play which will be "performed." Perhaps this exterior setting is the more important of the two. It must not only suggest the disordered images of a mind approaching collapse but also, correspondingly, the phantasmagoria of the nightmarish world that all of us live in at present, not just the subjective but the true world with all its dismaying shapes and shadows . . .

When the interior is lighted, it should seem to be filled with the benign light of a late summer afternoon: the stage surrounding should have a dusky violet light deepening almost to blackness at its upstage limits.

Of the unassembled set pieces which clutter this backstage area, the most prominent is a (papier-mâché) statue of a giant, pedestaled, which has a sinister look.

At curtain rise, FELICE, *the male star of an acting company on a tour which has been far more extensive than was expected, comes out of a shadowy area, hesitantly, as if fearful of the light. He has a quality of youth without being young. He is a playwright, as well as player, but you would be likely to take him for a poet with sensibilities perhaps a little deranged. His hair is almost shoulder length, he wears a great coat that hangs nearly to his ankles; it has a somewhat mangy fur collar. It is thrown over his shoulders. We see that he wears a bizarre shirt—figured with astrological signs—"period" trousers of soft-woven fabric in slightly varying shades of gray: the total effect is theatrical and a bit narcissan.*

He draws a piano stool into the light, sits down to make notes for a monologue on a scratch pad.

FELICE [*slowly, reflectively, writing*]: To play with fear is to play with fire. [*He looks up as if he were silently asking some question of enormous consequence.*] —No, worse, much worse, than playing with fire. Fire has limits. It comes to a river or sea and there it stops, it comes to stone or bare earth that it can't leap across and there is stopped, having nothing more to consume. But fear—

[*There is the sound of a heavy door slamming off stage.*]

Fox? Is that you, Fox?

[*The door slams again.*]

Impossible! [*He runs his hands through his long hair.*] Fear! The fierce little man with the drum inside the rib cage. Yes, compared to fear grown to panic which has no—what?— limits, at least no'n short of consciousness blowing out and not reviving again, compared to that, no other emotion a living, feeling creature is capable of having, not even love or hate, is comparable in—what?—force?—magnitude?

309

CLARE [*from off stage*]: Felice!

FELICE: —There is the love and the—substitutions, the surrogate attachments, doomed to brief duration, no matter how—necessary . . .—You can't, you must never catch hold of and cry out to a person, loved or needed as deeply as if loved —"Take care of me, I'm frightened, don't know the next step!" The one so loved and needed would hold you in contempt. In the heart of this person—him-her—is a little automatic sound apparatus, and it whispers, "Demand! Blackmail! Despicable! Reject it!"

CLARE [*in the wings*]: Felice!

FELICE: Clare! . . . What I have to do now is keep her from getting too panicky to give a good performance . . . but she's not easy to fool in spite of her—condition.

[CLARE *appears in the Gothic door to the backstage area. There is a ghostly spill of light in the doorway and she has an apparitional look about her. She has, like her brother, a quality of youth without being young, and also like* FELICE *an elegance, perhaps even arrogance, of bearing that seems related to a past theatre of actor-managers and imperious stars. But her condition when she appears is "stoned" and her grand theatre manner will alternate with something startlingly coarse, the change occurring as abruptly as if another personality seized hold of her at these moments. Both of these aspects, the grand and the vulgar, disappear entirely from the part of* CLARE *in "The Performance," when she will have a childlike simplicity, the pure and sad precociousness of a little girl.*

[*A tiara, several stones missing, dangles from her fingers. She gives a slight startled laugh when she notices it, shrugs, and sets it crookedly on her somewhat disheveled and streaked blonde head. She starts to move forward, then gasps and loudly draws back.*]

Now what?

CLARE [*with an uncertain laugh*]: I thought I saw—

FELICE: Apparitions this evening?

CLARE: No, it was just my—shadow, it scared me but it was just my shadow, that's all. [*She advances unsteadily from the doorway.*] —A doctor once told me that you and I were the bravest people he knew. I said, "Why, that's absurd, my brother and I are terrified of our shadows." And he said, "Yes, I know that, and that's why I admire your courage so much . . ."

[FELICE *starts a taped recording of a guitar, then faces downstage.*]

FELICE: Fear is a monster vast as night—

CLARE: And shadow casting as the sun.

FELICE: It is quicksilver, quick as light—

CLARE: It slides beneath the down-pressed thumb.

FELICE: Last night we locked it from the house.

CLARE: But caught a glimpse of it today.

FELICE: In a corner, like a mouse.

CLARE: Gnawing all four walls away.

[FELICE *stops the tape.*]

CLARE [*straightening her tiara*]: Well, where are they, the ladies and gentlemen of the press, I'm ready for them if they are ready for me.

FELICE: Fortunately we—

CLARE: Hmm?

FELICE: —we don't have to face the press before this evening's performance.

CLARE: No press reception? Artists' Management guaranteed, Magnus personally promised, no opening without maximum press coverage on this fucking junket into the boondocks.—Jesus, you know I'm wonderful with the press . . . [*She laughs hoarsely.*]

FELICE: You really think so, do you, on all occasions?

CLARE: Know so.

FELICE: Even when you rage against fascism to a honking gaggle of—crypto-fascists? . . . With all sheets to the wind?

CLARE: Yes, sir, especially then.—You're terrible with the press, you go on and on about "total theatre" and, oh, do they turn off you and onto me . . . *Cockroach! Huge!* [*She stamps her foot.*] *Go!*—I read or heard somewhere that cockroaches are immune to radiation and so are destined to be the last organic survivors of the great "Amen"—after some centuries there's going to be cockroach actors and actresses and cockroach playwrights and—Artists' Management and—audiences . . . [*She gestures toward the audience.*]

FELICE: Have you got an "upper"?

CLARE: One for emergency, but—

FELICE: I think you'd better drop it.

CLARE: I never drop an upper before the interval. What I need now is just coffee. [*She is struggling against her confusion.*] —Tell Franz to get me a carton of steaming hot black coffee. I'm very annoyed with Franz. He didn't call me . . . [*She laughs a little.*] —Had you forbidden him to?

[*There is no response.*]

So I'm left to while the long night away in an unheated dressing room in a state theatre of a state unknown—*I have to be told when a performance is canceled!*—or won't perform! [*Her tiara slips off. She crouches unsteadily to retrieve it.*]

FELICE: The performance has not been canceled and *I* called you, Clare.

CLARE: After *I'd* called you.

FELICE: I have some new business to give you, so come here.

CLARE: I'll not move another step without some—Oh, light, finally something almost related to *daylight*! But it's not coming through a window, it's coming through a—

FELICE [*overlapping*]:—There's a small hole in the backstage wall. [*He crosses to look out at the audience.*] They're coming in.

CLARE: Do they seem to be human?

FELICE: No.—Yes! It's nearly curtain time, Clare.

CLARE: Felice! Where is everybody?—I said, "Where *is* everybody?"

FELICE: Everybody is somewhere, Clare.

CLARE: Get off your high horse, I've had it!—Will you answer my question?

FELICE: No cancelation!

CLARE: No show!

FELICE: What then?—In your contrary opinion?

CLARE: *Restoration* of—*order*!

FELICE: What order?

CLARE: Rational, rational! [*Her tiara falls off again.*]

313

FELICE: Stop wearing out your voice before the—

CLARE: Felice, I hear gunfire!

FELICE: I *don't!*

CLARE [*sadly*]: We never hear the same thing at the same time any more, *caro* . . . [*She notices a throne-chair, canopied, with gilded wooden lions on its arms: on the canopy, heraldic devices in gold thread.*] Why, my God, old Aquitaine Eleanor's throne! I'm going to usurp it a moment— [*She mounts the two steps to the chair and sits down in a stately fashion, as if to hold court.*]

FELICE [*holding his head*]: I swear I wouldn't know my head was on me if it wasn't aching like hell.

CLARE: What are you mumbling?

FELICE: An attack of migraine.

CLARE: You'd better take your codeine.

FELICE: I've never found that narcotics improve a performance, if you'll forgive me for that heresy, Clare.

CLARE: —Is this tour nearly over?

FELICE: It could end tonight if we don't give a brilliant performance, in spite of—

CLARE: Then it's over, *caro,* all over . . . How long were we on the way here? All I remember is that it would be light and then it would be dark and then it would be light and then dark again, and mountains turned to prairies and back to mountains, and I tell you honestly I don't have any idea or suspicion of where we are now.

FELICE: After the performance, Clare, I'll answer any question you can think of, but I'm not going to hold up the curtain to answer a single one now!

314

CLARE [*rising*]: —Exhaustion has—symptoms . . .

FELICE: So do alcohol and other depressants less discretely mentioned.

CLARE: I've only had half a grain of—

FELICE: Washed down with liquor, the effect's *synergistic.* Dr. Forrester told you that you could have heart arrest—*on stage!*

CLARE: Not because of anything in a bottle or box but—

FELICE [*overlapping*]: What I know is I play with a freaked out, staggering—

CLARE [*overlapping*]: Well, play with yourself, you long-haired son of a mother!

FELICE [*overlapping*]: Your voice is thick, slurred, you've picked up—vulgarisms of—gutters!

CLARE [*overlapping*]: What you pick up is stopped at the desk of any decent hotel.

FELICE [*overlapping*]: *Stop it!* I can't take any more of your—

CLARE [*overlapping*]: *Truth!*

FELICE [*overlapping*]: *Sick, sick—aberrations!*

[*There is a pause.*]

CLARE [*like a child*]: When are we going home?

FELICE: —Clare, our home is a theatre anywhere that there is one.

CLARE: If this theatre is home, I'd burn it down over my head to be warm a few minutes . . . You know I'm so blind I can't go on without crawling unless you—

FELICE: Wait a minute, a moment, I'm still checking props
—bowl of soapwater but only one spool . . .

[CLARE *encounters the Gothic, wood figure of a Madonna.*]

CLARE: —You know, after last season's disaster, and the
one before last, we should have taken a long, meditative rest
on some Riviera instead of touring these primitive, God-
knows-where places.

FELICE: You couldn't stop any more than I could, Clare.

CLARE: If you'd stopped with me, I could have.

FELICE: With no place to return to, we have to go on, you
know.

CLARE: And on, till finally—here. I was so exhausted that
I blacked out in a broken-back chair.

FELICE: I'm glad you got some rest.

CLARE [*hoarsely*]: The mirrors were blind with dust—my
voice is going, my voice is practically gone!

FELICE: —Phone where? Piano top. No. Table.—Yes, you
never come on stage before an opening night performance
without giving me the comforting bit of news that your voice
is gone and . . . [*Imitaing her voice:*] "I'll have to perform in
pantomime tonight."

CLARE: Strike a lucifer for me.

[*He strikes a match and she comes unsteadily into the interior set: he gives her a despairing look.*]

FELICE: —Why the tiara?

CLARE [*vaguely*]: It was just in my hand, so I put it on my
head.

[*He gives a little hopeless laugh.*]

316

I try like hell—how I try—to understand your confusions, so why don't you make some effort to understand mine a little?

FELICE: Your variety's too infinite for me, Clare.

CLARE: —You still can't forgive me for my Cleopatra notices. Ran into columns of extravagance and your Anthony's were condensed as canned milk.

FELICE: —Do you hate me, Clare?

CLARE: I think that's a question I should be putting to you. The night we opened in . . . [*She tries to remember the place, can't.*] —you turned on me like a spit-devil and shouted—Oh, I'd rather not quote you!

FELICE: Do. Please.

CLARE: —You called me a drunken slut and said "Fuck off!"

FELICE: —You can't believe I said that.

CLARE: Oh, let it go, it's gone . . . [*She starts toward the proscenium.*] Think I'll have a look at the enemy forces.

FELICE [*seizing her wrist*]: You will not, you must never look at an audience before a performance. It makes you play self-consciously, you don't get lost in the play.

CLARE: Never catch hold of my wrist like that, it leaves blue bruises! [*She has struck his hand away.*] Why are you so—wildly distracted, *cher*?

FELICE: I'm living on my nerves and they're—I'll probably dry up several times tonight but— [*He quickly exits to light the interior set.*]

CLARE [*looking about*]: Oh, God, this is the set for "The Two-Character Play," but where's the stairs and—?

FELICE [*returning*]: So far only parts of the set have arrived.

CLARE: What will I do when I'm supposed to go upstairs for parasol and gloves?

FELICE: Face upstage and I'll say you've gone upstairs. Your parasol and gloves are on top of the piano.

CLARE: Are you serious? About playing it this way?

FELICE: Desperately.

CLARE: Are you going to throw new speeches at me tonight?

FELICE: Tonight there'll have to be a lot of improvisation, but if we're both lost in the play, the bits of improvisation won't matter at all, in fact they may make the play better. [*He smiles wryly.*]

CLARE: I like to know what I'm playing and especially how a play ends.

FELICE: When the curtain is up and the lights are on, we'll fly like birds through the play, and if we dry up, we'll use it.

CLARE: Felice, do you have a fever?

[FELICE *has crossed to the proscenium.*]

There you go peeking out again, and you won't let me.

FELICE: I have to see if they're in or—

CLARE: We have no communication with the front of the house? [*She coughs and spits.*]

FELICE: None.

CLARE: You mean we're—?

FELICE: Isolated. Completely.

CLARE: —I need a month at a little—Bavarian—spa.

FELICE: You know, that "high" you're on is going to wear off in about half an hour and you'll have the energy of a piece of seaweed at low tide . . . Immediately after this tour I suggest that you enter a clinic for withdrawal from—

CLARE [*shouting*]: *After this tour is when? When will there be an end to it?*

FELICE: Soon.

CLARE: Make it sooner! Cancel the rest and let's—*rest!*

FELICE: Do you want to cross back over forty, fifty frontiers on wooden benches in third-class coaches?

CLARE: —You mean that—?

FELICE: I mean that's the style we'd make our triumphant return in if we turned back now without playing a week in the black since—

CLARE: —How big a hole are we in?

FELICE: Big enough to bury an elephant team.

CLARE: Why haven't you told me these things?

FELICE: It's impossible to have a realistic discussion with someone who's—[*He holds up three fingers.*] How many fingers am I holding up?

CLARE: You know I don't have my—my God, yes, I do! [*she fumblingly removes a pair of "granny" glasses from a pocket in her cloak-lining. She crosses directly to Felice, head tilted back to peer into his face.*] Oh, Felice, you look so terribly tired!

FELICE: Those glasses make you look—

CLARE: Ancient? Well—they don't subtract many years from you either.—Do you mind if I make one more comment on your appearance—if it's tactfully worded?

FELICE: I've had no time to make up.

CLARE: This comment's on your hair, why, it's almost as long as mine.

FELICE: You know I wear a wig for the role of Felice.

CLARE: The part of Felice is not the only part that you play.

FELICE: From now on, it might be.

CLARE: Wouldn't *that* please the Company! What would they be doing?

FELICE: I don't have any idea or a particle of interest.

CLARE: Oh! How regal!

[FELICE *pounds the stage floor three times with a staff.*]

Listen to that!

FELICE: I hear it.

CLARE: It sounds like a house full of furious, unfed apes.

FELICE: Maybe it is.

CLARE: Felice—where is everybody?

[*He pounds the stage floor again.*]

I asked you where is everybody and I *insist* on an answer.

FELICE: Oh, you *insist* on an answer! You're sure you want an answer?

CLARE: Yes, I do, right now!

320

FELICE: Perhaps you'll find this more illuminating than I did. [*He hands her a piece of paper.*]

CLARE: Oh. A cablegram?

FELICE: Yes!

CLARE: I can't make it out in this sepulchral—

FELICE: —Never mind, Clare, give it back.

CLARE: Not if it has to do with—strike a match!

[*He does. She reads aloud, slowly, in a shocked voice.*]

"Your sister and you are—*insane!*—Having received no pay since—"

[*The match burns out.*]

Strike another!

[*He does.*]

"We've borrowed and begged enough money to return to—"

FELICE: Signed: "The Company." Charming? [*He blows the match out.*]

CLARE: My God! Well, as they say— [*She turns to the piano and strikes a note.*]

FELICE: What do they say?

CLARE: That sort of wraps things up!

FELICE: The Company's left us, except for two stage hands who came in without a word and put up this piece of the set before they—

CLARE: Deserted us, too?

FELICE [*again at the proscenium, looking out*]: Now, then, they're finally seated!

CLARE [*retreating from the proscenium*]: —Felice, I am going to the hotel, that's where you'll find me when you've recovered your senses, I am going straight there and collapse because I would rather collapse in my hotel room than on a stage before people stranger than strangers.

FELICE: What hotel did you think you were going to, Clare?

CLARE: —Whichever—hotel we—stay at . . .

FELICE: Do you recall checking into a hotel, Clare?

CLARE: —When?

FELICE: Yes, when? After we got off the train, before we came to the theatre, is that when?

CLARE: Are you telling me that Fox hasn't made hotel reservations for us?

FELICE: Fox has done one thing. No, two: he demanded his salary—which I couldn't pay him—and after that, disappeared.

[*She gasps.* FELICE *holds out his hand toward her. Looking desolately into space, she places her hand in his.*]

Clare, I was holding out my hand for your coat.

CLARE: Do you think I'm about to remove my coat in this ice-plant?

FELICE: We're in our home, Clare, in the deep South and in summer.

CLARE [*hugging her coat about her*]: Let's—synchronize—thermometers and—geographies.

[*He suddenly tears the coat off her, and she cries out*]

FELICE [*pointing downstage at the supposed curtain*]: Hush.

322

CLARE: You're a monster!

FELICE: Yes, if you wish. Take your place.

[*She snatches up her coat, which he had flung onto the sofa.*]

CLARE: I'll wait in my dressing room till you've announced the performance is canceled. *Where are you—?*

[*He is striding toward the wings.*]

FELICE [*turning to hiss at her furiously*]: Will you take your place? I'm going to open the curtains!—Now, this instant!

CLARE: Are you serious?

FELICE: Desperately!

CLARE: Impossible!

FELICE: Necessary.

CLARE: Some necessary things are impossible.

FELICE: And some impossible things are necessary. We are performing tonight.

[*She stares at him a moment: then strikes a sharp note on the piano.*]

CLARE: I told you that I would not perform again in *The Two-Character Play* until you had cut it. Have you? Have you cut it?

FELICE: [*evasively*]: Where my work is concerned—

CLARE: I said *have you cut it?*

FELICE: You're given cuts when I make them.

CLARE: I'm not going to be given cuts, I'm going to make them myself. Now can you hear this C-sharp on the piano?

323

[*She strikes a note on the piano.*] Whenever you hear this C-sharp struck on the piano it means a cut's coming at you, and don't try to duck it or I'll take a walk.

FELICE: This is—

CLARE: *Sacrilege?*

FELICE: —*Idiocy!*

CLARE: Total theatre is going to be total collaboration on this occasion, ducks.

FELICE: —Take your place.

CLARE: My place is here at the phone.

FELICE [*pointing to the window frame*]: Your place is—

CLARE: *Here* at the *phone!*

FELICE: You—*mother!*—May I have the tiara?

[*She smiles with fierce mockery: removes the tiara from her head and places it crookedly on his. He hurls it away.*]

You—castrating bitch, you—drunk—*slut!* Yes, I did call you that, I don't look at you on stage because I can't bear the sight of your—eyes, they're eyes of an—old demented—whore! Yes, a water-front whore! Lewd, degenerate, leering!

CLARE: I see!

FELICE: No, no, no, you don't see, you're *bl-i-i-nd!*

[*He stalks into the wings. She stands shocked motionless for a moment: then snatches up her cloak and throws it about her. She starts a few steps toward the opposite wings when the interior set is flooded with warm amber light and the curtains are heard jerking spasmodically open. She freezes. There are several guttural exclamations from the house: above them, a hoarse male laugh and the shrill*] *laugh of a woman.* CLARE's *eyes focus blazingly on the "house": She suddenly flings her cloak to the floor as if challenging the audience to combat.* FELICE *returns to the stage. He inclines his head toward* CLARE: *then toward the house.*]

The performance commences!

[*The performance. Clare is at the phone.*]

FELICE: Who are you calling, Clare?

[*She seems not to hear him.*]

Clare! Who are you calling?

CLARE: —Not a soul still existing in the world gone away . . .

FELICE: Then why did you pick up the phone?

CLARE: I just picked it up to see if it's still connected.

FELICE: The telephone company would send us a notice before they turned off the phone.

CLARE [*vaguely and sadly*]: Sometimes notices aren't—noticed.

FELICE: The house is—

CLARE: Still occupied but they might have the idea it wasn't, since it's not lighted at night and no one still comes and goes.

FELICE: We would have received a notice if one was sent.

CLARE: We can't count on that.

FELICE: We mustn't start counting things that can't be counted on, Clare.

CLARE: We must trust in things—

FELICE: Continuing as they've—

CLARE: Continued?

FELICE: Yes, as they've continued, for such a long time that they seem—

CLARE: Dependable to us.

FELICE: Permanently dependable, yes, but we were—

CLARE: Shocked when the—

FELICE: Lights refused to turn on, and it was lucky the moon was so nearly full that, with the window shades raised, it lighted the downstairs rooms.

CLARE: But we collided with things in the upstairs hall.

FELICE: Now we could find our way around in it blind.

CLARE: We can, we do. Without even touching the walls.

FELICE: It's a small house and we've lived in it always.

[CLARE *strikes C-sharp: he glares at her; she strikes it repeatedly. In a fierce whisper:*] *I will not cut into texture!*

CLARE: There's more about night. You tell me that I was indulging in a bit of somnambulism, last night?

FELICE: Clare, you had a sleepless night.

CLARE: And you did, too.

FELICE: In a small house when one of the occupants has a sleepless night, it keeps the other awake.

CLARE {*crying out*}: *Why do I have to sleep in that death chamber?*

FELICE [*controlled*]: We agreed that their room was just a room now. Everything about them's been removed.

326

CLARE: Except Father's voice in the walls and his eyes in the ceiling.—That night of the accident night I had to force my way past you to the room where—Mother opened the door . . .

FELICE [*cutting her off*]: Stop repeating, repeating!

CLARE: No sign of recognizing me at the door, no greeting, a look of surprise, very slight, till she opened her mouth on a soundless fountain of blood, and Father said, "Not yet, Clare," just as quietly, gently to me as *that,* before they went separate ways, she to the door of the bathroom where she fell and he to the window where he fired again looking out at—*out* . . .

[FELICE *strikes his fist on the piano keys.*]

And you tell me it isn't their room any more?

FELICE: I said: "LET IT REST!"

CLARE: Not in that room at night!

FELICE [*with forced quiet*]: You weren't in that room last night, you wandered about the house, upstairs and down, as if you were looking for something.

CLARE: Exploring the premises, yes . . .

FELICE: With a fine tooth comb as if you suspected there was a time bomb somewhere.

CLARE: I could almost hear it ticking.

FELICE: Well? Did you find it?

CLARE: No, but I did find something, this old memento, this token of—

FELICE [*starting the tape recorder*]: What?

CLARE [*lifting her hand*]: My ring with my birthstone, the opal.

327

FELICE: You haven't worn it for so long that I thought it was lost.

CLARE: Mother told me that opals were unlucky.

FELICE: Frigid women are given to little fears and superstitions, and—

CLARE: Opals do have a sinister reputation. And it was a gift from Father.

FELICE: That was enough to prejudice her against it.

CLARE: Sleepless people love rummaging. I look through pockets that I know are empty. I found this ring in the pocket of an old mildewed corduroy coat which I'd forgotten I'd ever owned and didn't care if the stone was unlucky or not.

FELICE: Nothing could be unlucky that looks so lovely . . .

[*He turns the ring on her finger—a sort of lovemaking. She strikes the piano key.*]

CLARE [*regaining her composure somewhat*]: Didn't you tell me you went out today?

FELICE: Yes, you saw me come in.

CLARE: I didn't see you go out.

FELICE: When you see somebody come in you know he's been out.

CLARE [*skeptically*] How far outside did you go? Past the sunflowers, or—?

FELICE: I went to the gate, and do you know what I noticed?

CLARE: Something that scared you back in?

FELICE: No, what I saw didn't scare me, but it, it—*startled* me, though. It was—

CLARE: What?

FELICE: Clare.

CLARE: What?

FELICE [*in a stage whisper*]: You know *The Two-Character Play*.

CLARE [*in a loud stage whisper*] The cablegram is still on the set.

FELICE: Clare, there wasn't, there isn't a cablegram in *The Two-Character Play*.

CLARE: Then take it off the sofa where I can see it. When you see a thing, you can't think it doesn't exist, unless you're hallucinating and you know that you are.

[*He picks up the cablegram, crumples it, and makes a gesture of throwing it out the window.*]

FELICE: There now, it never existed, it was just a moment of panic.

CLARE: What a convenient way to dispose of a panicky moment!

FELICE: Dismissed completely, like that! [*He snaps his fingers.*] And now I'll tell you what I saw in the yard when I went out.

CLARE: Yes, do that! Do, please.

FELICE: I saw a sunflower out there that's grown as tall as the house.

CLARE: Felice, you know that's not so!

FELICE: Go out and see for yourself.

[*She tries to laugh.*]

329

Or just look out the window, it's in the front yard, on this side.

CLARE: *Front* yard?

[*He nods but averts his face with a slight smile.*]

Now I know you're fooling.

FELICE: Oh, no, you don't or you'd go look out the window for yourself, it's shot up as quick as Jack's beanstalk and it's so gold, so brilliant that it—[*He sits on the sofa and seems to be musing aloud.*]—it seems to be shouting sensational things about us. [*He gives her a quick, sly look.*] Tourists will be attracted, botanists—you know botanists—will come to—marvel at this marvel, photograph it for the—the *National Geographic,* this marvel of nature, this two-headed sunflower taller than a two-story house which is still inhabited by a recluse brother and his sister.

CLARE: It would be a monster of nature, not marvel, if it existed at all, and I know that it doesn't.

[*She strikes a warning note on the piano. He snatches her hand off the keyboard and slams the piano lid shut; then sits on it, grinning at her mockingly.*]

FELICE: You know, I wonder if nature, that vast being and producer of beings, is satisfied with so many of its beings being so much like so many others of that kind of being or would actually be better pleased with more little—prodigies? Monsters? Freaks? Mute relations?—What's your opinion, Clare?

CLARE: No opinion, no comment, no recollection of lines!

FELICE: My opinion is that nature is tolerant of and sometimes favorable to these—differentiations if they're—usable? Constructive?—But if you're not, watch out you!

330

CLARE: You watch out.

[*She snatches up her cloak. He rises from the piano lid.*]

FELICE: —Why don't you go to the door? Don't you hear them knocking?

CLARE: Who?

FELICE: I can't see through the door.

CLARE: I don't hear any knocking. [*He drums the piano lid with his knuckles.*] —Oh, yes, now, I do, but—

FELICE: See who's there.

CLARE: I can't imagine.

FELICE: You don't have to imagine, you can go to the door and—

CLARE: *You* go.

[*There are audible whispers.*]

You're closer to it than I am, and—

[*He knocks the table harder.*]

—They're very—insistent, aren't they?

FELICE: It must be something important, go on, see what it is.

CLARE: I'm—not dressed for callers.

FELICE: You're prefectly dressed and look extremely well.

CLARE [*retreating further from the door*]: So do you aside from your hair.

FELICE: I don't have a tie on, and this old shirt of father's, I've sweated through it.

331

CLARE: That's, uh, excusable on a—hot afternoon. You, uh, let them in and say you'll call me down if it's *me* they— want to see *me*.

FELICE: Have you reached the point where you're scared to answer a door?

CLARE: Reached and—the knocking's stopped.—I think they've gone away, now.—No! Look! They're slipping a piece of paper under the door!

[*They stare fearfully at the supposed piece of paper on the doorsill.*]

FELICE: —They've left.

CLARE: Yes! Pick up the—

[*He crosses to the door, and makes the gesture of picking up a card, then frowns at it.*]

—What is—?

FELICE: A card from something called "Citizens' Relief."

CLARE: Then people know we're still here?

FELICE: Naturally, yes, where would we be but still here? —"Citizens' Relief"—I've never heard of it. Have you?

CLARE: No, and I think it's wise to be cautious about things you've—

FELICE: Never heard of.

CLARE: It might be a trick of some kind.

FELICE: It might be an excuse to intrude on our—

CLARE: Privacy, yes. Shall we destroy the card or keep it in case of a desperate situation?

FELICE: The case of a desperate situation isn't a thing we have to wait for, is it?

CLARE: Oh, but all the questions we'd have to—

FELICE: —Answer . . .

CLARE: Yes, there'd be interviews and questionnaires to fill out and—

FELICE: Organizations are such—

CLARE: *Cold!*

FELICE: Yes, impersonal things.

CLARE: I'll put the card under grandmother's wedding picture, just in case a desperate situation—

FELICE: Increases in desperation . . .

CLARE: Anyway, here it is, at least we—know where it is—What's next on the agenda? Do I pick up the phone? No, no, I pick up this sea shell, hold it to my ear, and remember the time that Father took us to the sea coast.

FELICE: It was the Gulf coast. [*He starts the tape again.*]

CLARE: The Gulf connects with a sea, it has gulls, tides, dunes—

FELICE: Much against Mother's objections, he took us there one summer when we were children, before we had started to school—

CLARE: Mother refused to stay at The Lorelei on the beach, we had to stay at the Hotel Commerce, back of the business district, and walk to the Municipal in bathing suits that hung down to our knees, and Mother never stopped nagging: "I checked with the cashier at the hotel. We can only afford a day more."

FELICE: Father would grin up lazily from the sand but finally shout out furiously at her: "Go back to the Hotel Commerce, continue your mathematical talk with the cashier, subtract, divide if you can, but don't multiply, and don't stay here in the sun, it disagrees with you!"

CLARE: And he'd snatch us up and away we would race, away . . .

FELICE: —Away from the Municipal, past the lighthouse tower and into the sand dunes where he tore off his suit and looked so much more elegant without it that we tore off ours, and he carried me into the water on his smooth gold shoulders and I learned to swim as if I'd always known how to . . .

CLARE [*pointing out toward the audience*]: Felice—someone's talking out there with his back to the stage as if he were giving a lecture.

FELICE: That's the interpreter.

CLARE: Oh, my God, he's telling them what we're saying!?

FELICE: Naturally, yes, and explaining our method. That's what he's here for.

CLARE [*half sobbing*]: I don't know what to do next—I . . .

FELICE: —I know what to do.

CLARE: Oh, do you? What is it? To sit there staring all day at a threadbare rose in a carpet until it withers?

FELICE: Oh, and what do you do? What splendid activity are you engaged in, besides destroying the play?

CLARE: None, none, nothing, unless it's something to pace about the house in a maze of amazement all day and sometimes in the night, too. Oh, I know why!

FELICE: Why?

CLARE: I want to go out! *Out, out, human outcry, I want to go out!*

FELICE: You want to go out calling?

CLARE: Yes, out calling!

FELICE: Go out!

CLARE: *Alone?*—Not *alone!*

FELICE: Ladies go calling alone on such nice afternoons.

CLARE: You come out calling with me.

FELICE: I can't, I have to stay here.

CLARE: For what?

FELICE: —To guard the house against—

CLARE: What?

FELICE: *Curious—trespassers!* Somebody has to stay on the premises and it has to be me, but you go out calling, Clare. You must have known when you got up this morning that the day would be different for you, not a stay-at-home day, of which there've been so many, but a day for going out calling, smiling, talking. You've washed your hair, it's yellow as corn silk, you've pinned it up nicely, you have on your blue-and-white print that you washed to go out in today and you have the face of an angel, Claire, you match the fair weather, so carry out your impulse, go out calling. You know what you could do? Everywhere you went calling you could say, "Oh, do you know how idiotic I am? I went out without cigarettes!" And they'd offer you one at each place and you could slip them into your purse, save them till you got home, and we could smoke them here, Clare. So! Go! [*He opens the door for her.*]

CLARE: Why have you opened the door?

FELICE: For you to go out calling.

CLARE: Oh, how thoughtful yes, that's very gentlemanly of you to open the door for me to go outside without parasol or gloves, but not very imaginative of you to imagine that I'd go out alone.

[*They stand a moment staring at each other near the open door: her hands and lips tremble; the slight smile, mocking and tender, twists his mouth.*]

—Suppose I came home alone, and in front of the house there was a collection of people around an ambulance or police car or both? We've had that happen before . . . No. I won't go out alone. [*She slams the door shut.*] My legs wouldn't hold me up, and as for smiling and talking, I'd have on my face the grimace of a doll and my hair would stick to the sweat of my forehead. Oh, I'd hardly sit down for this friendly call on—*what* friends?—before I—staggered back up, that is, if, if—the colored girl had been allowed to admit me.

FELICE: It was your idea. *You* shouted: "Out!" Not me.

CLARE: I'd never dream of going out without you in your —disturbed—*condition.*

FELICE: And *you* in *yours.*

CLARE: Me, calling, a fire engine shrieks, a revolver— bang!—discharges! Would I sit there continuing with the smile and the talk? [*She is sobbing a little: her trembling hand stretches toward him.*] No, I'd spring up, run, run, and my heart would stop on the street!

FELICE [*his smile fading out*]: I never believed you'd go out calling.

CLARE: Right you were about that if you thought alone— but calling? Yes, I'll do that! Phone calling is calling! [*She rushes to the telephone and snatches up the receiver.*]

336

FELICE: Calling, who are you——? *Careful!*

CLARE [*into phone*]: Operator, the Reverend Mr. Wiley!
Urgent, very, please hurry!

[*Felice tries to wrest the phone from her grasp: for a
moment they struggle for it.*]

FELICE: Clare!

CLARE: Reverend Wiley, this is Clare Devoto, yes, you
remember, the daughter of——

FELICE: What are you? Out of your——?

CLARE: You'll have to let me go on or he'll think I'm——
[*into the phone again:*] Excuse me, Riverend Wiley, there
was——an interruption. My brother and I still live in our parents' home after, after the——terrible accident in the house
which was reported so maliciously falsely in *The Press-Scimitar.* Father did *not* kill Mother and himself but——

FELICE: Tell him *we* shot them why don't you?

CLARE: The house was broken into by some——

FELICE: Favorite of nature?

CLARE: Housebreaker who murdered our parents, but I
think *we* are suspected! My brother Felice and I are surrounded by so much suspicion and malice that we almost
never, we hardly ever, dare to go out of the house. Oh, I
can't tell you how horrifying it's been, why, the neighbor's
child has a slingshot and bombards the house with rocks, we
heard his *parents* give the slingshot to him and *tell* him to——
——*Ha! Another rock struck just now!*——It goes on all through
the daytime, and in the nighttime people stop and linger on
the sidewalk to whisper charges of——anomalous letters of obscenities are sent us, and in *The Press-Scimitar*——sly allusions
to us as the deranged children of a father who was a false

mystic and, Reverend Wiley, our father was a man who had true psychic, mystical powers, granted only to an Aries whose element is cardinal fire. [*She is sobbing now.*]—Why? We're gentle people, never offending a soul, trying to still live only, but—

[FELICE *wrests the phone from her hands.*]

FELICE: Mr. Wiley, my sister has a fever.

CLARE: No, I—!

FELICE: She's not herself today, forget what, excuse and—[*He hangs up, wipes the sweat off his forehead with a trembling hand.*] Wonderful, that does it! Our one chance is privacy and you babble away to a man who'll think it his Christian duty to have us *confined* in—

[*She gasps and stumbles to the piano.*]

Clare!

[*She strikes a treble note repeatedly on the piano. He snatches her hand from the keyboard and slams the lid down.*]

CLARE: You shouldn't have spoken that word! "Confined"! That word is not in the—

FELICE: Oh. A prohibited word. When a word can't be used, when it's prohibited its silence increases its size. It gets larger and larger till it's so enormous that no house can hold it.

CLARE: Then say the word, over and over, you—*perverse monster,* you!

[FELICE *turns away.*]

Scared to? Afraid of a—?

338

FELICE: I won't do lunatic things. I have to try to pretend there's some sanity here.

CLARE: Oh, is that what you're trying? I thought you were trying to go as far off as possible without going past all limits.

[*He turns to face her, furiously. She smiles and forms the word "confined" with her lips; then she says it in a whisper. He snatches up a soft pillow.*]

Confined, confined!

[*He thrusts the pillow over her mouth, holding her by the shoulder. She struggles as if suffocating.*]

FELICE: All right? O.K., now? Enough?

[*She nods. He tosses the pillow away. They stare at each other silently for a moment. She has forgotten the next bit of business. He points to the piano. She turns and strikes a chord on it.*]

An interval of five minutes.

CLARE: *Fifteen!*

FELICE [*rushing into the wings to lower the curtain*]: Ten!

CURTAIN INTERVAL

ACT TWO

During the interval, there has obviously been a physical struggle between the stars. She is still clutching an elbow and wincing with pain: a scratch is visible on his face. Both of them are panting.

FELICE [*in a whisper*]. Ready?

[*She nods: the performance is resumed.*]

A bowl of soap water and one spool are for blowing soap bubbles.

CLARE: Yesterday you said, "There's nothing to do, nothing at all to do."

FELICE: When we were children we blow soap bubbles on the back steps, not in the parlor.

CLARE: Can you imagine us sitting back there now, exposed to public view, blowing soap bubbles? We can't turn back to children in public view, but privately, in the parlor window . . .

FELICE: Soap bubbles floating out of the parlor window would not indicate to the world that we were in full possession of our senses.

[*She crosses to him and dabs his scratched cheek with a bit of cotton. His eyes shut as if this tender gesture were creating a sensuous sleepiness.*]

CLARE: Have you dried up, Felice?

[*He sways slightly.*]

I'm afraid I have, too.

FELICE: Improvise something till I—

CLARE: All right. Sit down. Breathe quietly. Rest a little, Felice, I'll—

[*He sits on the sofa and clasps the sides of his head.* CLARE *strikes a soft note on the piano, then leans against it, facing downstage.*]

—When Father gave up his psychic readings and astrological predictions, a few days before the *un-, in-explicable*—accident!—in the house—Well, he didn't give them up, exactly.

FELICE: No, not exactly by choice.

CLARE: Mother had locked up his quadrant and chart of night skies and his psychic paraphernalia.

FELICE: Except for this worn-out shirt of his I have on, which bears his sign of the zodiac on it and his rising sign and a chart of the sky as it was on the hour before daybreak of the day of his nativity here in New Bethesda!

CLARE: You know, he seemed to—accept. At least he said nothing. Not even when she spoke of State Haven to him. "Yes, I can see your mind is going again. Check yourself into State Haven for a long rest—voluntarily, or I'll—" He became very quiet. But restlessly quiet. He sat almost continually where you're sitting and stared at that threadbare rose in the carpet's center, and it seemed to smolder, yes, that rose seemed to smolder like his eyes and yours, and when a carpet catches fire in a wooden house, the house will catch fire, too. Felice, I swear that this is a house made of wood and that rose is smoldering, now!

[*She strikes a C-sharp on the piano. He glares at her furiously but she strikes the note again, louder.*]

FELICE [closing his eyes]: —Line?

CLARE: Didn't you tell me you'd thought of something we have to do today?

FELICE: —Yes, it's something we can't put off any longer.

CLARE: The letter of protest to the—

FELICE: No, no, letters of protest are barely even opened, no, what we *must* do today is go out of the house.

CLARE: To some particular place, or—

FELICE: To Grossman's Market.

CLARE: *There?*

FELICE: Yes, *there!*

CLARE: We tried that before and turned back.

FELICE: We didn't have a strong enough reason and it wasn't such a favorable afternoon.

CLARE: This afternoon is—?

FELICE: Much more favorable—And I simply know that it's necessary for us to go to Grossman's Market today since— I've kept this from you, but—sometimes the postman still comes through the barricade of sunflowers and that he did some days ago with a notification that no more—

CLARE: —Deliveries?

FELICE: Will be delivered to the steps of—

CLARE: I knew! Payment for costlies has been long—overdue.

FELICE: So out we do have to go to Grossman's Market, directly to Mr. Grossman's office and speak personally to him.

CLARE: His office! Where's his office? Probably tucked away in some never-discovered corner of that shadowy labyrinth of a—

FELICE: We'll ask a clerk to tell us, to take us, to Mr. Grossman's office.

CLARE: If the clerk saw us, he'd pretend that he didn't.

FELICE: Not if we enter with some air of assurance—
We're going to enter Grossman's Market today like a pair
of—

CLARE: Prosperous, paying customers?

FELICE: Yes, we'll say to the clerk, "Please show us the
office of Mr. Grossman." We are going to tell him convinc-
ingly that in spite of all spite and, and—contrary—accusa-
tions—Father's insurance policy will be paid to us by the
Acme Insurance Company on, say, the first of next month,
yes, on September the first.

CLARE: But we know that it won't be!—Why, they wrote
only three sentences to us in reply to the twelve-page appeal
that we wrote and rewrote, for a week—

[*They have crossed downstage to opposite sides of the
interior set, facing out.*]

CLARE [*at a fast pace*]: We've been informed by the—

FELICE [*at a fast pace*]: Acme Insurance Company—

CLARE [*at a fast pace*]:—that the insurance money is—

FELICE [*at a fast pace*]: Forfeited.

CLARE [*at a fast pace*]: Yes, the payment of the insurance
policy is forfeited in the—

FELICE [*at a fast pace*]: Event—

CLARE [*at a fast pace*]: Yes, in the event of a man— [*She
stops, pressing her fist to her mouth.*]

FELICE [*at a fast pace*]: In the event of a man killing his
wife, then himself, and—

CLARE: Unkindly forgetting his children.

343

FELICE:—That's what's called a legal technicality . . .

[*They turn again to each other.*]

CLARE: What do you know about anything legal, Felice?

FELICE: I know there are situations in which legal technicalities have to be, to be—disregarded in the interests of human, human—We must say that what we saw, there was only us to see and what we saw was *Mother* with the revolver, first killing Father and then herself and—

CLARE: A simple lie is one thing, but the absolute opposite of the truth is another.

FELICE [*wildly*]: *What's the truth in pieces of metal exploding from the hand of a man driven mad by—!* [*There is a pause.*] Well? Well? Do we do it or forget it?

CLARE: Sometimes our fear is—

FELICE: Our private badge of—

CLARE: —Courage . . .

FELICE: Right!—The door is still open. Are we going out?

[*After a pause, she backs away from him a step.*]

CLARE: See if there are people on the street.

FELICE: Of course there are, there are always people on streets, that's what streets are made for, for people on them.

CLARE: I meant those boys. You know, those vicious boys that—

FELICE: Oh, yes. You stopped on the walk and shouted "Stop!" to the boys. Covered your ears with your hands and shouted: "Stop, stop!" They stopped, they crossed the street. I said: "For God's sake, what did you think they were doing? Why did you shout 'Stop!' at them?"

CLARE [*overlapping*]: They were staring and grinning at me and spelling out a—

FELICE [*overlapping*]: You said they were spelling out an obscene word at you.

CLARE [*overlapping*]: Yes, an obscene word, the same obscene word that somebody scrawled on our back fence.

FELICE [*overlapping*]: Yes, you told me that, too. I looked at the back fence and nothing was scrawled on it, Clare.

CLARE [*overlapping*]: If you heard nothing the last time we went out, why wouldn't you go on alone to the grocery store? Why did you run back with me to the house?

FELICE [*overlapping*]: You were panicky. I was scared what you might do.

CLARE [*overlapping*]: What did you think I might do?

FELICE [*overlapping*]: What Father and Mother did when—

CLARE [*overlapping*]: Stop here, we can't go on!

FELICE: Go on!

CLARE: Line!

FELICE: A few days ago you—

CLARE: No, you, you, not I! I can't sleep at night in a house where a revolver is hidden. Tell me where you hid it. We'll smash it, destroy it together—line!

FELICE [*calmly*]: I removed the cartridges from the revolver, and put them away, where I've deliberately forgotten and won't remember.

CLARE: "Deliberately forgotten!" Worthless! In a dream you'll remember. Felice, there's death in the house and you know where it's waiting.

FELICE [*wildly*]: *So!*—Do you prefer locked doors of separate buildings?

CLARE: You've been obsessed with locked doors since your stay at State Haven!

FELICE: Yes, I have the advantage of having experienced, once, the comforts, the security, the humanizing influence of—

CLARE: Locked doors!

FELICE: At State Haven!

CLARE: I'm sorry but you had allowed yourself to lose contact with all reality.

FELICE: What reality was there left in this—?

CLARE: Stopped speaking! Stared without recognition!

FELICE: Yes, being dumb-struck and blinded by—!

CLARE: Was *I? I* was here, too!

FELICE: Oh, I don't think you knew where you were any more! You—

CLARE: I knew enough to get out of bed in the morning instead of crouching under covers all day!

FELICE: Was that a sign of clearer—?

CLARE: It was a sign of ability to go on with—

FELICE: Customary habits!

CLARE: An appearance of—!

FELICE: *Fuck appearances!*

CLARE: *Hush!*—You've hidden the revolver, give it up. I'll take it down to the cellar and smash it with the wood-chopper, and then be able to sleep again in this house!

FELICE: —People don't know, sometimes, what keeps them awake . . .

[*He starts to lapse. The pace slows from exhaustion and they retreat from their opposite sides of the downstage interior.*]

CLARE: The need to search for—

FELICE: The contents of empty pockets?

CLARE: Not always empty! Sometimes there's a birthstone in them that isn't lucky!

[*There is a pause: they stare, panting, at each other. Very slowly, with lost eyes, he closes the door—nearly.*]

FELICE: —You have the face of an angel—I could no more ever, no matter how much you begged, me, fire a revolver at you than any impossible, unimaginable thing. Not even to lead you outside a door that can't be closed completely without its locking itself till the end of—I haven't completely closed it.—Clare, the door's still open.

CLARE [*with a slight, sad smile*]: Yes, a little, enough to admit the talk of—

FELICE [*overlap*]: Are we going out, now, or giving up all but one possible thing?

CLARE: —We're—going out, now. There never really was any question about it, you know.

FELICE: Good. At last you admit it.

[*There is a pause.*]

CLARE [*assuming a different air*]: But you're not properly dressed. For this auspicious occasion I want you to look your best. Close the door a moment.

FELICE: If it were closed, it might never open again.

CLARE: I'm just—just going upstairs to fetch your fair-weather jacket and a tie to go with it. [*She turns upstage.*] Oh, but no stairs on the set!

FELICE: The set's incomplete.

CLARE: I know, I know, you told me. [*She faces upstage.*] I have gone upstairs and you are alone in the parlor.

FELICE: Yes, I am alone in the parlor with the front door open.—I hear voices from the street, the calls and laughter of demons. "Loonies, loonies, loonies, *loooo-nies!*"—I—shut the door, remembering what I'd said.

CLARE: You said that it might never be opened again. [*She turns abruptly downstage.*] Oh, there you *are!*

FELICE: Yes. Of course. *Waiting* for you.

CLARE: I wasn't long, was I?

FELICE: —No, but I wondered if you would actually come back down.

CLARE: Here I am, and here is your jacket and here is your tie. [*She holds out empty hands.*]

FELICE: The articles are invisible.

CLARE [*with a mocking smile*]: Put on your invisible jacket and your invisible tie.

FELICE: —I go through the motions of—

CLARE: Ah, now, what a difference! Run a comb through your hair!

FELICE: —Where is—?

CLARE: The inside jacket pocket. I put it there.

FELICE: —Oh?—Yes.—Thanks . . . [*He makes the gesture of removing a comb from his invisible jacket.*]

CLARE: Oh, let *me* do it! [*She arranges his hair with her fingers.*]

FELICE: That's enough. That will do.

CLARE: Hold still just one moment longer.

FELICE: No, no, that's enough, Clare.

CLARE: Yes, well, now you look like a gentleman with excellent credit at every store in the town of New Bethesda!

FELICE: Hmmm . . .

CLARE: The door is shut.—Why did you shut the door?

FELICE: —The wind was blowing dust in.

CLARE: There is no wind at all.

FELICE: There *was,* so I—

CLARE: Shut the door. Will you be able to open it again?

FELICE: Yes. Of course. [*He starts the tape recorder again. Then, after a hesitant moment, he draws the door open.*]

CLARE: —What are you waiting for?

FELICE: For you to go out.

CLARE: You go first. I'll follow.

FELICE: —How do I know you would?

CLARE: When a thing has been settled, I don't back out.

FELICE: That may be, but you are going out first.

CLARE: Will you come out right behind me or will you bolt the door on me and—

349

[*He seizes her hand and draws her forcibly to the door. She gasps.*]

FELICE: Out!

CLARE: See if—!

FELICE: There are no boys on the street!

CLARE: May I set my hat straight please?

FELICE: Stop this foolishness. Afternoons aren't everlasting, you know.—OUT!

[*He thrusts her through the open door. She cries out softly. He comes out, shutting the door and faces the audience.*]

Now there is, there must be, a slight pause in the performance while I slip offstage to light the front of the house. [*He starts offstage.*]

CLARE [*terrified whisper*]: Oh, God, don't leave me alone here!

FELICE: For a moment, one moment. [*He goes into the wings. An amber light is turned on the area around the door. He returns to her side, takes her hand and leads her forward a little.*] It's a nice afternoon.

CLARE [*tensely*]: Yes!

FELICE: You couldn't ask for a nicer afternoon, if afternoons could be asked for.

CLARE: No!

FELICE: I don't know what we're waiting here for. Do you?

[CLARE *shakes her head and tries to laugh.*]

We're waiting here like it was a car stop. But it's only a block and a half to Grossman's Market.

350

CLARE: I don't know why, but I'm shaking, I can't control it. It would make a bad impression on Mr. Grossman.

FELICE: You're not going to back out now. I won't allow you.

CLARE: Felice, while you're gone, I could, could, could—make a phone call to "Citizens' Relief," you know, those people we wouldn't let in the house. I could tell them to come right over, and answer all their questions, and we would receive their relief even if Mr. Grossman doesn't believe the story.

FELICE: Clare, quit stalling. Let's go now.

CLARE: —I left something in the house.

FELICE: What?

CLARE: I left my—my—

FELICE: You see, you don't know what you left, so it can't be important.

CLARE: Oh, it is, it's very—it's, it's the—cotton I put in my nose when I have a nosebleed, and I feel like I might have one almost any minute. *The lime dust!*

[*She turns quickly to the door, but he blocks her, stretching his arms across the doorway. She utters a soft cry and runs around to the window. He reaches the window before she can climb in.*]

FELICE: You're not going to climb in that window!

CLARE: I am! Let me, I have to! I have a pain in my heart!

FELICE: Don't make me drag you by force to Grossman's Market!

CLARE: The moment I get back in I'll call the people from "Citizens' Relief"!—I *promise!*

FELICE: *Liar! Liar, and coward*

CLARE: Oh, Felice, I—

[*She runs back to the door. He remains by the window. She enters the interior set and stares out at him, hands clasped tightly together. He steps over the low windowsill and they face each other silently for a moment.*]

FELICE: If we're not able to walk one block and a half to Grossman's Market, we're not able to live in this house or anywhere else but in two separate buildings. So now listen to me, Clare. Either you come back out and go through the program at Grossman's or I will leave here and never come back here again and you'll stay on here alone.

CLARE: You know what I'd do if I was left here alone.

FELICE: Yes, I know what she'd do, so I seize her arm and shout into her face: "Out again, the front door!" I try to drag her to it.

CLARE: I catch hold of something, cling to it! Cling to it for dear life!

FELICE: Cling to it!

CLARE: It's not on the set, the newel post of the stairs. I wrap both arms about it and he can't tear me loose.

FELICE: Stay here, stay here alone When I go out of this house I'll never come back. I'll walk and walk, I'll go and go! Away, away, away!

CLARE: I'll wait!

FELICE: For *what?*

CLARE: For *you!*

FELICE: That will be a long wait, a longer wait than you imagine. I'm leaving you now. *Good-bye!* [*He steps out over the low sill of the window.*]

CLARE [*calling out after him*]: Don't stay long! Hurry back!

FELICE: Hah! [*He comes forward and speaks pantingly to the audience.*] The audience is supposed to imagine that the front of the house, where I am standing now, is shielded by sunflowers, too, but that was impractical as it would cut off the view. I stand here—move not a step further. Impossible without her. No, I can't leave her alone. I feel so exposed, so cold. And behind me I feel the house. It seems to be breathing a faint, warm breath on my back. I feel it the way you feel a loved person standing close behind you. Yes, I'm already defeated. The house is so old, so faded, so warm that, yes, it seems to be breathing. It seems to be whispering to me: "You can't go away. Give up. Come in and stay." Such a *gentle* command! What do I do? Naturally I obey. [*He turns and enters by the door.*] I come back into the house, very quietly. I don't look at my sister.

CLARE: We're ashamed to look at each other. We're ashamed of having retreated—surrendered so quickly.

FELICE: There is a pause, a silence, our eyes avoiding each other's.

CLARE: Guiltily.

FELICE: No rock hits the house. No insults and obscenities are shouted.

CLARE: The afternoon light.

FELICE: Yes, the afternoon light is unbelievably golden on the—

CLARE: The furniture which is so much older than we are—

FELICE: I realize, now, that the house has turned to a prison.

CLARE: I know it's a prison, too, but it's one that isn't strange to us.—Felice, what did I do with that card from "Citizens' Relief"?

FELICE: I think you put it under—

CLARE: Oh. Grandmother's wedding picture. [*She takes the card and goes to the phone.*]—I'm going to call them!

FELICE: —I suppose it's time to.

[*She lifts the phone hesitantly.*]

CLARE: I lift the receiver and it makes no sound. I feel like screaming into the phone: "Help, help!"

FELICE: —Is it—?

CLARE [*hanging up the receiver*]: Sometimes a phone will go dead temporarily, just for a little while, and come back to life, you know.

FELICE: Yes, I know. Of course.

CLARE: —So we stay here and wait till it's connected again?

FELICE: We might have to wait till after the Relief Office closes. It might be a better idea to ask the people next door if we can use their phone since something's gone wrong with ours.

CLARE: That's right. Why don't you do that?

FELICE: *You* do that. It's the sort of thing you could do better. Look! [*He points at the window.*] The woman next

door is taking some clothes off her wash line. Call her through
the window.

[CLARE *catches her breath. Then she rushes to the window
and calls out in a stifled voice.*]

CLARE: Please, may I, please, may we—!

FELICE: Not loud enough, call louder.

CLARE [*turning from the window*]:—Did you really imagine that I could call and beg for "Citizens' Relief" in front of
those malicious people next door, on their phone, in their
presence? Why, they gave their son a slingshot to stone the
house!

[*There is a slight pause.*]

FELICE: You asked me what people did when they had
nothing at all left to do.

CLARE: I asked you no such thing. [*After a moment, she
dips a spool in the soapy water.*]

FELICE: Instead of calling the woman next door through
the parlor window, you blow a soap bubble through it. It's
lovely as your birthstone.—But it's a sign of surrender, and
we know it.—And now I touch her hand lightly, which is a
signal that I am about to speak a new line in *The Two-
Character Play.* [*He touches her hand.*] Clare, didn't you tell
me that yesterday or last night or today you came across a box
of cartridges for Father's revolver?

CLARE: No! No, I—

FELICE: Clare, you say "yes," not "no." And then I pick
up the property of the play which she's always hated and
dreaded, so much that she refuses to remember that it exists
in the play.

CLARE: I've said it's—*unnecessary!*

[FELICE *has picked up a revolver from under the sheet music on the piano top.*]

Has it always been there?

FELICE: The revolver and the box of cartridges that you found last night have never been anywhere else, not in any performance of the play. Now I remove the blank cartridges and insert the real ones as calmly as if I were removing dead flowers from a vase and putting in fresh ones. Yes, as calmly as—

[*But his fingers are shaking so that the revolver falls to the floor.* CLARE *gasps, then laughs breathlessly.*]

Stop it!

[CLARE *covers her mouth with her hand.*]

Now I—[*He pauses.*]

CLARE: Have you forgotten what you do next? Too bad. I don't remember.

FELICE: I haven't forgotten what I do next. I put the revolver in the center of the little table across which we had discussed the attitude of nature toward its creatures that are regarded as *unnatural* creatures, and then I—[*After placing the revolver on the table, he pauses.*]

CLARE: What do you do next? Do you remember?

FELICE: Yes, I—[*He starts the tape recorder.*]—I pick up my spool and dip it in the water and blow a soap bubble out the parlor window without the slightest concern about what neighbors may think. Of course, sometimes the soap bubble bursts before it rises, but this time please imagine you see it rising through gold light, above the gold sunflower heads.

Now I turn to my sister who has the face of an angel and say to her: "Look! Do you see?"

CLARE: Yes, I do, it's lovely and it still hasn't broken.

FELICE: Sometimes we do still see the same things at the same time.

CLARE: Yes, and we would till locked in separate buildings and marched out at different hours, you by bullet-eyed guards and me by bullet-eyed matrons. [*She strikes a note on the piano.*] Oh, what a long, long way we've traveled together, too long, now, for separation. Yes, all the way back to sunflowers and soap bubbles, and there's no turning back on the road even if the road's backward, and—[CLARE *looks out at the audience.*]—The favorites of nature have gone away.

[FELICE *does not respond.*]

Felice, the performance is *over*. [*She stops the taped guitar.*]

[*After the performance.*]

CLARE [*continued*]: Put on your coat. I'm going to put on mine.

[*He stares at her, stupefied.*]

Felice, come out of the play. The audience has left, the house is completely empty.

FELICE:—Walked? Out? All?

CLARE [*she has picked up their coats from behind the sofa*]: You honestly didn't notice them get up and go?

FELICE: I was lost in the play.

CLARE: You were but they weren't, so they left.

FELICE: You made cuts in the play that destroyed the texture.

357

CLARE: I cut when the house sounded like a t.b. ward.

FELICE: If you'd been concentrating you would have held them.

CLARE: Christ, did I try! Till the seats banged up and—

FELICE: —I hear no sound from the house when I'm lost in a play.

CLARE: Then *don't* get lost in a play! Get lost in *woods,* among *wolves!*

FELICE: HA!

CLARE: Oh, let's stop this silly bitching, taking our rage at those idiots out on each other, it's pointless. Here, here, put this on you!

[*She has jerked a torn, discolored white silk scarf from his sleeve, and tries to stuff it under his mangy fur collar.*]

FELICE: Stop that! Don't put things on me I can put on myself if I want them on me! This scarf goes into the wardrobe for *The Lower Depths* . . .

[*He throws it to the floor. She picks it up and now he permits her to place the dirty scarf beneath his collar; he is still panting and staring desolately out.*]

CLARE [*she opens her cigarette case*]: Only three smokables left.—*Gentle man,* be seated.

[*She gestures toward the sofa upstage and they move unsteadily toward it. She stumbles; he clutches her shoulders; they sit down. She offers him a cigarette; he takes it.*]

—Lucifers?

[*Mechanically he removes a scant book of matches from his coat pocket, strikes one and holds it before him: for a couple of moments both of them seem unconscious of it; then she slowly turns her look on it.]*

—Did you strike it to light our cigarettes, dear, or just to relieve the gloom of the atmosphere?

FELICE [*lighting her cigarette*]: Sorry . . . [*He starts to light his own cigarette, the match burns his fingers.*] Mmmmmmmmm!

[*She blows the match out and lights his cigarette with hers; they smoke together quietly for a moment.*]

CLARE: The first time I turned downstage I simply couldn't help seeing those—

FELICE: Clare, let it go, they're gone.

CLARE: —fur-bearing mammals out there, went into panic, didn't come out till this moment. Ahhh . . .

FELICE: Hmmm . . .

CLARE: Now call Fox. See if there's money enough to get us out of this place.

[*There is a pause.* FELICE *is afraid to call Fox, suspecting he's long gone.*]

Well, for God's sake, call him!

FELICE [*calling into the house*]: Fox!—*Fox!*

CLARE: Perhaps the audience caught him and fed him to their dog teams—*Fox, Fox, Fox!*

TOGETHER: *Fox!*

[*There is an echo from their call; they listen, with diminishing hope, for a response. Finally:*]

CLARE: I feel like falling into bed at the nearest hotel and sleeping the next thousand years.

FELICE: Well, go get your things.

CLARE: Get what things?

FELICE: Your purse, your handbag, for instance.

CLARE: I don't have one to get.

FELICE: You've lost it again?

CLARE: This still seems like a performance of *The Two-Character Play*. The worst thing that's disappeared in our lives is not the Company, not Fox, not brandy in your flask, not successes that give confidence to go on—no, none of that. The worst thing that's disappeared in our lives is being aware of what's going *on* in our lives. We don't dare talk about it, it's like a secret that we're conspiring to keep from each other, even though each of us knows that the other one knows it. [*She strikes a piano key. There is a pause.*] Felice, is it possible that *The Two-Character Play* doesn't have an ending?

FELICE: Even if we were what the Company called us in the cable, we'd never perform a play that had no end to it, Clare.

CLARE: It never seems to end but just to stop, and it always seems to stop just short of something important when you suddenly say: "The preformance is over."

FELICE: It's possible for a play to have no ending in the usual sense of an ending, in order to make a point about nothing really ending.

CLARE: I didn't know you believed in the everlasting.

FELICE: That's not what I meant at all.

CLARE: I don't think you know *what* you meant. Things do end, they do actually have to.

FELICE [*rising*]: Up! Hotel! Grand entrance! We'll face everything tomorrow.

CLARE: Everything will face *us* tomorrow and not with a pretty face. No, Sir. And as for right now, we don't have fares for a dog sled to the hotel, and just before the performance you told me that Fox hasn't made us hotel reservations here, wherever here is!

FELICE: I think I remember seeing a hotel across the plaza from the theatre when we came from *the station. We'll go there, we'll enter in such grand style that we'll need no reservations. Wait here while I—[*He rushes into the wings.*]

CLARE: *Where are you——?*

[*She follows him as far as the giant's statue, and stops there. The cold, stone vault of the building is no longer silent. We hear running footsteps, the hollow, unintelligible echo of shouitng, metal clanging, etc. Clasping the pedestal of the statue,* CLARE *faces downstage, moving spasmodically at each ominous sound, sometimes catching her breath sharply. The sounds stop: there is total silence. She starts toward the door far upstage, then retreats to the statue.*]

Giant, he'll come back, won't he? You don't look sure about that. It's so terribly quiet after all those noises.—*Felice!*

FELICE'S VOICE [*distant*]:Yes!

CLARE: Hurry back! I'm alone here!—turning to a frozen supplicant at the feet of a merciless—poor Felice. He lost his argument about the impossible being necessary tonight. The impossible and the necessary pass each other without recognition on streets, and as for *The Two-Character Play,* when he read it aloud I said to myself, "This is his last one, there's nothing more after this."—Well, there are festivals to remember. Riding a fiacre, you driving the horses, drunk across

Rilke's Bridge of Angels over the Tiber, a crack of thunder and suddenly a sleet storm, pelting our laughing faces with tiny marbles of ice. *Un mezzo litro. Una bottiglia. Une bouteille de. Frutta di mare. Comme c'est beau ici! Como bello! Maraviglioso!*—"Your sister and you are insane."—How ridiculous! Clinging for protection to the pedestal of a monster . . .

[*There is the sound of footsteps.*]

He's coming back, thank God!

[FELICE *returns, as if blind, to the stage.*]

What luck, Felice?

[*He crosses past her as if he didn't see her, enters the interior set, and sinks, panting, onto the sofa. She follows him slowly, drawing her coat close about her.*]

Well? Another disaster?

FELICE [*without facing her*]: Clare, I'm afraid we may have to stay here a while.

CLARE: In this frozen country?

FELICE: I meant here in the theatre.

CLARE: Oh?

FELICE: Yes, you see, the stage door and the front doors are all locked from outside, there isn't a window in the building, and the backstage phone is lifeless as the phone in *The Two-Character Play* was, finally was.

CLARE: Do you notice any change in the lighting?

FELICE: Yes, the lights have dimmed.

CLARE: They're still dimming.

FELICE: And I haven't touched the light switch.

CLARE [*shouting*]: *Out, out, out! Human outcry!*

FELICE: It's no good screaming, *cara.*

CLARE: I wasn't screaming, I was shouting!

FELICE: The firing of a revolver in this building wouldn't be heard outside it.

CLARE: Does this mean we'll have to stay here freezing till they open up the building in the morning?

FELICE: Clare, there's no assurance they'll open up the building in the morning or even in the evening or any morning or evening after that.

CLARE [*with an abrupt flash of hope*]:—Oh, Felice, the hole in the backstage wall . . . [*She points upstage.*]

FELICE: Sometimes the same idea still occurs to us both. [*He looks at her with a "dark" smile. He is breathing heavily from his exertion.*] I tried to increase the width of that— crevice, it's narrow as those vents in old castle walls that— arrows were shot through at—besiegers, and all I accomplished for my labors was *this* . . . [*He lifts the bloodied palms of his hands.*]

CLARE [*cutting in*]: Are you working on some neo-Elizabethan historical drama, Felice? If you are, write me out of the cast and, and—wipe your bloody hands on something clean.—Stop grinning at me like that!

FELICE: It's not you I'm grinning at, Clare.

CLARE: You're looking at me with a savage grin!—Do you *hate* me, Felice?

FELICE: Of *course* I do, if I *love* you, and I think that I do. [*He moves a little downstage: his next line should be underplayed.*]—"A garden enclosed is my sister . . ."

[*There is a pause.*]

I think fear *is* limited, don't you, Clare?

CLARE: —Yes. I do.

FELICE: Isn't it limited to the ability of a person to care any more?

CLARE: —For anything but—[*She means for "one other person"; but that touch of sentiment, is better left spoken by just a glance between them*] —So it's a prison, this last theatre of ours?

FELICE: It would seem to be one.

CLARE [*objectively, now*]: I've always suspected that theatres are prisons for players . . .

FELICE: Finally, yes. And for writers of plays . . .

[*She moves downstage.*]

CLARE: So finally we are—the prohibited word . . .

[*He strikes a note on the piano. They are almost smiling, wryly: there is no self-pity.*]

And, oh, God, the air isn't cold like ordinary cold but like the sort of cold there must be at the far, the farthest, the go-no-more last edge of space!

FELICE: Clare, you're not frightened, are you?

CLARE: No, I'm too tired to be frightened, at least I'm not yet frightened.

FELICE [*placing the revolver under the sheet music at the piano*]: Then you will *never* be frightened.

CLARE: It's strange, you know, since I've always had such a dread of—prohibited word!—it's the greatest dread of my life.

FELICE: And of mine, too.

CLARE: But, no, right now what I feel is—[*She crosses to the sofa and sinks exhaustedly onto it.*]—is simply bone-tired and bone-cold.

[*Her rigid hands tremble in her lap. He sits beside her and takes hold of one of her hands and rubs it.*]

—Otherwise I'd get up and see for myself if these mysteries that you've reported to me are exactly as you've reported, or—

FELICE: Do you think I've imagined them, dreamed them, Clare?

CLARE: —Sometimes you work on a play by inventing situations in life that, that—correspond to those in the play, and you're so skillfull at it that even I'm taken in . . . [*She withdraws one hand and offers him the other.*] Circulation has stopped in this hand, too.

[*He rubs her other hand, looking into her eyes as if presenting her with a challenge: She doesn't return the look.*]

—About our cholera shots, they may not be so tolerant on the way back . . . And with my passport missing . . .

FELICE: Your mind's wandering, Clare.

CLARE: —Going back . . .

FELICE: Going back's reversing a law of—

CLARE: Nature?

FELICE: About that likely, Clare.

[*There are clanking noises.*]

CLARE: —What's—?

FELICE: Pipes expanding with—

CLARE: Metal contracts with—

FELICE [*Gently*]: Clare, your mind's going out.

CLARE: That shows it's—wiser than God . . .

FELICE: —When there's a thing to be done—

CLARE: There's nothing to be done.

FELICE: There's always something to be done. There's no such thing as an inescapable corner with two people in it. What's necessary is to know that there is a thing to be done, and then not think about it, just know it has to be done and—

CLARE: You have a dark thought in your head and I think I know what it is.

FELICE: Sometimes we still have the same thought at the same time, and that could be an advantage to us now.

CLARE [*drawing her cloak about her*]: Will it get any colder?

FELICE: It's not going to get any warmer.—You know, during the performance, even under hot lights, the stage was cold, but I was so lost in the play that it seemed warm as a summer afternoon in . . .

[*During this speech he has crossed to the tape recorder and turned it back on at a low level. The selection could be Villa-Lobos'* Brasilianas *and should continue through the curtain.*]

CLARE: —You are suggesting that we—?

FELICE: Go back into the play.

CLARE: But with the stage so dim—

FELICE: If we can imagine summer, we can imagine more light.

CLARE: If we're lost in the play?

FELICE: Yes, completely—in *The Two-Character Play*.

[*She nods and struggles to rise from the sofa but topples back down. He draws her up.*]

CLARE: *Back into the play,* try it, give it a Sunday try!

FELICE: Other alternatives—

CLARE: Lacking!—Can we keep on our coats?

FELICE: We could but I think the feeling of summer would come more easily to us if we took our coats off.

CLARE: *Off coats! Put the cablegram back on the sofa!*

[*They remove their coats and fling them over the sofa. He places the cablegram against the back of it.*]

Do we stop where we stopped tonight or do we look for an ending?

FELICE: I think that you will find it wherever you hid it, Clare.

CLARE: Wherever *you* hid it, not me. [*She looks at him and gasps, lifting a hand toward her mouth.*]

FELICE: Is something wrong?

CLARE: No!—no . . .

[*He smiles at her, then removes the revolver from under the sheet music on the piano.*]

—Was it *always* there?

FELICE: Yes, in every performance. Where would you like me to place it?

CLARE: Under a sofa pillow? By the Company's cable?

FELICE: Yes, but remember which one and snatch it up quickly, quickly, and—[*He thrusts the revolver under a pillow.*]

CLARE [*Her smile glacial, now*]: Hit hard and get out fast?

FELICE: Yes, that's the cry!

CLARE: Do we start at the top of the play?

FELICE: With your phone bit, yes. *The performance commences!*

CLARE: When a performance works out inevitably, it works out well. [*She lifts the telephone.*]

FELICE: Who are you calling, Clare?

CLARE [*very fast*]: Not a soul still existing in the world gone away.

FELICE [*very fast*]: Then why did you pick up the phone?

CLARE [*very fast*]: To see if it's still connected.

FELICE [*very fast*]: We would have been notified if—

CLARE [*very fast*]: It's a mistake to depend on—notification. Especially when a house looks vacant at night. [*She hangs up the phone.*]

FELICE [*very fast*]: Night, what a restless night.

CLARE [*very fast*]: Wasn't it, though?

FELICE [*very fast*]: I didn't sleep at all well and neither did you. I heard you wandering about the house as if you were looking for something.

CLARE [*very fast*]: Yes, I was and I found it. [*She pauses.*] Are you lost in the play?

FELICE: Yes, it's a warm August day.

CLARE [*raising a hand, tenderly, to his head*]: Felice, your hair's grown so long, you really must find the time somehow to.—We mustn't neglect appearances even if we rarely go out of the house. We won't stay in so much now. I'm sure they'll believe that Mother shot Father and then herself, that we saw it happen. We can believe it ourselves, and then the insurance company will come through with the policy payment, and livables, commendables, and necessities of persistence will be delivered through the barricade of—

FELICE: Go straight to the tall sunflowers.

CLARE: Quick as that?

FELICE: That quick!

CLARE: Felice, look out of the window! There's a giant sunflower out there that's grown as tall as the house!

[FELICE *crosses quickly to the window and looks out.*]

FELICE: *Oh, yes, I see it. Its color's so brilliant that it seems to be shouting!*

CLARE: *Keep your eyes on it a minute, it's a sight to be seen!*

[*She quickly retrieves the revolver from beneath the sofa cushion, and resolutely aims it at* FELICE, *holding the revolver at arm's length. There is a pause.*]

FELICE [*harshly*]: *Do it while you still can!*

CLARE [*crying out*]: *I can't!*

[*She turns convulsively away from him, dropping the revolver as if it had scorched her hand. As it crashes to the floor,* FELICE *turns from the window, his motion as convulsive as hers. Their figures are now almost entirely lost in dark but light touches their faces.*]

369

Can you?

[*He moves a few steps toward the revolver, then picks it up and slowly, with effort points it at* CLARE. FELICE *tries very hard to pull the trigger: he cannot. Slowly he lowers his arm, and drops the revolver to the floor. There is a pause.* FELICE *raises his eyes to watch the light fade from the face of his sister as it is fading from his: in both their faces is a tender admission of defeat. They reach out their hands to one another, and the light lingers a moment on their hands lifting toward each other. As they slowly embrace, there is total dark in which:*]

THE CURTAIN FALLS

CPSIA information can be obtained
at www.ICGtesting.com
Printed in the USA
LVOW12*0953190317
527713LV00006B/19/P